Academic Janus

The Private College and Its Faculty

Reece McGee

Foreword by Theodore Caplow

ACADEMIC JANUS

Jossey-Bass Inc., Publishers
615 Montgomery Street · San Francisco · 1971

ACADEMIC JANUS
The Private College and Its Faculty
　　Reece McGee
　　Foreword by Theodore Caplow

Library of Congress Catalog Card Number 70-149913

International Standard Book Number ISBN 0-87589-097-0

Manufactured in the United States of America
　　Composed and Printed by York Composition Company, Inc.
　　Bound by Chas. H. Bohn & Co., Inc.

JACKET DESIGN BY JANE OKA, MILL VALLEY

FIRST EDITION

Code 7116

THE JOSSEY-BASS SERIES IN HIGHER EDUCATION

General Editors

JOSEPH AXELROD
*San Francisco State College
and University of California, Berkeley*

MERVIN B. FREEDMAN
*San Francisco State College
and Wright Institute, Berkeley*

Foreword

In 1958 Reece McGee and I published *The Academic Marketplace,* a study of how vacancies occurred and replacements were made in university faculties. It focused on the institutional consequences of academic mobility: we interviewed everyone except the persons who moved. (Hamlet without the prince, several critics remarked.) Describing the major universities from which our sample had been drawn, we said:

> Not only our own data but a great accumulation of other writings provide us with information about the major universities and their departments. We have not been able to discover a single scientifically oriented investigation of a nonmajor institution. The smaller universities and the independent liberal arts colleges are far too important, intellectually and numerically, to be neglected in this way. Descriptive studies of their institutional patterns are badly needed.

Some of this uncharted territory has since been explored in studies related to ours. Theodore N. Farris studied vacancies and replacements in a sample of community colleges. Diana Crane compared the careers of research scientists at major and minor universities. Hope Klapper drew a sample of "quality" liberal arts colleges across the country for a study of faculty roles. Earl McGrath's monograph on predominantly Negro colleges and universities describes their institutional patterns in some detail.

And now comes *Academic Janus: The Private College and Its Faculty* to examine the academic mobility of college faculties from the standpoint of the protagonists themselves, describing their working lives and career choices with an inimitable mixture of irony and respect. All these studies agree that academic men, by and large, are

as happy and productive as any other body of professionals and that
corruption and malfeasance are remarkably rare among them. The
study you are about to read, the most careful of them all, is most em-
phatic on these points.

Taken in themselves, these findings are interesting. Against the
background of yesterday's headlines and today's editorials, they are
astonishing and enigmatic. While this study was being planned, carried
out, and written up, the institution of higher education was shaken by
the greatest convulsions it had experienced since the Reformation and
its whole future became doubtful. The excitement was not confined to
the United States; the universities of France, Germany, Japan, and
several other countries were hit even harder, but the surprise was
greater here than elsewhere. The development of American undergraduate education had been an unbroken success story from the
founding of Harvard College in 1636 to the proliferation of community colleges in the early 1960s; nothing in that long history of peace-
ful expansion foreshadowed the mobs of students and the faculty juntas
who, by 1968, were denouncing higher education from coast to coast
and arguing about whether the existing establishments should be de-
stroyed or only drastically reformed. Admittedly, the private colleges
were less affected by this upheaval than were the public colleges or
the universities because the private colleges were more amenable to
structural change and in closer touch with their students. But they
were severely shaken nevertheless.

The contrast between McGee's portrait of the academic man,
secure and at ease in his modernized ivory tower, and those other
academic men who help students to draft their nonnegotiable demands
is almost grotesque, and the reader of *Academic Janus* will be tempted
to look for some easy explanation to reconcile these jarring images.
Perhaps a study undertaken a year or two later would have shown
different results. Perhaps McGee, although he is a dissenter of long
standing, sees the academic life through rose-colored glasses. I am convinced that such explanations do not resolve a paradox that is quite
real and that it is peculiar but quite true that academic men are generally contented in the midst of the confusion into which their institutions have fallen.

We may obtain some insight about this odd condition by
examining some of the changes that occurred in American higher
education in the decade between the field work for *The Academic
Marketplace* (1956–1957) and the field work for *Academic Janus*

(1966–1967). There was a vast increase in institutional scale. (Most of the statistical assertions here are based on the *Digest of Educational Statistics 1968,* especially Tables 80, 81, 82, 103, 110, and 129.) Enrollment in institutions of higher education rose from 2.918 million in the fall term of 1956 to 5.885 million in the fall of 1966, that is, it doubled in a single decade. Even the private institutions, which grew much more slowly than the public institutions, increased by about 60 per cent. As a necessary consequence of this growth, undergraduate colleges became less intellectual. A third of the total population aged eighteen to twenty-one in 1956 was enrolled in institutions of higher education. By the fall of 1966 this proportion had risen to nearly a half, from which it necessarily follows that great numbers of students of average intelligence (and a considerable number of less than average intelligence) were in college. The colleges also became less exclusive during this period. The enrollment of women increased much faster than the enrollment of men, the enrollment of blacks much faster than the enrollment of whites, and the enrollment of the poor much faster than the enrollment of the middle class. More people not only sought higher education but sought much more of it. The number of bachelor degrees awarded in the United States almost doubled from the spring of 1957 to the spring of 1967, but the number of higher degrees almost tripled. This enrollment boom was accompanied by an even more impressive financial boom. The income of institutions of higher education rose by about 15 per cent annually and faculty salaries by about 6 per cent. In 1956–1957 the median professor earned $8072. Ten years later his salary had risen to $14,713, more than keeping pace with the average improvement of personal income throughout the labor force. Federal grants and loans for higher education and related activities rose from less than $500 million in 1956–1957 to $3.5 billion in 1966–1967.

In sum, times were good in Academia in 1966–1967, and the trouble just over the horizon was a cloud no bigger than a man's hand. In the ensuing years, prosperity continued but several unexpected things happened. The control that American colleges and universities had traditionally exerted over the daily lives, habits, and manners of students was simultaneously challenged in a hundred places, and in response to the challenge this ancient system of private law crumbled away. The selective biases that the colleges had always taken for granted in carrying out their mission to train an elite were challenged from all sides. Universities began to recruit black freshmen as eagerly as high school football players, sometimes happily combining the two searches. City colleges began to admit high school dropouts. Vigorous attempts were made to extend the benefits of higher education to housewives, migratory workers, and mid-career executives. Within the ivied walls, dozens of schemes were hatched to modify the grading system that formerly made every course part of a competitive contest and to reduce prerequisites and requirements at every level from freshman English to the defense of a dissertation. At the same time, student interest shifted from laboratory to descriptive science, from the study of languages to the study of social problems, from the learning of history to the discussion of current events.

One of the most important and startling changes that occurred in the late 1960s was the disappearance among students of what might be called the alma mater cult, the body of beliefs and sentiments that had inspired previous generations with a certain chauvinism about their college, led them to participate worshipfully in its rituals and ceremonies, and fostered a lifetime sense of obligation for benefits received. The students who exploded a charge of dynamite under the statue of Alma Mater on the Columbia campus in the spring of 1970 were expressing with unusual vigor a sentiment that had become commonplace among their contemporaries. In addition to the minority who viewed the college as an agency of the military-industrial complex, there was an apparent majority to whom the college spirit seemed archaic, childish, and consummately irrelevant. Superficially, this decline represents lost ground for professors in their dealings with students since one of the major components of the cult was the veneration of faculty saints and heroes. In some colleges, the denial of faculty charisma by students has been explicit and unequivocal. Elsewhere it hovers beneath the surface.

Yet, by and large, the academic profession is less troubled by these developments than might be expected. The steady improvement of wages and working conditions has not been materially affected by widespread campus disorders, although there are innumerable portents that the public in general and state legislatures in particular are beginning to question the motives of higher education and to support it less willingly. In other respects, the weakening of conventional patterns has not been entirely disadvantageous for faculties. Throughout *Academic Janus* the reader will be reminded that professors often hate the harried exprofessors who administer colleges and universities ("the dirty, damn deans") and find solace in their discomfiture. The student revolt that slightly reduces the prestige of a faculty has shattering effects on the authority of vice-presidents and deans. In academic power struggles (which, as Courtney Brown once remarked, are terribly bitter because the stakes are so low) the students somtimes pull down the administrative aristocracy for the eventual benefit of shrewd faculty politicians.

Another euphoriant factor has been the liberation of faculty members from conventional norms that weighed as heavily upon them as upon undergraduates and for a much longer term of years. The trivial freedoms to wear sweaters and sandals to class, to court nubile undergraduates without public censure, to use obscenities in lectures and correspondence, and to cultivate underworld acquaintances in the community are no less heady than the major freedoms to express dissident political opinions, to espouse radical causes, and, above all, to challenge the judgment of one's seniors about one's professional merits. The competitive grading system to which students object is no more galling than the competitive mechanism within each academic discipline and department—a mechanism which measures scholars for eminence or obscurity. It is no wonder that behind nearly every SDS chapter in its heyday stood a devoted little band of faculty advisors. And there is no further wonder that, by and large, academic men seem to be relatively untroubled by the confusion into which academic institutions have fallen. There is objective evidence on this point. For example, the rate of voluntary resignation from the Berkeley faculty has fallen to a negligible level during the extended time of troubles on that campus.

While the problems that obsess intellectuals in the United States and in comparable societies, from Japan to Italy, are real enough and serious enough to threaten unspeakable calamities if technological culture does not learn to lift itself by its bootstraps, I think nevertheless that McGee's report about American liberal arts colleges can be trusted despite its favorable view of academic institutions. His love of the teaching trade, which he practices so admirably himself, is apparent on every page together with his deep respect for academic men and their style of life. I invite the reader to discover for himself that McGee's bias in favor of teaching and learning has not contaminated this admirable piece of sociological research.

Charlottesville, Virginia   THEODORE CAPLOW
January 1971

For Betty, with love

Preface

Academic Janus reports a sociological study of that peculiarly American institution, the private liberal arts college. Of course, similar educational structures exist elsewhere and the roots of the American college are firmly embedded in the European past. However, the privately supported, four-year, undergraduate institution specializing in a liberal arts curriculum has a development in this country which has set such colleges apart from their counterparts elsewhere and has produced a structure unique to the United States and to American education. The liberal arts colleges occupy a special place in American higher education. It is not the purpose of this work to present even a brief history of the private colleges or to describe how they came to be what they are today. Neither is it the purpose here to fully analyze the colleges or to predict their future. It is, rather, to describe some facets of such colleges as they exist today, to explore their workings as social systems, and to investigate the professional careers of their faculties, as segments of the larger institution of American higher education.

This report, however, has a double role. The research was sponsored by the Hill Foundation of St. Paul in the expectation that it would reveal facts of immediate practical value concerning the faculty labor market for the private liberal arts colleges of the upper Midwest. The book is in part, then, a research report to the foundation describing the academic labor market in which those colleges operate and the professional and personal norms which guide the faculties of such colleges in making their employment decisions. In this respect, it is factual reporting of the way things are. I have endeavored to go beyond this factual statement, however, to try to suggest why things are the way they are and to put my findings into the larger context of higher education in the United States.

Some definitions and explanations are in order. By the term *private* I mean supported mainly by sources other than public funds and directed by private persons rather than public officials. There remain few, if any, institutions of higher education in the United States which are purely private in the sense of having nowhere in their budgets some funds from public sources; almost all do, in fact, receive funds of some sort from federal agencies (scholarships, funds for construction of dormitories or purchase of scientific equipment, etc.). Many also receive such monies from states, counties, or municipalities, and I know of none of the type considered here which are not state supported in the sense of being tax-exempt. Nonetheless, it is a valid distinction among the several forms of institutions of higher education. The colleges with which I am concerned in *Academic Janus* are private in the sense of having governing boards appointed by and responsible to sources other than the state or public and in receiving most of their financial support from sources other than taxes.

The term *liberal arts college* is, if anything, even looser in meaning than *private,* and there are endless discussions in faculty lounges and in professional journals as to what a liberal arts college is or ought to be. For my purpose I define it as a four-year institution of higher education devoted mainly to undergraduate instruction, the principal degrees from which are baccalaureates, and the curricula of which is mainly nonvocational and nonprofessional. The degree to which each of these criteria may apply to a specific institution which calls itself a liberal arts college varies. Many of the schools sampled for this study, for example, provide some graduate instruction and grant some graduate degrees, typically the master of education or the master of arts in teaching. Some offer courses in nursing, and two have ROTC curricula. Several offer preprofessional curricula in law, medicine, dentistry, and the ministry. All, however, are mainly four-year undergraduate institutions offering the bachelor's degree as the terminal degree for the majority of their graduates who take courses of instruction not specifically vocational or preprofessional. In this they are similar to most of the institutions in the United States which call themselves liberal arts colleges.

The reader must understand, however, that a college is not a university, the institution with which it is most frequently compared in this country (and sometimes confused) and with which it often is contrasted in the following pages. A university is defined by the presence in it of graduate and professional schools of instruction. These, together with the organizations for undergraduate instruction within the institution, are, it is true, often called colleges, as in "college of law" or "college of arts and sciences" or even "college of liberal arts." (And two of the colleges in the sample also include the word *university* in their names.) Nonetheless, despite similarities in nomenclature, universities and liberal arts colleges are essentially different, although related, institutions.

One of the signal differences between the college and the university, both in my own experience and in the eyes of the college faculties, is in the roles of the student and of teaching. The colleges are primarily teaching institutions, although research is accomplished in them too. In almost every college the student and his welfare and the means for his instruction are paramount considerations, the college sees itself as organized to perform instructional and other services for students, and the faculty member accepts the definition of his role which imposes teaching and counseling of students as the primary obligation. This is perhaps the major differentiating characteristic between colleges and universities. Colleges have only one fundamental or basic function to perform—teaching undergraduates. Universities usually have at least three—teaching undergraduates, teaching graduate students, and performing basic (and sometimes applied) research. The difference, then, is one of emphasis rather than of kind. It is, nonetheless, quite real and has important implications for the natures of the two institutions. In many ways, the college and the university are alike, but their differences in emphasis and function markedly distinguish them; they are different institutions established for different reasons and performing different jobs. As in so many other areas of American life, we probably have good reason to be grateful for the diversity. It may be that, in some improbable future, we could get along without the colleges (we could not continue to exist as a civilization without the universities). But equally our collective life would be poorer without them, and we should all have cause to bemoan their passing. With their emphasis on the instruction of the young, but without the bureaucratization and the stultification of professional education in the public schools, they remain the stronghold of enlightenment liberalism, and they enrich us all, graduates and nongraduates alike.

Acknowledgments

It is conventional to preface one's literary debts by remarking that of course it is impossible to name the numberless persons who contribute to the final production of a book. The reason for the convention is that it is entirely true. All readers should be aware of my numerous debts to many persons who in one way or another forwarded this project or the manuscript resulting from it, but who are not named herein. Most prominent among these are the faculties and administrative officers of the eleven colleges which are the subjects of *Academic Janus,* in particular those faculty members who consented to give their precious time to be interviewed. Without their generous cooperation, there would be no subject matter for this book.

For financial assistance in support of the research, I am indebted to the Louis W. and Maud Hill Family Foundation of St. Paul, Minnesota, which funded the project producing the data reported here and throughout the work gave valuable assistance, encouragement, and advice. Specifically I acknowledge the assistance of Al Heckman, executive director of the foundation, and of Donald Hughes and John Taylor, his assistants. Lesser but invaluable financial support was also given the project in embryonic stages by the University Research Institute of The University of Texas and the Hogg Foundation for Mental Hygiene of that institution, and I am indebted to W. G. Whaley, dean of the Graduate School of The University of Texas, the late J. A. Burdine, formerly dean of the College of Arts and Sciences, and Robert Sutherland, director of the Hogg Foundation, for this assistance. President Harvey M. Rice and Vice-President Lucius Garvin of Macalester College made it possible for me to undertake the pilot study at that institution, and I am grateful for their help and the cooperation of that faculty. Theodore Caplow of the University of Virginia was a participant in the original definition of the study and made valuable suggestions; indeed the original work from which the present enterprise evolved was to have been a joint one between him and me.

I am indebted to the Institute for the Study of Social Change of the Department of Sociology of Purdue University, under the direction of Richard J. Hill, for statistical and secretarial services, to Jean Hicks and Karen Tate for data processing, to Loretta Chu and Louise Sabin for help with project operation and bookkeeping, and to Jean Wehr, Julia Beard, Pat Hobson, and Jackie Stringer for manuscript typing and other clerical services of high order. For coding and methodological criticism (see Appendix B), thanks are owed to Kathleen Stones Crittenden of the University of Illinois at Chicago Circle. The quotation from Veblen's *The Higher Learning in America: A Memorandum on the Conduct of Universities by Business Men* (New York: Viking) is used by permission of the publishers. The quote from Barzun is reprinted from *The American Scholar*, 1964, 33 (2), copyright 1964 by the United Chapters of Phi Beta Kappa, and is used with permission of the publishers. The quotation from Arrowsmith is contained in Calvin B. T. Lee, *Improving College Teaching* (Washington, D.C.: The American Council on Education, 1967), and is used with permission of the publisher.

Finally, I am deeply indebted to the following academic men who read the manuscript in draft and to whose wisdom, advice, and critical commentary it owes a great deal: Paul M. Berry, Department of Sociology and Anthropology, Macalester College; Kenneth P. Goodrich, dean of Macalester College; G. Theodore Mitau, chancellor of the Minnesota State College System; J. R. Smiley, president of The University of Texas at El Paso.

Lafayette, Indiana   REECE MCGEE
January 1971

Contents

APPENDICES

Academic Janus

*The Private College
and Its Faculty*

ONE

Why This Book?

How the Study Came About

I undertook this work for several reasons, some substantive, some empirical, some theoretical or methodological. The general purpose was to investigate the labor market for faculty members in the small American college. Much information has been accumulated concerning the American university and the social, psychological, economic, and political contexts in which it operates. The labor market for university faculty has been thoroughly, if not intensively, studied. Much less is known about the smaller college. Specific aspects of small college operation have been investigated, and occasional surveys of single institutions have been made. There remained to be accomplished, however, an investigation of faculty turnover and the market for teaching personnel in the private college. But to know the purpose of the study is not necessarily to understand its rationale. When the project was first conceived, such an investigation appeared to be useful in light of the then rapidly increasing college enrollments and accelerating competition among institutions of higher education for faculty members. Such competition was believed by administrators of small colleges, and by other observers as well, to pose serious problems in institutional staffing for unprestigious colleges or for those without the financial resources to compete with publicly supported institutions. This intense

1

competition for faculty and the activity of faculty members in a labor market where they stood in short supply have now (1971) ended, at least temporarily, in response to national financial recession and to political backlash against student radicalism, demonstrations, and violence. There is some reason to believe—as I will argue later—that for the private colleges, at least, this cessation of competition may be only temporary and that the eventual end of the teacher shortage forecast by Cartter (1967) may be delayed longer than for other kinds of institution.

Furthermore, the small colleges, whether publicly or privately supported, have an important and valued role to play in American education and have contributed to the national well-being out of proportion to the number of students they enroll. For example, excessive numbers of successful scientists originate in small colleges rather than in large universities. Any information which might enable such institutions successfully to compete for faculty members would be of considerable value.

The research investigation reported here, then, concerned the private college labor market. It was designed, however, in the certain knowledge that such research always reveals a great deal about the anatomy of the organization investigated and this, in fact, was the purpose of the undertaking. For institutions of higher education the faculty labor market and the behavior of professors in response to it represent the intersection of a number of significant planes, institutional, disciplinary, personal, and interpersonal. The natural history of a labor market interaction for a particular individual reveals his professional and personal value systems, his perceptions of himself and his colleagues, the organizations with which he is affiliated, and the institution employing him. A collection of such histories thus details the social reality, the reality in action, of a social institution. This is what is reported here.

David Brown's works (1965a; 1967) are the definitive studies of the labor market for American academics. Brown, a labor economist, surveyed two thousand college and university presidents and thirteen thousand faculty members by mailed questionnaire. Some of his conclusions are particularly germane to our consideration here (1965a): Vacancies occur for various reasons—decisions to expand staff, switches from one college to another which leave a vacancy at the first, persons leaving the teaching profession to enter careers with business or government or to retire, and professors going on leave. Most vacancies occur in the poorest schools, which also have the greatest difficulty in retaining staff and are expanding most rapidly. To fill these vacancies, college teachers expect to and do switch jobs several times during their careers. Most of these moves are voluntary. Involuntary mobility is concentrated among the less qualified teachers and at the lower ranks. Market entry is often not obvious, however, since the most acceptable method of job seeking is to do nothing or to look informally by using friends or former teachers. Thus, in general, professors must be recruited for jobs. Even those actively seeking jobs, possibly through formal intermediaries such as college placement offices and teacher placement bureaus, are not always visible. Traditionally a professor does not inform his employer of his intention to leave until he has found another job. In addition, several major factors decrease the extent and effectiveness of mobility—the ethics of the labor market, the policy of promotion from within, seniority and tenure provisions, the nontransferability of some fringe benefits, ignorance about both job vacancies and the desirability of known openings, the costs of finding and switching jobs, the economically irrational preferences of faculty and institutions, and the extreme specialization among faculty and institutions.

This last factor points to the fact that there is no single academic labor market, but rather a balkanization of the market, with many submarkets differing according to institutional size and specialization and according to discipline. Brown is the only writer who has explored empirically this balkanization of "the" market. It is a point which cannot be overemphasized. "The" market for college teachers does not exist. Instead there are numerous overlapping markets, the rules for operation in which differ rather widely. It should be emphasized, therefore, that the present work reports not on the entire academic labor market, but on the workings of that market for private college faculties only. Mobile professors operating in this system tend to move between schools of similar size. This tendency probably arises from the different emphases of large and small schools and from the consequent differences in responsibilities such as teaching and research.

Another nationwide survey of labor market practice was made by Howard Marshall in 1964. This questionnaire study covered 150 institutions of different types and was based on replies from chairmen in economics, chemistry, and English regarding their recent experiences with vacancies and replacements in their departments. Four hundred and twenty teaching economists who had recently taken new positions were also questioned. Marshall's conclusions were that the market was very active at the time surveyed and that turnover in faculty positions was so considerable as perhaps to be excessive. He found that faculty members changing positions were importantly, although not dominantly, motivated by economic considerations. (This is flatly contradicted by the present study. The incongruity seems to be explained, however, by the fact that Marshall's sample was heavily weighted with economists who do seem to be influenced in their decisions by economic factors.) Although the larger (and better financed) universities had an edge on the colleges in recruiting faculty, Marshall saw no reason for despair on the part of the small college, for hope was offered by the small college practices of promotion from within and of giving younger men opportunity to teach in their specialties and by the warm, personal friendships which are more easily developed in a small college community than in the more anonymous university.

John Gustad (1960) sampled 1665 faculty members and 121 administrators at more than 150 southern colleges and universities to determine why people elect college teaching as a career and why some later leave the profession. One of his major conclusions was that faculty personnel policies, typically designed by administrators, are ineffectual because administrators and faculty members have quite divergent views of their jobs; major discrepancies exist between their value hierarchies and reward systems, and communication between two classes of academic personnel is poor. Gustad also agreed that mobility was high. Among his sample of professors of chemistry, English, and psychology, he found averages of 38 per cent of college faculty and 40 per cent of university faculty unsure whether they would remain in their current jobs, and 18.6 per cent and 12.7 per cent certain that they would not.

More limited than Gustad's study, but more centrally focused on the concerns of the present work was John Stecklein's (1961) report of questionnaires answered by and interviews conducted with four groups of faculty members associated with the University of Minnesota—newly appointed faculty, persons who received job offers from the university but rejected them, persons resigning their Minnesota positions to move elsewhere, and persons fired or let go by the university. Germane to our considerations and largely supported by my data are Stecklein's conclusions that faculty who were offered positions at Minnesota but rejected them did so because they were happy where they were and because the offers were insufficiently attractive to make them move; the offers were inferior in salary or rank to their existing positions or the duties and requirements of their existing positions were preferable to those offered at Minnesota. Minnesota faculty who resigned in order to take other positions reported that they did so either because the duties or salaries offered, or both, were preferable to those at Minnesota (and the university presumably unwilling or unable to match them) or because they preferred to live in the geographic area of the other institution.

Allen Cartter (1967), a labor economist and provost of New York University, surveyed academic manpower needs and growth and came to a conclusion startling to many teaching faculty: the academic labor shortage, which has been very marked since World War II and which, with burgeoning enrollments, has created a hectic (and, for faculty, a highly favorable) market for years, is coming to an end. Since this prediction flies in the face of every other one of recent years, it behooves us to examine it carefully and to attempt to estimate its significance for the private liberal arts colleges. Cartter first showed that the great shortage of college teachers expected for the latter part of the sixties did not occur because of errors in interpretation of the data on which the predictions were based and in assumptions about such matters as the net loss of Ph.D.'s from the teaching profession each year. (The loss rate was less than one-third of that usually expected.) In addition, most forecasters were unduly pessimistic in their estimates of the future production of doctoral degree holders, in part because they could not foresee (in the fifties and early sixties) the coming massive federal support of graduate education.

Cartter suggested that the demand for college teaching staff of all kinds will slow down in the seventies because of a decrease in the rate of expansion of student enrollment (as enrollments approach 100 per cent of the college age population, the rate at which they expand will level off). Indeed, Cartter predicted that if other factors (such as teacher-student ratio and the proportion of college teachers holding doctoral degrees) remain constant, by 1977 45 per cent of new doc-

torate holders annually will find jobs in academics. Even allowing for
an improvement of 1 per cent a year in proportions holding the doctorate, by 1980 an adequate supply of highly trained teachers seems
assured. (Radical changes in quality demands, radical decline in the
relative pay for academic work, or increased demands from nonacademic fields for the Ph.D. could change these predictions considerably.)

What is the meaning of these predictions for the liberal arts
colleges? Was the current study based on a false assumption that the
private colleges were operating in a tight market which was not likely
to loosen very much? The answer to the latter question is probably no.
Although by 1980 the supply of doctorate holders may exceed the
nationwide demand, the small colleges still have the seventies to get
through, and faculty supply for private colleges will probably not expand as rapidly as it will for universities. In addition, the quality of
private college faculties, as indicated by the proportion of full-time
staff with the doctoral degree, still lags behind that of the universities,
so the demand for Ph.D. holders will remain greater among the colleges for longer. The supply of trained academic manpower may, indeed, be much better by 1980, but during the seventies the labor shortage will probably keep the market for the private college more or less
as great as that during the sixties and will keep it operating under rules
like those described here.

One other factor makes Cartter's speculations difficult to apply.
Cartter must, perforce, deal with doctoral degrees of all sorts at a national level. But the academic labor market does not deal only in doctoral degrees and only nationally. An increase in doctoral degrees in
education does not benefit the private colleges very much, for example,
because their education faculties are small. In the same way, a shortage
of teachers of physics cannot be made up by a surplus of artists. Nor
is the private college market as much a national one as is that of the
multiversities. The existence of openings in the Midwest does not automatically attract or draw a supply of labor from a surplus in the
Southeast. Indeed a liberal arts college may be desperately seeking
faculty in some field at the same time that a nearby university department is equally desperately attempting to place a surplus of graduates
in that discipline without either institution's seriously considering the
other as a source of remedy for their problems—the college because it

defines the university graduates as research-oriented rather than teaching-oriented, and the university because it regards liberal arts teaching as a dead end for professionally promising graduate students. We must conclude, then, that although Cartter's work is extremely valuable in pointing out the fallacy of some universally held assumptions, it does not pertain to the specific situation in which we are interested.

The eleven institutions studied in the present research are probably representative of better American liberal arts colleges. This contention is impossible to prove without a strenuously contested definition of *better,* but there is little question that the sample institutions are typical of private liberal arts colleges in their organization, support, size, and departmental array. I contend, too, that barring the great colleges of the country (Williams, Vassar, Antioch, Swarthmore, Reed, and Oberlin, to name only a few), the sample institutions as a class are qualitatively as good as any others and may be better, in fact, than most; my respondents—who are not all midwesterners in origin—believe that the better colleges of the Midwest (of which the eleven are a good sample) are probably among the best in the country, the great colleges excepted.

The names of the participating institutions cannot be revealed since all were asked to cooperate on the assurance of anonymity. It betrays no confidences, however, to describe some of their institutional characteristics, from which the reader may make his own judgments of their typicality if not of their quality. All eleven are private liberal arts colleges in the upper Midwest. All are coeducational. They do not all belong to the same conference, whether *conference* is taken to mean athletic association (not all engage in intercollegiate athletics) or interinstitutional consortium. Their students come from every state and from many foreign lands as well. Numbers of students range from 1150 full-time students to 2450, with an average of 1499 for the group; regular, full-time faculties average 109, with a range from 73 to 162. All are organized with governing boards which act as immediate overseers to the executive officer (in each case, as it happens, called the president), but their forms of control are various: five describe themselves as "church-related," three are "independent," two are "church-controlled," and one describes itself as "nominally affiliated with" a Protestant denomination. All are accredited by the North Central Association of Colleges and Secondary Schools, and all maintain various other accreditations and affiliations with professional, denominational, and other agencies.

The eleven colleges are all endowed in various degrees, which means they receive income from invested capital. The church-related, -affiliated, and -controlled institutions also receive support in varying amounts from their denominations. All make annual appeals to their surrounding communities and to business enterprises for funds, and all rely on alumni contributions for some support. In all cases income from student tuition is an important source of operating (as distinguished from investment) funds, although the significance of this income varies considerably from school to school. At one college it was claimed that the institution was in such serious financial condition it would admit any student who could manage to find the campus without assistance; in others income from student fees, while needed and important, was the source of less than half of the annual operating budget. Although several of the eleven are prestige schools, at least in the Midwest, none are expensive. Comprehensive fees in 1967 ranged from $985 to $3000 a year and averaged $2248.

Considerable variation appears in the academic programs of the colleges in the sample, but all follow rather typical patterns of offerings. Some confine themselves strictly to traditional liberal arts curricula, while others have somewhat emulated the universities by offering various vocational and preprofessional programs as well. Only faculty members in traditional liberal arts disciplines were surveyed, although professors of education were included when they belonged to a department within the liberal arts framework rather than to a separate school. Departments surveyed in the eleven institutions included anthropology, architecture, art, astronomy, biology, botany, business administration (only when combined with economics), chemistry, classics (or classical languages or ancient languages), drama or theater, economics, education, English, geography, geology, government or political science, history, mathematics, modern languages or foreign languages (or separate departments for particular languages or language groups), music, philosophy, physics, psychology, religion, sociology, speech, and zoology. None of the eleven institutions has departments in all these areas, but all have course offerings in all of them, except architecture; allowing for the vagaries of departmental organization and nomenclature, with that one exception all could have such arrangements without much affecting their curricula. In several of the colleges nursing, accounting, ROTC, and preprofessional programs for law, dentistry, the ministry, and medicine are also represented.

The institutions studied are typical of the private liberal arts colleges of the country. They offer typical curricula concentrating in the liberal arts to a more or less select student body; they are fully accredited, and, judging by the destinations of their products (in no case do fewer than half their graduates go to graduate and professional schools; in one instance as many as 90 per cent do), they do a good job of preparation. They are squarely in the liberal arts tradition as it is known in this country, and they have been there for a long time— several are in their second century of continuous operation. Although their names are probably not household words for most Americans, they are well known and universally respected in their region, and some, at least, are reasonably well known among the academic and intellectual communities from coast to coast. In support, organization, curriculum, and student body, they are very much like most other American colleges of their type. Finally, among the faculty members interviewed were many who had taught elsewhere in liberal arts colleges. In no case, while discussing either the faculty member's provenance or the institutions from which he had experienced probes, did any individual assert that the institution where he was then teaching was essentially different from the norm.

Once the promise of cooperation had been secured from institutional officers, the process of visiting the eleven institutions and interviewing faculty members was not difficult but contained numerous small hazards and problems. It was my habit, for this research, to arrive at an institution without specific previous announcement. Coming on the campus, I simply called the president or dean with whom negotiations for cooperation had been conducted and made arrangements for the trivial facilities required to conduct the work. I needed from the college only access to a telephone and a faculty telephone directory. Armed with my roster of market-active faculty (derived from a mailed inquiry), I simply called men on the list, reminded them of the earlier correspondence, and requested an interview. I was able to reach and interview 81 per cent of the individuals shown as eligible by my rosters, but the proportion of true eligibles reached was actually somewhat higher because some individuals turned out to be inappropriately included. An informed guess is that 88 to 94 per cent of true eligibles were finally interviewed.

The term *men* is used in the paragraph above rather than *men and women* because married academic women cannot be responsive to offers unless their husbands are simultaneously mobile and willing and able to move to the same place. As a matter of fact, of course, a kind of obverse is true in overwhelming fashion: married academic women are virilocal. If married to other academics, they seek employment in the institutions or areas where their husbands take jobs. If married to nonacademics, they seek any academic employment they can get within striking distance. These facts are reflected in their much lower mobility and mobility potential: although the faculties of the institutions in this survey included seventy-four women (10.4 per cent of the total) only three were eligible for interview (2.1 per cent of the potentially mobile). Further, all three were unmarried. Some job immobility on the part of academic females is also probably accounted for by sex discrimination.

Making contact with the subjects was usually not difficult and my request for an interview was typically received graciously. As a rule my explanation of the study over the telephone was brief; in the respondent's office I established initial rapport through introducing it at greater length. Once committed to being interviewed in this way, most respondents spoke freely and answered my questions fully and, I believe, frankly.

I used a tape recorder in almost all interviews. Considerable editing must be done, however, before taped material is fit to print, because the spoken language is not the same as the written one. Literal quotation of conversation is frequently unreadable and sometimes unintelligible, and the matter does not seem to be much affected by education or social station. The reader should understand, therefore, that while I hold all material quoted in the following pages to be accurately quoted, I have edited it somewhat for grammar and legibility, and the quotations are not, in most instances, *exactly* what the respondents said. In addition, throughout the interviews, respondents made constant references to their own schools and to other institutions in ways which would permit the knowledgeable reader to identify at least the institutional source of the quotation if not the faculty member quoted.

I have, therefore, used two devices to insure institutional and individual anonymity. First, throughout the quoted interview material, respondents' professional affiliations have been changed so that references made, let us say, to physics, appear as references to some other natural science or, in some cases, to a different subject area entirely. Second, throughout the quoted material, all references to the institution employing the faculty member at the time he was interviewed are given as Shadyside College and all references to the institution proffering him a position or with which he was negotiating are given as Fairlawn College. When institutions are mentioned by real name in the quoted material they either are not relevant to individual or institutional identification or have been changed to the names of similar actual schools. Thus the statement "He was a man I knew in graduate school at Harvard" may be rendered ". . . at Yale" or, simply, ". . . in graduate school." These conventions have been applied throughout and no material otherwise so idiosyncratic as to permit identification has been quoted without permission of the interviewee. At the same time the anonymity devices have been employed in such ways as not to distort the meaning or significance of the quoted material. I have not used quotations which did not prove amenable to this form of disguise or quotations from the several persons who asked not to be quoted.

What Is a College?

Social Structure of the College

This book has a double audience in mind: the academic public, which may be supposed already to be familiar with much of the ground here covered, and the nonacademic public for which no such supposition may be made. For those unfamiliar with the way liberal arts colleges work and how they go about their day-to-day affairs, a survey of the social structure and organization of the American college may prove useful.

Formal Authority and Control

The governing body of the college corporation is a board of regents, overseers, or trustees, who may be prominent lay members or clerics of the denomination at church-related institutions, or equally prominent "friends of the college" or alumni. This board is legally responsible for the institution's operation and financial solvency. The degree to which the board actually influences or is aware of the college's day-to-day operation varies considerably. Some boards restrict themselves to financial affairs and very long range planning. Others meet on campus with considerable frequency and regard the college administration merely as their mouthpiece to the students and faculty;

12

their agenda include such matters as student morals and complaints about food service. Most boards probably fall between these extremes, with the board largely concerning itself with matters of finance and policy but occasionally acting on operational details. Board members are most often businessmen, but professionals such as physicians, lawyers, and clerics appear frequently.

Faculty complaints concerning board interference with everyday affairs are probably usually exaggerated. Although complaints about the boards' attitudes appeared in our interviews, no respondent charged there was actual board interference in matters deemed the faculty's province. The authority of the governing boards to govern is unquestioned by our respondents, although their competence to do so is sometimes impugned. Some faculty complaints echoed Thorstein Veblen's comments on boards.

> There is, indeed, a visible reluctance on the part of these businesslike boards to expand the corporation's income for those intangible, immaterial uses for which the university is established. These uses leave no physical, tangible residue, in the way of durable goods, such as will justify the expenditure in terms of vendible property acquired; therefore, they are *prima facie* imbecile, and correspondingly distasteful, to men whose habitual occupation is with the acquisition of property. By force of the same businesslike bias the boards unavoidably incline to apportion the funds assigned for current expenses in such a way as to favour those "practical" or quasi-practical lines of instruction and academic propaganda that are presumed to heighten the business acumen of the students or to yield immediate returns in the way of a creditable publicity (1957, p. 59).

However, in only one institution in our sample were similar charges made by professors.

> Let's say, first of all, that this college has an established reputation as a conservative college. Its outlook is conservative and, by whatever means, discussions of issues on this campus are discouraged. . . . The essential problem . . . is the way it's constructed. The board of trustees, there are about thirty-five of them, are almost to a man industrialists, bankers, institutional managers. Not a great many of them are college graduates, although some are. Why they're trustees is anybody's guess. Why anybody's a trustee is anybody's guess. But they carry over from their own

private professions a kind of conviction that a college can be operated as though it were a bank or an industry, that the books must balance in some fashion. In other words, what goes out must be accounted for by what comes in. So, on the simplest level, there's an absolutely close tie-in between tuition and expenses, so that as the college's expenses have gone up, tuition has gone up and up also. . . . The only people who can really afford to come here—current costs for these kids, aside from clothing and incidentals, is $2900, that's a *lot* of money, and a great many youngsters who could use an education can't begin to touch it, and we don't have a decent scholarship program—the only people who can afford it are well-heeled, upper-middle-class families, and many of these are not, strictly speaking, interested in education. They want the status, they want the degree so they can become junior executives or the women want to get married properly.

The college president reports directly to the board and is sometimes the only institutional agent authorized to do so. Together with any vice-presidents for various affairs, or a provost, he is responsible for preparing budgets for the college, supervising the expenditure of board-approved budgets, and carrying out in detail and through delegation board-approved policies in many areas of college life (curriculum, admissions, athletics, student worship, and so on). The president is the executive officer of the college and usually operates as the head of faculty government as well. He normally has final approval, at least formally, on faculty appointments and curriculum, policy on student discipline and requirements, and so forth, and more than one president in our sample exercises these authorities in more than merely formal ways. The president often has considerable responsibility for fund raising and always devotes much time and energy to acting as the institution's front man and ambassador to the outside world, giving speeches to civic groups and appearing as the college's first citizen on numerous ceremonial occasions both within the academic community and outside it.

Some presidents act as their own deans, recruiting faculty and dealing with them directly on matters of salary, promotion, and discipline, while others are rarely seen by working faculty members. (Indeed, some are off their campuses on institutional business more than they are present on them.) Some regard faculty members as hired hands or line employees and have little patience with their problems or urgings; others see themselves as faculty and, when possible, treat faculty members as colleagues in a shared enterprise. This is, however, not always possible, for the president is sometimes the only figure on campus who has real authority over the individual faculty member. The only real power over faculty is the power of the budget, for academic institutions have few coercive sanctions to bring to bear, and the very active market for faculty manpower of recent years has reduced what little they have. Since many academic men are unwilling or loath to exercise their freedom to take another job, however, a host of lesser sanctions are employable, and the files of the American Association of University Professors are filled with cases where both these and essentially illegitimate budget or appointive sanctions have been used. In this way, too, deans and chairmen sometimes are able to wield tyrannical authority over diffident, or immobile, faculty members. It is necessary to recognize another side to this coin, however: institutions sometimes need to have use of sanctions against faculty which they may find difficult to apply. Faculty members are too often unwilling to admit that a few of their number are flagrantly incompetent, malicious, dishonest, or mentally disturbed. Such problems are likely to end up on the president's desk and, given the absolute necessity for academic freedom for professors along with the insufficient discrimination with which demands for it are sometimes made by faculty, problems of institutional control can become very difficult indeed. Faculty members also have a general paranoid tendency toward administrative officers which is usually unnecessary as well as naive. Although the foregoing qualifications are necessary, there are altogether too many instances of continuing misuse of administrative authority and position, as the AAUP reports show, to permit us realistically to expect much overall improvement in communication between the two academic classes.

What role the president plays in a particular institution at a particular time is not solely a matter of his own choosing. Roles are always reciprocal, and, while the presidency is always in some degree a leadership role for the institution, it always involves a high degree of coordinating activities as well. The president is not a free agent, able to work his will by command, and the degree of individual leadership and direction he is able to provide is, in part, a function not of his personality and desires but of faculty cooperation and of his ability to harness the energies and acquiescence of his hierarchical subordinates, as well as of extrainstitutional figures such as the board, influential alumni, or donors. It seems reasonable to suppose that the processes of institutional metabolism demand emphasis on leadership roles at one period and on coordinating roles at another. A college in intellectual—and perhaps financial—receivership may require a strong president to put things in order through example and tight control. That same institution some years later, however, once more back on its feet and operating smoothly, may find correctly that the same president is intolerably dictatorial and interfering in matters more properly left in the hands of faculty or others. From the institutional point of view, matching the requirements of the college with the capacities of the president is a critical problem. It is not assisted by the faculty who rarely recognize the need for authority over them. A competent faculty, devoted to their jobs and intelligently aware of institutional needs, can, with a few campus statesmen among them to provide leadership, adjudication, and coordination with administration, be trusted to run the place themselves in great degree. An incompetent or parochial faculty cannot, although they may seldom be expected to recognize either the condition or the reasons for it.

The dean, like the president, has multiple roles and, also like the president, he must react to power both above and below him. He is the senior faculty member in the college, although he seldom teaches. Presidents are sometimes not academics; deans are always former faculty members. The areas of the dean's authority almost universally include curriculum and degree requirements, student discipline and allied matters (usually handled through subsidiary officers such as the dean of students), and matters of faculty personnel, welfare, and assignment. The dean is far more centrally concerned with the academic or teaching operation of the institution than is the president, who is more apt to center his activities in finances and public relations. The dean is usually the high administrator best known to the faculty. In some cases he may be responsible for faculty appointments and discharges, and he is commonly, although not universally, involved in raises and promotions and faculty discipline when required. The reciprocity between his role and the president's is considerable; those executive functions which the president, from inclination or custom, does not exercise, the dean does. Since his role is so greatly defined by the extension and limits of the president's role, the duties of the office vary more considerably among different institutions than do those of the presidency.

One of the dean's principal duties in most colleges is the supervision of the teaching program and of most or all activities directly subsidiary to it. He is thus in continuous contact with department chairmen and, with them, he is deeply involved in budget and curricular problems, which necessarily involve him equally deeply with faculty. Depending on the strengths and inclinations of the president and of the various chairmen, he may act over faculty members with nearly total authority or appear to them as a rather distant figure who merely ratifies departmental decisions and requests. It is not unusual to find both aspects of the deanship in operation simultaneously at the same institution, because a wise dean does not interfere much with a strong department which is doing its job while he more or less runs the weaker ones himself. University deans are frequently somewhat obscure figures while departmental faculties and chairmen occupy the foreground of institutional action. In smaller colleges the dean is more important, for the task of the college is less specialized, less esoteric, and more subject to effective central control. Regarding labor market phenomena, many respondents reported that all negotiations were carried on with the dean, and it is not unusual for deans to act as chairmen for their departments in the recruitment and hiring process. Nor is this resented by faculty members. Comments in interviews indicate this is the dean's expected and accepted role. Deans almost invariably have veto power over prospective recruits and frequently select them themselves, sometimes traveling about the country on recruiting trips to do so. (This function is sometimes performed by the president as well.) In many respects the role of the dean in the smaller college is similar to that of the chairman of the large and prestigious university department except that the college dean (unless the president preempts it) exercises greater discretionary influence, not having to worry so much about a faculty prestige order which is noninstitutional in locus.

As in universities, the lowest level of academic organization in the college is the department headed by a faculty chairman or head. In universities the chairmanship is sometimes a position of great influence; in the small colleges it typically is not and is often described as consisting largely of paper shuffling, that is, of the essentially clerical and coordinative labor of working out faculty class schedules, ordering supplies, keeping student records, arranging for examinations, and so on. Where this is the case the dean will be found to be exercising executive influence in the department. In this arrangement, the chairmanship carries with it little power but often has a measure of prestige which gives its incumbent some weight in faculty affairs and acts as an attraction to the position.

The department, of course, is the basic unit of affiliation for academic men everywhere (some professional schools excepted) and, while emotional and professional identification with the department is less strong in small colleges than it is in universities (where professors may experience little sense of belonging to the parent institution at all), it remains their basic allegiance. Departmental sizes in the colleges of our sample range from one or two persons to twenty-five. (Large university departments may number over two hundred.) Feelings of attachment to the department as an academic unit probably have something to do with size, for the larger the department, the greater the proportion of one's social, emotional, and work requirements which may be met within its confines. Thus, in colleges where average departmental sizes are around five or six, greater attachment to the college itself is to be expected among faculty members than at a university since most faculty must go beyond the limits of their departmental colleagues for friendships and social and professional interactions and since the department is less an operating agency of the college than a convenience for classifying the subject matter offered in the catalogue and the classroom.

In the university the department is the embodiment of the professional discipline and represents a total work unit. In the college it is a teaching instrument and the task its faculty define for it is deeply involved with its classes and its students. The total work unit, in their view, is the institution. Departmentalization, however, creates a sense of close identification with students who have chosen to major or minor in the department's teaching area, and competition among departments for brighter students is keen. Competition among university departments is apt to center around the distribution of funds. In colleges, where the departments have few sources of outside or extrainstitutional power and the dean correspondingly represents a larger figure and controls fiscal distribution himself, funds are apt to be tied closely to student load and presumed teaching performance. The recruitment of capable students as majors and their postgraduate careers, particularly in graduate and professional schools where the departmental contribution to their growth may be assumed, therefore become of great interest to departmental faculty members.

The individual faculty member has little authority over institutional policy and operation. He votes at faculty meetings on those issues which the administration sees fit to bring before the faculty, but it is not uncommon for such expressions of opinion legally to be "for information only" and not considered binding by the administration. The faculty does, as a rule, determine the curriculum, and it retains its ancient power to recommend candidates for degrees, although the latter function is, in some cases, actually performed by the dean. Within the department the faculty member usually has the right to decide what classes he will teach and what texts he will use, and he normally has considerable freedom in the classroom. He may or may not be consulted in the selection or removal of his chairman, and he usually has little to say with regard to the assignment of classrooms or teaching hours except as may be informally arranged with the chairman.

An exception to this generalization is the matter of committee responsibility, particularly with regard to student affairs, where the faculty members of the committee may have in fact what amounts to absolute authority. It is probably significant that both individual and collective faculty autonomy seem to increase proportionately to the distance or removal of their concerns from questions of what to do and how to pay for it and the proximity of those concerns to how to accomplish some end or activity already decided on. Thus, the report of a faculty committee calling for the establishment of a college-owned bookstore, complete with suggested alternative sites and estimates of conversion costs may, although unanimously endorsed by the faculty, languish for years, while faculty committee decisions on whether the religious requirement shall be satisfied by one or two courses in biblical history plus attendance at chapel can be expected to be implemented instantaneously. It is always possible for faculty members individually or collectively to make recommendations as to appointments, promotions, and institutional policy or operation, but the final authority over such matters rests elsewhere. Even in highly democratized institutions with committees which review personnel recommendations, the veto of which is tantamount to refusal, the power to appoint or refuse remains in the hands, finally, of the president and is subject to the approval of the board.

It would be a mistake to conclude, however, that the small college is a tyranny and the faculty member there a helpless pawn. The possibility for tyranny is always present, of course, as it is in any structure where all authority is vested at the top and where no legal specification of the authorities and rights of subordinate offices exists. Some colleges do have constitutions defining rights and obligations of faculty members (and sometimes of students) to which their boards have subscribed; others do not. It is doubtful that observable differences in treatment of faculty could be found to distinguish them. Good colleges treat their faculties and students well, bad colleges treat them badly, and formal statements of constitutional authority are not apt to be the characteristic distinguishing them. In general it is probably fair to say that the greater the actual authority exerted over faculty by administration, the poorer the faculty and, hence, the weaker or lower in quality the school. Really competent scholars who are also competent teachers can usually leave one position for another and, thus, remove themselves from arbitrary or tyrannical authority. The competent administrator recognizes this fact of academic life, and, if he is sophisticated, recognizes also that his own ability to do his job well is dependent on the quality of his faculty. An academic institution is not an army, in other words, and, if possible, should not be run like one. Sometimes, however, it is not possible. When that occurs it may be concluded that the institution is probably not performing well the function for which it exists, having failed to attract, or having driven out, the better qualified (and, hence, most mobile) teachers. But matters are rarely that simple. While it is probably true that administrative incompetence or tyranny results in a Darwinian selection of the less fit among the faculty remaining in an institution, it must also be recognized that, among the lesser colleges of the nation, there exist what appear to be a good many schools the administrations or boards of which do not wish to strive for academic excellence as their primary goal. Many regard their first imperative as conformity with religious or even political orthodoxy, and the community service ethic of some is easily translatable into a slavish worship of the local status quo. "Education for life" dogmas in some teacher-training curricula are interpreted to mean giving the students what the chamber of commerce wants them to hear and, under such conditions, faculty devoted to the pursuit of intellectual superiority may be neither desired nor retained. That administration in such institutions truly may not perceive the distinction between their goals and academic excellence does not affect the outcome, it only confuses the matter.

Faculty Government

Our discussion of the social organization of the college has turned, as any such discussion necessarily must, to considerations of power within the college, and its sources. These latter are diffuse and will be described at various places as we proceed, but it is useful at this point to lay to rest a pleasant myth: the belief of many faculty members that they are self-governing and that the faculty government has power. All academic institutions except the most unabashedly tyrannical have some form of faculty government. Such structures are typically charged with determination of curriculum, degree requirements, committee structure, grading, standards of scholarship, and so on. Their authorizations, in other words, principally concern students. This is, indeed, a form of power, but it is not the power of self-determination, and it is amazing how rarely this distinction is enunciated. In most colleges, almost all authority to finally determine matters pertaining to the faculty lies with the board, president, and dean and not with the faculty themselves. Real power in academic institutions is the power over budget, for budget decisions determine who is to be hired and who is not and what he will be paid, what programs will be encouraged or shut off from further support, and what lines of endeavor will be rewarded. Perhaps only second in influence to the power over budget is the power to allocate time and space, and the authority to make these decisions also lies outside faculty purview since class loads, research leaves and offices, extra-classroom assignments, and so on are all administrative decisions. What classes an instructor teaches are usually decided within the department in discussions between him and the chairman. The normal load for the college, however, is again a budget matter, and permission for him to depart from it may require presidential approval. Even the sabbatical leave is almost universally considered a privilege rather than a right, and is not infrequently hedged with restrictions which demand that the instructor must justify the leave in terms of service to the college or to his field before it will be granted and that he will return to the institution for a year or two after the leave. A faculty perquisites committee may recommend the granting or withholding of the leave, but the authority to do so is the president's. (Which is not to say that faculty agencies may not influence administrative decision a great deal.)

The pertinent point is that the real power of faculty government is over students, and much of its organization and activity is directed toward students. Most faculty government organizations also have the statutory right to advise the president and to make recommendations to him and requests of him. In many instances, of course, such recommendations or requests are given every consideration and are frequently granted automatically so that certain of the president's powers may be said to have come to the faculty de facto if not de jure. But de facto delegated authority, or influence, is not real power, for it may always be withheld, and changes in personnel at either end of the transaction may disturb its allocation. Power, in the lexicon of sociology, is the ability to control or determine the activities of another, whether legitimately or illegitimately, and the power of the faculty over its own affairs exists either as a reciprocal from an administration which respects or fears its faculty or as an administrative loan made for convenience but which might, sometime, be called due.

It should be noted, however, that regardless of the statutes or articles of incorporation under which an institution operates, all colleges are social systems and can only be fully understood as such. That a president has the statutory authority to be a tyrant does not mean that he will be one or even that he could exercise the authority that is legally his if he so desired. Strong presidents can be strong only if they are backed by boards which are supportive or indifferent, which means boards suspicious of or hostile to the faculty or, for one reason or another, enamored of the president. A president who has difficulty securing the backing of his board may find his power to influence affairs diminished or even given over to the faculty, the college constitution notwithstanding. Faculties, likewise, have a certain ineradicable minimum of influence simply because they are necessary for the institution to operate and, acting in concert, faculty members may attain a great deal of delegated authority from their administrations. Thus, while a conflict model is a useful one for understanding much which occurs within a college simply because there is likely to be so much conflict within them, it is conflict within the confines of a social system, which means an unstable equilibrium of mutual and reciprocal needs, interests, and accommodations. Like workers and management in industry, the interests of all parties in the system are neither entirely coincidental nor mutually exclusive, and each is necessary to the other. The genius of successful college administration lies in the adjudication of conflict about divergent interests and the promotion of mutual cooperation in pursuit of shared goals.

 If we exclude from consideration for the moment the influence of administration and direct our attention only to faculty government as such, we may observe that even within the domain of the faculty the range seems to run from oligarchy to anarchy and that while a more or less democratic model seems to be the norm, too much democracy is sometimes as bad as too little. At the institutions in the sample, considerable faculty self-governance is the rule, as must be the case in schools of better quality. In most of them, however, respondents complained mightily of the costs in time that such self-direction imposes and, indeed, for some men, committee burdens are staggering. While such complaints are standard throughout academic life in the United States, they may be particularly common in high quality liberal arts colleges where constant concern with students and their needs, and with curriculum, leads to constant dissatisfaction with the status quo and constant experimentation with "better ways of doing it." When these dissatisfactions and experiments concern only one man and his own classes, they involve no extra work for anyone but himself and, perhaps, his students. But when they will affect graduation requirements or plans of study or the budget, they are likely to become matters of sometimes endless committee study, recommendation, and debate. And it is in this regard that too much democracy may be as bad for a faculty's welfare as too little, for working democracy assumes the intelligent concern of the participating voter and implicitly as sumes, furthermore, that his concern and his vote will be directed to the welfare of the society or community of which he is a part rather than to his own self-interest. The degree to which real faculty democracy works for the benefit of the college, then, becomes a function of the vision and personalities of faculty members. A faculty composed of relatively strong men, professionally competent, secure in their positions and devoted to the college, may be better suited to its governance than their board. A relatively weak faculty, composed in significant part of less professionally competent and less secure individuals, is less likely to adopt necessary changes with their risks and to seek instead to maintain forever the status quo. The result, if democracy is truly practiced, is to hold everyone's standards and practice to that tolerable by the weakest members. Such behaviors are particularly devastating among hiring and promotion committees which then act to exclude the very personnel the college should be seeking. Self-perpetuation of incompetence is a standing danger in faculty self-governance.

Institutional Roles and Statuses

Social stratification occurs in every society. An obvious source of stratification in a college faculty is the structure of academic rank. The four ranks are firmly institutionalized in American academic life and everywhere are associated with differential, although frequently overlapping, pay scales and prestige. It is clearly better to be a full professor than an instructor or assistant professor. However, it is also necessary to recognize that rank has little material significance at the liberal arts college. As in the universities, promotions are largely status symbols and, while generally not unconnected with salary, do not by any means have a direct and firm connection with it either. In many colleges it is the practice, in effect, to guarantee a faculty member a continuous salary progression as long as his work is satisfactory, regardless of rank, the assumption being that before he absolutely runs off the pay scale for his present rank he will be promoted. The fact that scales for ranks frequently have a considerable overlap—sometimes more than 50 per cent—makes this possible.

Instructor is the lowest academic rank and the first step on the academic ladder. Among major universities it has been the practice for a decade to use this rank mostly for men who have not yet ac-

quired the Ph.D. but who teach full time as regular members of the
faculty. While still not so common in the colleges as in the universities,
this usage is now rather widely adopted. In most colleges most assistant
professors are young men or women beginning their professional careers with the doctoral degree. The associate professorship is normally
given after four to seven years of service and represents recognition by
the college of fully mature professional commitment and accomplishment. It usually represents a commitment by the institution to permanent appointment of the individual, because it is almost invariably
accompanied by the granting of tenure. In most colleges, eventual promotion to full professor is probably guaranteed once the individual has
been made associate, endurance and good behavior being all that will
finally be required to assure the transition. Because rank is primarily
symbolic, however (increasing rank carries with it neither increase in
authority nor change of job as in industry), the rapidity with which
the transition from associate to full professor is made has considerable
impact on status in the institution and on self-image. It is one matter
to be promoted to the final rank after only three or four years' tenure
as associate professor. It is quite another to mark time for twenty years,
receiving the promotion only the year before retirement. Rank is probably most important to faculty members who lack professionally acquired symbols of status to represent success, perhaps because professional (that is, extrainstitutional) rewards are likely to guarantee
satisfactory escalation in rank. High rank is meaningful in the eyes of
students (and in the smaller colleges, they know about it), and conveys
a sense among colleagues of arrival and acceptance. It is loosely correlated with salary and conveys a somewhat nebulous prestige but carries with it little in the way of access to the world's goods. Much of its
symbolic reward can be enhanced or spoiled by the manner in which
it is given.

More important than rank in determining social stratification
on the campus is a matter which can be called institutional personality
and which operates in such a way as to confer local, or institutional,
status on individuals. More than universities, liberal arts colleges have
personalities—characteristic values and emphases—of their own. Among
the eleven sampled for this study, startling differences were immediately visible. One campus was characterized by students strolling on
the lawns playing musical instruments and a casual attitude among

the faculty apt to express itself in long coffees in the union and frequent participation in student activities and outdoor functions. Another— of equally high student quality—had a studious atmosphere among both faculty and student body best exemplified by empty lawns and busy libraries and laboratories. These personalities express themselves in stratification by throwing up for reward in institutional prestige certain roles and character types for faculty members to play: research man or dedicated scholar, poet, beatnik, student's man (advocate against authority), dilettante, political activist, intellectual sophisticate, and so on. Institutions which encourage and reward involvement in student activities and teaching convey prestige on men defined by students as exciting classroom personalities and "interested in us." Campuses where an apprentice relationship with faculty is encouraged, on the other hand, are more likely to grant prestige not to teachers who are "merely" popular but to those whose patronage guarantees success in graduate or professional school. In some colleges, faculty prestige is assured by active involvement in institutional politics; in others it is refused to "committee bureaucrats who waste their time in busywork instead of devoting it to their research or teaching."

The role of the committee in faculty politics and in the prestige order on the campus deserves special note. All faculties have governments and all faculty governments are structured around committees, even in those institutions small enough, and with faculties careless enough of their own time, to try to accomplish most of their business as a committee of the whole. There are, typically, one or two committees which, because of their closeness to the administration, involvement in policy matters, or influence on the dean or president (or even, on rare occasions, on the board), are perceived by the faculty in general as important and powerful. Committees believed to be powerful are automatically prestigious, and election or appointment to one is viewed as both reflecting and conveying personal prestige to the nominated individual. Indeed in some institutions it is possible to identify members of the faculty with local prestige simply by checking off past and present committee assignments. Perhaps the height of prestige is conveyed by special appointment to presidential ad hoc advisory committees; lowest, but still on the scale, by colleague election to committees which perform routine administrative tasks such as student admissions. Persons who are never on committees are either those universally regarded as incompetents or fools or else individuals of such reputation as to guarantee them freedom from committee chores.

The reason committees are important in the stratification of the campus is that they do influence local politics and are, thus, purveyors of institutional power. To sit on the president's advisory committee is to have some small hand in determining the direction and quality of college life and, thus, to assist in directing one's own future. Opportunities are offered to do favors for a friend or a friendly department or to ward off unfavorable alternatives, and, for those members of the faculty whose futures for one reason or another are intimately tied to the particular institution, what goes on in committees and who is permitted to sit on them thus becomes a matter of some importance. For some few, indeed (those without possible extrainstitutional futures), committee assignments may represent extreme importance as one of the few measures of their standing with their colleagues and as rare opportunities to influence their own fates. Under these circumstances it is not surprising that the apparatus of faculty government is apt to be perceived by most faculty members as having more significance, more real power, than it does, and that presidential "interference" with faculty recommendations (that is, failure to adopt them) will be more bitterly resented than the situation often warrants. The fact that the president, as budget officer of the college, will somehow have to find money to pay for what he may regard as a harebrained scheme with little chance of success seems often to the faculty member to be a poor excuse for not adopting an exciting new experiment in instruction or institutional direction.

A second source of local prestige in the liberal arts college, although not normally in the university, is teaching. The colleges are teaching institutions and perceive themselves as such, and this definition of their function is shared by their faculties. A man who becomes known as an interesting or exciting teacher among his students will rapidly be so identified by his colleagues, for faculty-student relations are close in small colleges and students quickly spread the word of men to seek out or avoid in the classroom. In large universities excessive popularity with students is a dubious virtue because it is presumed to suggest clowning, striving for popular appeal at the sacrifice of intellectual content in instruction, or, at best, excessive attention to teaching at the expense of research diligence. This is not so in the small college.

Experienced college teachers are able to distinguish between those of their colleagues who are popular because they have something to say and an appealing manner in which to say it and those who are merely seeking student approval. In the first place, small college students are apt to be better and better prepared and more critical of their instruction than the massive and amorphous student bodies of the universities. In the second place, their instructors know them better and can make more discriminating judgments concerning student reports. Third, and perhaps most important, in a faculty of perhaps a hundred, inevitably one man's students become another's and permit the second to observe what the first has taught them. Thus, an individual who really is an interesting and successful teacher is apt to become identified as such and, because of the values of the college, is likely to be rewarded for it. The system actually does reward good teaching for two reasons or in two ways. First, in most liberal arts colleges, the institutions mean it—good instruction is their job and their reason for existence and everyone involved agrees on the matter. (Again unlike the university where much of the attention paid to undergraduate instruction is ritual lip service.) Second, in the small college word gets around rapidly among the students so that an exciting new course or instructor is likely to be identifiable by rising enrollments, changes of major, student coteries, and so on. This, in turn, reflects credit on the department or chairman astute enough to initiate the program or appointment and provides a base to build on for further program which, in turn, means further expansion, and increased budget. The prestige of being a successful teacher is desirable to the individual faculty member because it conveys emotional rewards from students and colleagues alike and because it is likely to be recognized by administration in the form of promotion, salary, and emoluments. The immediacy and magnitude of the reward may, it is true, lag somewhat behind what might be expected from reading the college public relations organ, but in most institutions there is a connection and the faculty recognizes its existence.

Extralocal Influences

Status on the college campus has significant other components which are essentially extrainstitutional or, at least, off-campus. Clearly the most important among these is disciplinary prestige, that is, the status conveyed to an individual by his professional reputation in his academic discipline. Disciplinary prestige is largely acquired by the production and publication of research or scholarly work but has as important subcomponents the possession of the right connections, that is, of friends powerful or influential in the affairs of the disciplinary professional organizations and of contacts or wide acquaintance with other scholars in the same fields and, where relevant, in government agencies and foundation bureaucracies. The importance to the individual of professional reputation is twofold: It promotes his scholarly work by making accessible research and travel monies and invitations to give papers at scholarly meetings or to contribute to the anthologies of others, and it frees him from total dependence for the determination of his future on the institution where he happens to be teaching. It has been remarked that mobility is the academic man's substitute for the strike; if he does not like it where he is, he moves elsewhere—if he is able to move, that is, if he is able to secure the offer of a position at least equally attractive from another institution. The significance of a wide professional reputation is obvious: the more widely a man is known as a desirable acquisition, as a good man in his field, the more easily he can set in motion a network of contacts for job seeking and the more attractive he will appear to institutional recruiters. From the perspective of the individual, the principal significance of disciplinary prestige is that it is extralocal: it cannot be significantly influenced by anything the institution does or fails to do, as it is based entirely on factors beyond institutional control, and, while it does not convey immunity from local social controls or even from harassment, it permits the individual to escape them if he so desires.

The possession of disciplinary prestige conveys status on the college campus because it is real; all academic men, in colleges and in universities, share a value structure in which scholarship is respected, if not universally practiced. The prestigious individual also possesses symbols of his success in the commonly valued enterprise, and the symbols are likely to stand for real rewards. Behind and beneath these more obvious sources of status there probably always stands to some degree the knowledge that the individual need not be "caught" if things go sour where he is. Disciplinary prestige, in other words, conveys and connotes freedom, and freedom to determine one's own conditions of work is always mentioned in surveys of academics as being among the most important characteristics of the enterprise.

The local status of the individual with disciplinary prestige is also enhanced by what he does, or is presumed to do, for the college. His presence there is presumed to serve notice on other scholars of similar quality that the institution is not only intellectually respectable but indeed admirable, a place, in other words, which might be suited to themselves. He is thought to be an ornament. But his ornamental value is, or should be, secondary. Through his contacts in his field he should be able to secure placement for the college's graduates in prestigious graduate and professional schools and to advise them knowledgeably concerning graduate applications. He also should be useful in recruiting younger men who will, presumably, be attracted there by his presence; his work, in addition to spreading the college's fame, should also attract research support and grants for student aid and equipment. This latter is no small item in this day of the technological revolution in teaching and research in many fields of academic endeavor. Few private colleges have inexhaustible funds and many, even of very high quality, must watch their budgets closely. But, pushed by the public institutions which have had good fortune in access to the public purse, they must keep up in their teaching with the latest advances which, in the sciences for example, often means heavy investment in equipment. Private foundations and the federal government have recognized these problems, and there are available to institutions a variety of grant programs which assist them in the purchase of such hardware as computers or accelerators, but the college must be able to demonstrate that it can use them constructively. To do this, it must have people on its faculty who can be shown to be competent to do the job, and the possession of a few "name scholars" in the appropriate fields is at least believed to be valuable in convincing granting agencies that their investment will not be wasted.

The reasons that disciplinary prestige is convertible to institutional prestige thus become obvious. What is not so obvious, and the source of one of the private college's most pervasive problems, is that such prestige not only is readily convertible, but is more desirable and significant to many academic men than anything the institution can offer. It supersedes institutional prestige entirely since the institution must reward the disciplinarily prestigious individual in order to keep him, yet it has little in the way of unique reward to offer. Whatever it can do for him, presumably, another can do equally well if not better. Local or institutional status thus becomes a sort of counterfeit coin or, at least, one struck from base metal and loses much of its value to reward or punish. In this way institutional loyalty, sentimental attachment to Old Shadyside, may be the only hold Shadyside retains on the individual and, to the degree that he has been thoroughly professionalized, he has been trained to ignore such attachments or not to let them become fixed in the first place.

Another source of higher than average status on the campus is what faculty members usually refer to as "outside money," that is, support from noninstitutional sources whether or not incorporated in the college budget. This special standing may accrue to either departments or individuals. The scientist who is able to secure long-term grants for the support of his research, perhaps complete with secretarial and laboratory assistance, or the department which manages to fund some of its operations or equipment needs through foundation, industrial, or government largesse is perceived to have gained some freedom from institutional control thereby. Being able to "budget oneself," in other words, conveys status.

Stratification on the campus is, in sum, affected by two kinds of phenomena—power, which is desired because it permits men more effectively to control their own destinies, and professional considerations such as teaching ability, rank, and professional reputation. "Position" of certain kinds sometimes intrudes itself on the ordering because it conveys power or is presumed to do so, although the access of the incumbent to such power may be regarded as illegitimate. But discussions of theoretical possibilities, and the structural means to high status present a distorted view of the way in which the stratification system actually works. A generalized description of the prestige structure probably provides a picture more typical.

In general, on most private college campuses, the faculty members with highest prestige will be older full professors with some professional reputation in their disciplines for scholarly activity or research whose activities have also fitted into the model provided by their institution's personality. It is rare for a man who is scorned by his students to have high status among his faculty colleagues. The most prestigious individuals among the faculty are likely to be full professors who have gained additional stature as a result of outside money or proximity to institutional power from the administration, board, or alumni. Middling positions of prestige will be held by "hotshot young research men" of senior rank and by other full and associate professors or senior assistant professors who have been members of the faculty for several years and have status as a result of varying mixtures of disciplinary prestige, teaching popularity, and faculty politics. Lowest status rankings will be occupied by older men kept permanently as associate or assistant professors and by youngsters so recently out of graduate school they have not had time to establish either professional or institutional reputations. The status structure of the typical private college is essentially a benign one. There are feuds among the faculty, but rarely does the "struggle" for power or preferment become so desperate as to ruin careers or personalities. High status is there to be had for any who choose to seek it, and the avenues for its attainment are broad and most of them are more or less intrainstitutional, which means they are within the grasp of most faculty members. While in many colleges highest prestige probably accrues only to men who are professionally active in their fields, what by university standards would be relatively moderate professional activity goes a long way at Shadyside. The fact that teaching and amicable relations with students is highly valued permits men of even very modest professional attainment to become successful simply because good or successful teaching is difficult to define (unlike poor teaching which becomes known very quickly), and success in pleasing students may result from widely disparate classroom styles. Thus, almost anyone whose needs for status in the eyes of his colleagues are modest may expect to have them fulfilled within the context of the private college and may look forward with reasonable assurance to retirement with the comforting expectations that he will be deemed to have served well and will be missed. There are many jobs and many institutional structures which offer less.

Social Organization

No discussion of the social organization of the American liberal arts college can be complete without recognition that the institution, if it is of any quality at all, is Janus-faced. In many respects the colleges exist as a race apart, for themselves and their own constituencies, loyal to their traditions, and independent of the forces that shape—or rack—the multiversities. But in one great way they are schizophrenic, bifurcated, and torn within themselves by problems not of their own making but rather a result of the structure of higher education in the United States itself. That bifurcation is that connoted by the century long controversy which goes under the inaccurate label *teaching versus research*. This label is inaccurate because, while the controversy takes shape in arguments of that form, the structural problem which lies behind it is in the nature of the academic profession in America. Fundamentally the problem is that our colleges and universities are organized to employ members of a profession—college teaching—which does not exist. Due to accidents of scientific and intellectual history, what does exist, and what in the decades since World War II has come into ever greater prominence in higher education, is a variety of professions rooted in the various scholarly disciplines. The immense technical specialization imposed on American scholars by the national adoption in the last century of the German institutional model has determined that they will not be college teachers but, rather, teachers of some specialty. This, in turn, means that their preparation is directed at mastery of the subject matter of that specialty and, with the development of specialist professional organizations and the increasing research emphasis which subject matter specialization necessarily imposes on its practitioners, college teachers of the subject become, willy-nilly, not just teachers of physics but physicists. (Certainly that is what they will be trained for in the graduate schools.) This is not, of course, as is sometimes foolishly suggested, the result of some great plot among the graduate schools to swallow liberal education. Nor is it some mechanic of history which, by recognizing, we can find the levers for and turn to another direction; it is not a matter which is much amenable to directed change. The trend toward specialization in subject matter came about in this country as a result of the adoption of the German university model, true, but the reasons this model rather than another was adopted when we built our universities in the nineteenth century were cultural. The United States was and is an industrialized, materialistic, pragmatic national culture. The Greek academy was not suited to our national needs; the nineteenth century German university was and probably remains so. The ideal of the academy is still enshrined in our notions of the liberal arts, and it has enriched our higher education beyond calculation. But structurally the academic professions are the outgrowths of the library and the laboratory, not of the forum, and where the academies and seminaries of the early nineteenth century taught rhetoric and logic, our colleges and universities today are, like it or not, essentially vocational institutions. Disciplinary specialization is structured into American higher education and probably cannot be removed by any means now known for good and sufficient reason: it does something which our culture believes needs doing and for which we have found no substitute. Americans, like other western European cultures, are heirs of the Enlightenment—positivist and rationalist. We believe the world can be manipulated, and we have sought and found the means of attempting it. Our educational system transmits those means. And while it is true that some students are raising profound questions as to whether such orientations should be continued, they are a minority and, since their thrust is countercultural, it will probably be unsuccessful in terms of "turning higher education around."

In graduate school, which, in the United States, is the accepted preparation for college teaching, men are trained to be specialists in their respective fields. This specialization necessarily implies the demand for carrying investigation of those fields ever further, for pushing back the frontiers of the known. Scholarly research, in other words, is an inevitable consequence of the commitment to specialization, for the discipline if not for every individual within it. As the products of our graduate schools, every academic in the United States recognizes in one way or another this authority of the disciplines: activity in one's field is the reason for existence; the colleges exist to teach the disciplines. With the further development of the disciplinary organizations, further allegiance to the discipline is fostered and, finally, with the explosion of research emphasis in higher education since World War II, the great rewards of fame and material fortune have accrued almost entirely to disciplinary rather than to institutional activity and loyalty. It is possible for the American academic today to choose from two quite different career lines while still remaining in academics and still being popularly labeled a college teacher. (He is more likely to label himself a chemist or a classicist.) He can choose a career essentially in the discipline, pursuing as his major goals research or scholarship while teaching in one institution or another as such affiliation advances his research interests or professional career as a chemist or a classicist.

Or he can choose to teach his field while remaining otherwise relatively inactive in it, which much more greatly commits him to a career within a single institution, or a very few of them, and keeps him out of the major universities where "teachers" are expected primarily to be research men. But even with this second choice his training holds him true: having selected another road for himself, he recognizes and honors the scholars in his field as those who really count in it.

Almost all academic men support themselves by teaching. Very few, even in the greatest universities, are employed solely for research activities. But there is, thus, built into the structure of academic life a dualism which becomes problematic in the private colleges which exist only for undergraduate instruction. The colleges are teaching institutions and the men who staff them do so, by and large, because they want to teach. Yet the professional rewards of their fields are gained by research activity, and the colleges, in order to secure trained personnel, have had to adopt the disciplinary reward structure. It is impossible for an institution of quality to decide it will not reward scholarly activity in order to secure a greater commitment to teaching from its staff. It must reward it in order to get and hold a staff of competence in the first place, and it must have such a staff in order to perform its function: the transmission of accurate, up-to-date information and skills to its students. But this, in turn, has the effect of freeing the individual from institutional controls by taking the assignment of reward out of institutional hands. The institution has no control over the professional reputation of its members; it can only react and adjust to the demands that such a reputation places on it, for if it does not, the individual will be able to satisfy them elsewhere. Thus, to some degree (that to which he is professionalized), even the most dedicated teacher will be working for noninstitutional rewards which are defined by noninstitutional sources and for which he qualifies by noninstitutional activity, although it is the responsibility and requirement of the institution actually to bestow the rewards on him.

This ambiguous situation is nearly universal in academics, and its ambiguity is probably maximized for the faculties of the liberal arts colleges, for in such colleges, where the teaching function is the most important one the institution recognizes, the instructor is, in essence, hired to do one job (for the institution) while he must, to some degree, be selected and rewarded according to his success at another (for the discipline). The degree to which the circumstances are recognized as problematic varies among men and among institutions. The recognition is probably more common among working teachers than among administrators. (The teachers have to face almost daily decisions about the budgeting of time and energy; the administrators can either pretend there is no inconsistency or ignore the matter in the hope that it will go away.) The problem may be less painful for the college teacher than for his colleague in the university. (The college teacher came to teach and will, at least, not be punished for doing so unlike the university professor who may be.)

The reader may have noted that I have slipped from speaking of activities which are rewarded by the institution and the discipline, respectively, to talking specifically of teaching and research although it was earlier called inaccurate to speak of teaching *versus* research. The distinction is a subtle one, but it is important. Research activity has no inherent capacity which unfits one for the classroom, nor vice versa, but more important than accepting this commonsense conclusion is acknowledging that teaching *time* and research *time* are, in fact, mutually exclusive. And it is not always true, as the defenders of research in the universities are wont to say, that research activities sooner or later always transmute into teaching. Many academic men have teaching specialties rather different from their research interests and even if the two are similar, the research may be uninteresting, or irrelevant, or even unintelligible, to undergraduate students at least. Furthermore, in the small college, the teaching job does not end in the classroom. Office hours are generally kept with liberality (many faculty members express the feeling that they need, or are expected, to "keep their doors open" at all times, that is to be available to students at any time they are in their offices, and informal bull sessions with students frequently occupy much time in the library, student union, or lounges. Although student bodies and student-teacher ratios are smaller at the college than at the university, the faculty member of the college is far more surrounded by students and by concern for them than is the university faculty member. The smaller colleges do not, as a rule, except for administrators, build office buildings separate from classrooms and laboratories, and, because of space problems and burgeoning faculty size, offices are sometimes scattered haphazardly all about the campus, thus making the faculty member, as one respondent put it, "excessively accessible." But while there is almost universal complaint of lack of time for adequate classroom preparation, for reading, and for research, most college teachers seem to accept their total involvement in college and student life as a normal and acceptable condition of the job, and do not seek escape from it. Teaching is what they wanted to do, and many find rich rewards in close relationships with students and involvement in student affairs and activities. It is not unusual for warm friendships to be formed between students and faculty members, relationships which may be kept up throughout life, and many faculty are able to recall fondly the successes in the postgraduate world which generations of their students have attained.

Finally, as many men have discovered when they tried to perform really well at both activities simultaneously, good, serious teaching and good, serious research are both full-time jobs. It is difficult even to just "keep one's hand in" at one while working hard at the other, and for the liberal arts college teacher, with a three to five class load and very heavy student advising chores and committee work as well, it is next to impossible. The typical resolution is to devote full time during the regular term to teaching and institutional chores and vacations to the demands or requirements of one's discipline. This is not a poor compromise for individuals whose expectations for professional or disciplinary recognition are modest, and it is one which seems to work quite well for most liberal arts college teachers. But it is, nonetheless, fraught with frustration even for those insightful individuals who recognize the nature of the dilemma which besets them. The frustration is heightened by the habit of the institutions (a necessary one, as I have said) of paying greater lip service to teaching and institutional chores than to scholarly pursuits while nevertheless rewarding scholarly attainments more richly.

Inevitably, the bifurcation of academic life produces a similar bifurcation among the faculty. *The Academic Marketplace* (Caplow and McGee, 1958) dealt with this phenomenon attitudinally, calling attention to the existence of disciplinary and institutional *orientations* in men. Alvin Gouldner, in work published almost simultaneously, was describing academic men possessing latent identities as locals and cosmopolitans (1957, 1958). Locals are those individuals whom Caplow and I called institutionally-oriented and whom Gouldner describes as "high on loyalty to the employing organization, low on commitment to specialized role skills, and likely to use an inner reference group orientation." Cosmopolitans (the discipline-oriented) are described as being "low on loyalty to the employing organization, high on commitment to specialized role skills, and likely to use an outer reference group orientation" (Gouldner, 1957, p. 290). In a study of "Co-op College," a private liberal arts college, he was able to identify groups of cosmopolitans and locals according to these criteria and found them to be significantly differentiated from one another by a wide variety of behavior and attitudes. One of his most interesting findings is that cosmopolitans were significantly more ready than were locals to consider leaving their jobs at Co-op College for other positions. They were also more interested in research and found it of greater personal importance to them, published more, and were professionally better trained as evidenced by proportional possession of the Ph.D. degree. In more refined analysis of his data (1958), Gouldner was able to define two different types of cosmopolitans (essentially, the established at the college and the itinerant) and four of locals. It is not necessary for our purposes to distinguish among them further, or to belabor characteristics which differentiate the two major groupings; the faculty in the liberal arts college (and, probably to a lesser extent, in the university as well) reflect the duality of the structure of American higher education, some primarily identifying themselves with the institutions in which they serve and others with the academic disciplines of which they are members.

But since institutions of the high academic quality of those sampled for this study must compete on a national market for students and must demonstrate success in training those students, they inevitably commit themselves to what are, at root, disciplinary criteria of accomplishment, because institutional success in education is largely rated, by academics themselves and by the middle-class parents who send their children to such schools, according to the proportion of the college's graduates who matriculate in graduate and professional schools on completion of the baccalaureate. And since admission to graduate and professional schools is likely to be in large part a function of academic performance as an undergraduate (and of skills learned then, although perhaps demonstrated on the Graduate Record Examination), thorough training in the academic disciplines necessarily becomes a central portion of even the most liberal curriculum if the college wishes to maintain its reputation for intellectual quality. This training, in turn, can only be offered by faculty members who are themselves competent in their fields. Thus, a bias toward seeking and rewarding discipline-oriented cosmopolitans is built into the institution whether or not it recognizes it. And, while it may hold with perfect honesty that teaching is its job and students its sole concern, it is likely to be felt even by men who choose to teach there for that reason, and by the administrators who judge and reward them, that somehow the better teachers in the institutions are those who show some signs of activity in their professional associations and in disciplinary pursuits.

There are those on the faculties who rage against such views and who regard individuals or institutions espousing them as traitors to the noble cause of liberal education. But for every man who advances the cause of teaching pure and uncontaminated by research, another will ask "teach what?" and turn away in disgust at his colleague's naivete. Janus faces are thus an integral part of the structure of the liberal arts college, one turned outward toward the wider arena of the world, responding to the standards imposed by professional allegiances, the other turned inward toward the campus community and its members, concerned with the quality of life there and the enrichment of the social, psychic, and moral lives of those with whom it interacts. The tension between the two, and the sometimes contradictions, touch every aspect of the faculty job; later chapters reveal in some ways how much.

The college is a Janus in yet another, although allied, way. It has long been a part of the credo of most of them that, in addition to providing vocational or professional training and skills, they also "build character" or "promote citizenship," and it is the proud and valid boast of some that, although large proportions of their graduates do not seek further degrees, they become decent men and women and parents and pillars of their communities. It is, of course, possible that, because of their selection procedures, they take in the first place only people who are likely to live such lives, but even if this is true, the education of solid if not particularly intellectual citizens is a goal at which few would cavil. Yet the college is a gatepost to the university as well, a removed or dislocated undergraduate division in a sense, and this function all of them have always recognized. So the dualism in their natures is no new thing, no product of the postwar years or the emergence in those years of college education as standard preparatory training for ever increasing proportions of our youth. It has always been there, in this century, at least, and its novelty now is only in its intensity, and in its wider recognition.

In the colleges in our sample, this recognition is likely to appear in the form of two rather different kinds of tensions: in disputes over the place in college life and faculty activity and reward structure of teaching as opposed to research, and in the identification of faculty members with, and tensions between, Old and New Guards on the campus. The Old Guard faculty, of course, are identified with teaching and its presumed values as apart from research and disciplinary activity with which the New Guard are identified. It is worthy of note that, while the distinction between Guards was made on every campus visited during the course of this study, it was also recognized on every one that membership in one or the other of the Guards was not necessarily a function of either age or tenure at the college. In general the Old Guard are older faculty members of long association with the college while the New Guard is principally composed of younger men of more recent vintage. In almost every college, however, examples can be cited of elderly faculty members who hold the values and promote the interests of the New Guard or of new young professors who enlist in the Old Guard in their first month on campus.

The Old Guard is usually perceived by the New as conservative and resistant to necessary change while they themselves are progressive, enlightened, and the real value-bearers for the college. The New Guard is perceived by the Old, on the other hand, as radical, immature, and heedless both of the wisdom of their elders and of the dangers to the college's great tradition with which their harebrained schemes are fraught. The relation to these perceptions of the teaching-research controversy in the light of the postwar emphasis on the latter is obvious.

What is painful, of course, to true Old Guard types among the faculty is the comparison of their own biographies of promotion and salary advancement with those of the younger men they see about them and what they honestly believe to be denigration of teaching and a dismissal of students in favor of personal advancement through research. Many older men worked twenty years before earning the salary a new Ph.D. can now command upon departure from graduate school, and older men may, typically, have taught even twenty years before attaining the full professorship now often reached before the age of forty. (Most academics leave graduate school with the Ph.D. at about the age of thirty.) But the world has changed and, while the New Guard, or even the Young Turks, can intellectually comprehend that "things were tougher in the racket then," they cannot appreciate the emotional gap which separates them from the older men. They come from different worlds. (The chasm dividing them may be the experience, as teachers, of the Great Depression.)

Faculty Goals

Another facet of the research question is the attitude toward it which faculty members hold. Local demands for research productivity and other professional activity are not high. On the better campuses it is expected that faculty members will attend local professional meetings with some frequency and national organizations occasionally. Activity in local societies (for example, the state or county historical association) is welcomed and encouraged, and some writing or other productivity in one's field is expected occasionally. The typical faculty member himself has internalized these expectations and tries to "keep his hand in" or "keep some research going" most of the time, although research may often become confused in his mind with professional reading and class preparation. Having been trained in a university graduate school (not uncommonly at one of the multiversities as our data show), he is well aware of the disciplinary norms of scholarly productivity and, while he may have adjusted to the fact that he is unlikely to attain university-level scholarly output, he feels that some continuing activity is necessary to prevent himself from "going dry." For men who, for one reason or another, are relatively unproductive of scholarly work for publication or display, professional ties may be maintained, and professional skills kept sharp, by activity in the disciplinary organizations or scholarly societies.

One major selling point of the liberal arts colleges is perhaps best described as the quality of life made possible to their faculties. Among men coming to the colleges from the universities, the tranquility, leisure, fraternal acceptance, and lack of competition among colleagues which seems to typify at least the better colleges are always remarked on. This is certainly in part a result of the fact that the vast majority of any college faculty are at some level aware of sharing a common purpose with their colleagues and is probably assisted as well by the relatively small salary differentiation among them and by the certainty of eventual institutional "success" for all but a very few. The better colleges pay quite well, and, since many are located in smaller towns, living costs are often low. Many, too, have excellent fringe benefit programs for faculty members and their families, and one such informal benefit often unappreciated until experienced is that of living within the confines of an institutional community where, for example, faculty wives and children are welcomed to athletic contests, swimming pools, and libraries without fee and without an elaborate system of forms, registration, or licensing. Faculty members themselves discover that they may use the gym without bother (it is never more than a block or two away from their offices) and many schools maintain houses for rental to faculty at lower than competitive rates. Many also finance mortgages for faculty members' purchase of homes, and the fact that vacations are frequent and work pressures relatively low permits men to enjoy their leisure in ways no longer common for other Americans. Another feature of "the good life" commonly remarked by faculty members newly arrived from universities is the absolute necessity for discourse between members of the various disciplines since, in most colleges, no department is large enough for the whole of an individual's intellectual life to be lived in it. The round of daily life in the private liberal arts college retains a nineteenth century flavor often associated by the public with academics in general but today to be found only at the smaller institutions. It is, for most faculty members, a life without access to the great rewards of fame and fortune, but one in which compensation in leisure, affectivity, and the bonds of close friendships and middle-class gentility do much to close the gap.

Conflict

The Academic Marketplace remarked that conflict was endemic on the campus of the university and that few departments did not sport at least one feud—sometimes of decades' standing—which frequently was at least a contributing factor in faculty mobility. The same observation seems to be valid for the liberal arts college, although to a considerably lesser degree. A certain degree of conflict, of course, is unavoidable in any system of scarce resources where the participants have some degree of influence over resource allocation; where more than one individual or department may benefit from a particular resource assignment, competition is to be expected. Where the resources are rather highly limited—as in annual budget or student enrollments—that competition may be expected often to turn into conflict. Any social organization, of course, also experiences conflict between personalities. We are not interested in this since it is not a function of the social structure of the institution at all, although it is my impression of the liberal arts colleges that there may be less of these interpersonal antagonisms active among their faculties than may be considered normal in a university.

Several different kinds of structural conflict also occur in the college. One of these, of course, is the three-cornered tension over policy and authority among faculty, administration, and board. Due to the nature of the collegiate authority structure this seldom breaks into open battle; the faculty does recognize the authority of the administration and board to govern the college. But constant issues of will and guile arise over the propriety of a given policy or action being undertaken either with or without faculty participation and over the specific areas of action which properly belong to one or the other of the groups. The wisdom of the board is frequently questioned by the faculty, and aspersions on the integrity of the administration are not uncommon. (It is a rare president indeed who has the complete confidence of the majority of his faculty, and deans, while better known and therefore perceived as less nefarious, are nonetheless mistrusted on principle since their authority is to such a large degree delegated from the president and, therefore, fragile.)

Within the faculty itself two structural conditions exist which seem invariably to breed conflict, and a third set of tension-producing factors is associated with ideologies and personality types. What we may call structural conflicts exist to a greater or lesser degree on every campus between scientists and humanists (with the representatives of the social sciences often split between the camps) and between departmentalists and interdepartmentalists in matters of curriculum. We need not linger on the tensions between scientists and humanists; C. P. Snow (1959) has described the reasons for its existence well and it is widely known and of long standing. For our purposes it is sufficient merely to note that the training of scholars in the two areas, the vocabularies and epistemologies of the two, and the values inherent in the pursuits which constitute the two, are so radically different, and, at times, so apparently inconsistent, that it is often impossible for their representatives to understand one another or for each to appreciate the value of what the other does. More specifically structural, the institutional needs of the two fields are sufficiently different that their interests frequently collide. The laboratory sciences, for example, must be able to claim blocks of time in the class schedule in order to hold laboratory hours for their courses; two, three, and four hour blocks are not uncommon. But, in an institution of limited enrollment where laboratory science is typically required of all or most students at some stage in their careers, this may mean that these hours of the week are unavailable for use by other areas, for example English, which may also have required courses which must be taken by the same students. The English teachers, who understand intellectually why two to four hours at a time are required for chemistry laboratories, may still resent emotionally the "dictation" of their own class schedules in this way by the scientists.

While conflicts between scientists and humanists may arise over a variety of issues, those between departmentalists and interdepartmentalists tend to focus on the curriculum and related matters. We may define departmentalists as those faculty members (from any department or intellectual area) who not only regard the department as the basic unit of academic structure but regard its subject matter as unique in itself and as having, therefore, unique value. Interdepartmentalists are those who regard all knowledge as one indivisible whole, see the standard subject areas into which it is divided, and the departmental organizations which teach those areas, as matters of intellectual convenience (or inconvenience), and hold that synthesis of knowledge, rather than the mastery of specific subject matter, is the aim of teaching. The interdepartmentalists frequently opt for courses taught by men from more than one area in the belief that synthesis is thus more readily achieved. Departmentalists tend to avoid and denigrate such courses on the theory that a historian, for example, cannot teach philosophy and a theologian is incompetent to render history accurately. The conventional form in which the conflict appears is dispute over whether there shall be interdepartmental required courses. ("Great Issues," "Common Learnings," and "Man and His World" are typical titles for such courses.)

Course requirements also offer fertile ground for disagreement. How many and, more specifically, which courses should be required of all students is a matter which can occupy a faculty for a year. And if science is to be required, is it of greater value to an English major to take a history of science offered in the philosophy department or the same introductory physics offered in the physics department to a physics major? Should there be a standard social science course with a common curriculum offered by teachers from various departments, or should the student merely take an introductory course in any departmental offering which appeals to him? The course hour requirements for majors and minors, levels of instruction to be required for various matters (is a three-hour course taught on the senior level intellectually equivalent to one taught for sophomores?), and similar questions all offer fertile fields for contention. And in every confrontation the issues will be essentially similar, with departmentalists arguing the necessity for thorough grounding in specific subject matters and the interdepartmentalists equally vociferous concerning the necessity for synthesis and broadening. Humanities professors are somewhat more likely to be interdepartmentalists than scientists, but the lines are far from hard and fast. Also complicating the issue is the fact that the conflict frequently splits along the lines of locals and cosmopolitans, Old Guard and New, or teaching versus research, although representatives of any of the groups named may be on either side of the controversy at any given institution. (Locals are not necessarily interdepartmentalists.)

The final, universal feud which may be expected, from time to time, to break forth on any college campus is more a matter of personality and ideology than of institutional structure. This is the ancient conflict concerning students and their treatment, the participants in which we may speak of as democrats and authoritarians. (The selection of these names, with their inescapable value implications, is deliberate, since I have definite ideas on the matter. "Permissives" and "paternalists" might be equally descriptive, but also carry some loadings.) Some of the differences expressed in this conflict are subtle and intelligent (there really is some question, for example, about how much discretion the typical freshman is able to handle without actually causing himself problems with it) ; some, on the other hand, are stupid and crass. ("It would be bad for our image in the community if there were an antiwar demonstration; therefore, we will penalize any student group which holds a meeting without having a dean's representative present.") While there are clearly many issues of student treatment and control by the institution where intelligent and reasonable men might reasonably and intelligently disagree, there are other common practices which automatically alienate some portions of the faculty. An example of the former case is the question of how much disciplinary discretion over students the institution should exercise over and above civil law, if any. One of the oldest of academic traditions is that of sanctuary on the campus for students; in medieval times local authorities were, by treaty with the universities, forbidden to come on the campuses to make arrests or even to keep the peace. This has come down to the American institution of higher education in the typical practice of police kid glove treatment of students, often resulting in the failure to arrest or book them for practices which would net a nonstudent at least a night in jail. The student is, instead, turned over to university or college authorities with the understanding that they will undertake appropriate discipline. This clearly works to the general benefit of the student body. But the distinction between civil law and institutional regulations, and the occasional substitution of the latter for the former, often results in situations in which students may be punished, even quite severely, for infractions of regulations which remain behavior perfectly legal under civil law, and, when civil law is involved, problems in double jeopardy are frequent, for it is often against institutional regulations for a student even to be arrested under the civil law, regardless of the eventual disposition of his case by the courts, if any. About situations of this kind, and the best means of handling them, reasonable men may reasonably differ.

Character Types

The Academic Marketplace used feudal analogies to describe some character types common among department chairmen. Principal among these were roles we called the robber baron, the lord of the mountain fief, the yeoman farmer and gentleman adventurer, with honest burghers, king's men and boy rulers also being observable occasionally (pp. 196–198). Such chairmen also exist on the college campus, but, in the same way that the department is a less important unit in the college, due to its small size, so do individual faculty members and their characteristics take on a greater importance on the small campus and, due to the differing circumstances, university character types may find themselves in different roles in the college. (The Gentleman Adventurer, for example, instead of becoming a department chairman, is more apt to be found as a higher administrator in the college.) If I may beg the reader's indulgence, I should like to suggest that many campuses offer the viewer examples of the following character-types among their faculties, and that their commonality may suggest some functional utility for them in the academic world.

All campuses, small and large, have official or unofficial campus poets-in-residence among their faculties as well as brash young scientists and campus iconoclasts. All three tend to be youngish, shaggy, casual in dress, and great favorites with the students, although the latter two may affect a disdain for their student followings. They are usually unimportant or inactive in campus affairs—perhaps they are *too* stereotypical—except that the brash young scientist may normally be counted on occasionally to denounce the blindness of his elders in faculty meetings. The iconoclast is frequently a professional failure whom his colleagues find unpleasant.

Every campus has among its senior full professors one or two who are—or imagine themselves to be—campus statesmen. The older faculty member who really is a campus statesman may be found either inhabiting or advising all the truly important committees, invited to dine with the president with some frequency, appearing before the Board as the spokesman for the faculty, and being approached continually by every faculty group which has an axe to grind and feels his ratification of their program will help to ensure its acceptance by the administration, the board, or the rest of the faculty. True campus statesmen are usually elderly, dignified, of long tenure at the institution, and have some record of professional accomplishment in their fields. Would-be statesmen, on the other hand, are sometimes only middle-aged, without solid professional accomplishment on which to base their local status, and presume to a dignity their presumptuous behavior only makes appear ridiculous to others. The would-be statesman is not invited to consult with the president but makes opportunities to offer his advice by writing him letters, calling on him in his office, and inevitably speaking up on every issue at faculty meetings. He campaigns incessantly for election to committees perceived as status-bearing on the campus and becomes an intolerable nuisance to his colleagues by attempting to impress his personality and ideas upon every group or project with which he is associated. He seems often to be abetted in his status-striving by a wife who is always both loquacious and birdbrained and whose ambitions for her husband are even more transparent than his own.

Perhaps a subvariety of the campus statesman (real) is the statesman who hides his influence over campus affairs by operating through influential others—the Cardinal Richelieu. Often a relatively obscure confidant of the president, he may or may not serve on influential committees but is always sure to know what happened in them within hours of the event itself as well as to have someone on the committee who may be counted upon to push his program. Like the statesman, he is likely to be a senior professor, although not necessarily an elderly one, and will surely have a professional standing in his field. His influence on the institution is apt to be benign, although it need not be, and it will invariably be mistrusted by some of those who envy it. It is likely to stem from a position as board's, angel's, or alumni's man.

All campuses have their old young men, professional marginals or incompetents who have managed to secure tenure through administrative oversight, through lying low and being useful in routine tasks, or through flattery of weak chairmen. Once assured of permanent appointment, they join the Old Guard of the institution, with whose members they have already become associated, and proceed to vote negatively on everything, particularly on changes or appointments which appear to them to threaten the image of success they strive desperately to project. Essentially insecure and defensive personalities, they can become immovable roadblocks to progress when elected to committees on personnel or policy since they are likely to perceive any alteration of the status quo as a threat. An institution with even a significant minority of them among its junior faculty just about has to become an oligarchy in order to escape their influence.

Relatively unknown in urban colleges, the agent of the local community may become a powerful influence indeed on a campus in a college town. The smaller the town and the weaker the college, the more important he is likely to be in faculty affairs. Agents of the local community may be campus statesmen of either variety or Cardinals Richelieu, but their influence on the institution is invariably pernicious. Locals with a vengeance, they have either never adopted or long since rejected academic values in favor of those of the Chamber of Commerce, the Lion's Club, the American Legion, or even the John Birch Society. Perceiving the institution as functioning to serve local needs primarily, they strive to fill the curriculum with vocational courses of the lowest order (typing, bookkeeping, meat cutting, hair styling, etc.) and the student body with respect for the economic and social values of corner merchants. In the Midwest they want to involve the colleges in religious revivals while in the Southwestern parts of the country anti-Communism seminars are their vogue. They rarely come from the standard academic departments and are most likely to be found in the college business office or departments of business administration, business education, or education. Occasionally they are athletic coaches. They are always authoritarian with respect to students and antiintellectual with respect to curriculum and requirements. They regard their campus bookstores as profit-making enterprises primarily and look with suspicion on English instructors because they fill the college library with dirty books which students may even be required to read. The agent of the local community gains his influence from his wide acquaintance among, and acceptance by, the Main Street commercial community of the town in which the college is located. Always known to the mayor, he can hint to the president of local unhappiness with the college which only his programs can correct (with the implied threat of the withdrawal of community financial support), and make dark suggestions concerning goings-on among students which are known to the police. A creature of institutional weakness, he will be summarily retired or adroitly sideslipped into obscurity by a canny president when the college's dependence on the local community is overcome or recognized as being less important than it had appeared.

Last but not least among our campus character-types is the plenipotentiary from a foreign power, the "high powered research man" brought in from one of the major universities for the principal purpose of adding lustre to the institution's reputation by his presence on the faculty. Since university professors with established reputations in their fields, particularly those of some eminence in them, are not easily persuaded to leave the university for the professionally dubious environs of a liberal arts college, they will always be among the most highly favored of the college's faculty, often with salary and perquisites far above the rest of the faculty, thus making them objects of some envy. And since, additionally, they represent a set of values which many other faculty members perceive as being part antithetical to those institutionalized in the college, their appearance on the campus is the signal for stirrings of restlessness and fear. And finally, since really "high-powered" research-oriented scholars are unlikely to accept permanent positions at liberal arts colleges, the individuals perceived by the college as being "high-powered" who are also available are likely in fact to be rejects from the university social system for one reason or another. (This varies by discipline, however. First-class research physicists or chemists are unlikely to be able to do their work in a liberal arts college and are rare there; eminent poets, painters, or literary scholars, on the other hand, may not be too uncommon. Another exception is the elderly scholar who retires from a university and is hired by a college for another few years of teaching.) Thus, the college faculty will be in part, at least, unwilling to accept the plenipotentiary on the campus and there is some probability that he will be unable to perform the function for which the administration hired him. As a foreigner, he may never feel at home in the culture of the college and the turnover among plenipotentiaries is likely to be high.

Role Ambiguity

I have indicated in several places already that the American private liberal arts college must exist, today, in a rather ambiguous condition; I have called it Janus-faced for having evolved or adopted some attributes of the university while maintaining unsullied other attributes of the nineteenth century academy. It appears that the world has changed about it more than it has itself been willing or able to change, and that, as a consequence, it now embodies functions and practices sometimes somewhat incongruous and occasionally even antithetical. A number of other phenomena further contribute to the dilemma in which the colleges find themselves. One of these is a declining proportionate share of the college population. In 1950, fully half of the college student population of the United States was enrolled in privately supported colleges or universities, which compose somewhat less than two-thirds of the total number of American institutions of higher education. In 1970, only 35 per cent of college students attended private schools, and the proportion will probably fall to 20 per cent before 1980 as tuitions inevitably rise in the private institutions in the face of increasingly severe competition from publicly supported schools for faculty salaries, nonteaching services, and specialized studies. It is true that although the proportion of students enrolled in private institutions is declining, the real number of such students has recently been at an all time high, and many schools have turned away more applicants for admission than they accepted. But it is also true that many more are beginning, for the first time in perhaps twenty years, to fail to fill the places they have open in the freshman class each fall.

A second problem contributing to their dilemma is, as suggested above, financial. Costs of college instruction have risen astronomically since 1950 and, while the public institutions are limited in their expenditures only by what their constituencies are willing to appropriate (and have had excellent expectations, in most instances, of getting what they needed if not entirely what they would have liked), the budgets of private institutions, even of the most prestigious, are distinctly finite and are severely handicapped in enlargement since they depend, in the end, on what amounts to a kind of charity and must compete with numbers of other interests among their donors. (All private institutions except the most marginal are endowed. Inflation, however, has reduced some of the real income realizable from investments, and it all comes in the first place from donations. Student tuitions represent a very important portion of the institutional financing for a private college, unlike most public institutions, which makes a reduction in enrollment doubly threatening.) College costs are skyrocketing while gifts have leveled off. Private colleges, furthermore, spend more per student than do public institutions of education. One report based on United States Office of Education figures estimates that the average expenditure of public institutions per student per year was $2,222 in 1966–67 and will be $2,575 in 1976–77. Comparable figures for private institutions are $3,414 and $4,870 (*U.S. News and World Report,* 1967, p. 58). Education is more expensive in the private institution because of smaller class sizes, smaller volume purchasing, less than full-time, year-round operation, fewer income opportunities (for example, patent royalties or intercollegiate athletics), reduced proportions of costs underwritten by federal and state governments through research contracts and grants, and a host of other factors. Some inefficiency of operation in many of the smaller private schools is also undoubtedly in part responsible. Whatever the reason, commentators are unanimous in their agreement that the financial state of private collegiate education in the United States is already critical and will become even more precarious within a very few years. Some colleges will have to close their doors in bankruptcy, merge with others, or permit themselves to become publicly supported schools within state systems. Examples of schools which have had to resort to each of these alternatives within the past few years can be cited from the pages of the press (*The Chronicle of Higher Education,* 1970).

But the private colleges face another kind of competition from the universities, too, regardless of support, and also from the high schools. Jacques Barzun, dean of the faculties and lately provost of Columbia University, discussed it in an address congratulating Hofstra on the first anniversary of its change from college to university status (1964). His view of the future of the independent college, private or public, is grim:

> But in all [the confusion of change in the educational system], what has happened to the American College? Well, there are more colleges than ever before, but I for one find it harder and harder to know what they do and why. There is a very fine sentence in the *Hofstra College Bulletin,* which discusses the difference between college education and university training . . . but what is the reality? The reality is that the best colleges today are being invaded, not to say dispossessed, by the advance agents of the professions, by men who want to seize upon the young recruit as soon as may be and train him in a "tangible salable skill."
>
> In short, both teachers and students are responding to the spirit of the times. They are impatient with everything that is not directed at the development of talent into competence . . . the meaning of this is plain: *the liberal arts tradition is dead or dying.* . . . The reasons are evident: the great movement for General Education, which began after the First World War, has in forty years transformed our entire precollegiate schooling. The

good high school now gives the historical surveys, the introductions to social science, the great books, that formed the substance of General Education. What is more, the Advance Placement Program has managed to fill in the old vacuum of the eleventh and twelfth grades with real work, so that more and more freshmen—even without Advance Placement—find the first year of college feeble and repetitious. . . . So that if we stand off and look at the silhouette of the American College . . . what we see is the thinning and flattening out of its once distinctive curriculum under pressure from above and below, the high school taking away the lower years; the graduate and professional schools the upper.

The private colleges are not unaware of this phenomenon, of course, and many of the better ones have taken steps to meet it by offering students services and quality they cannot hope to find in the public institutions. Counseling, years abroad, self-directed study, apprentice programs, and even general classroom instruction, are being beefed up to attract students and improve their college experience. But these programs cost extra money, too, and the colleges are right back where they started with more and more students unable to afford them despite work-study programs, scholarships (which, in the private institutions, must come from the same pockets which fund them in the first place), and work contracts for service to the college. Dean Barzun and the commentators are, I am very much afraid, correct: the general future for the private colleges as a class is grim.

This does not mean, however, that all is lost and that those who support the concept of the private liberal arts college must despair of its survival. It is extremely difficult, in fact, to doubt that the best among them will survive, for certain facts seem clear. One is that while it is true that the colleges cater essentially to only one segment of the American population, the upper middle class, that segment and the middle class of which it is a part are the most rapidly growing portion of the population. There is no danger, then, of the source of clientele disappearing. Second, even though rising costs are driving many students out of the private colleges and into state-supported institutions, there remains a reservoir in the upper middle class which can afford to send its children to private institutions if it wishes, and there seems no reason to believe it will cease to wish to do so. Third, and most important, while the proportion of the college population attending private schools may continue to diminish for some time, and while many marginal institutions may have to close or change their private character, the cold fact of the matter is probably that upper-middle-class students of some affluence can and do receive better general educations in the private liberal arts college than most of them would be likely to receive in the university. The reason for this is double: Undergraduate instruction, on the average, is probably better at a good private college than at a good university, and the student at the private college has a much greater chance of having it available to him and of absorbing some of it. It is, of course, impossible to prove or demonstrate any assertion concerning matters as broad and ambiguous as the general quality of instruction among great groups of similar institutions. Propositions of the kind are capable of demonstration but hardly of indisputable proof. Nonetheless, the argument has much to support it. In the first place, regardless of what its public relations organs may state, undergraduate instruction is not the first business of the university, and very few indeed pay a great deal of attention to it. The testimonies of their faculties and the conditions of employment among those faculties are sufficient to establish this. But undergraduate instruction is the first and, indeed, very nearly the only business of the liberal arts college, and the reader will learn from the words of its faculty members quoted in later chapters how seriously it is taken. In the second place, while no one who has ever been associated with one would argue that it was impossible for a student to receive a good, even an excellent, liberal arts education at a multiversity, it is largely left to the student to get it, and the university will not assist him very much simply because it is too large and perforce too bureaucratic to do so. His classes are large, even huge, and he rarely becomes acquainted with their instructors. His work, in many classes, is rarely if ever seen by the instructor of the class because it is graded by graduate assistants. If he gets in trouble, or feels the need of personal or vocational counseling, he is a stranger to his faculty and just part of the caseload of the university's counseling and guidance personnel whose strongest allegiances may be to the maintenance of order in the institution rather than to the troubled human beings who cross their paths. The university's requirements are, indeed, set up to expose the student to the rudiments of a basic liberal education. So when he graduates it is fair to judge that he has taken X hours of literature and Y of language or humanities and Z of social science. But since a D+ or C− average is all that is required for honorable discharge from the university, and the grades are always graded on a curve at least in the sense of being given relative to the instructor's estimate of what is average performance among the students who pass before him, and since the entrance requirements of most universities, at least public ones, are not really very high, the fact of having passed the requirements and graduated in no way contains the assurance that the individual has, in fact, received an education. It only gives assurance that he has had the opportunity to obtain one and has not completely rejected it.

The case is somewhat different in the liberal arts college. In the typical private college, class size may be as low as fifteen and, because of the diminutive (by university standards) size of both student body and faculty, faculty members come to know their students pretty well and vice versa. The teacher learns what to expect from the individuals before him, then, and when one fails to perform up to expectation the instructor can recognize it and call the student in to discover what the trouble is. And if a home situation or a psychiatric or financial problem appears to be at fault, the student can be assured of a referral to the appropriate college office by a sympathetic acquaintance who is likely to follow up on what happens to him there and what the outcome of the matter is. And that office, aware of its responsibilities to known individuals (the student, the professor, the parents), will do its best. Furthermore, since the business of the college is teaching, and the faculty is known and rewarded for it, the best talents and the major energies of the instructor are likely to find expression in the classroom. And since the private college is a private institution, and, for its own sake, has a real stake in student performance (as will be explained in Chapter Five), it tends to select students to be admitted as rigorously as it can. Both student and faculty members, thus, are forced to compete in the classroom not against a random segment of the college population, but against some of the best young minds in the country. Finally, of course, the environment of the private college is usually far more supportive of intellectual activity than is that of the undergraduate at the university. To remain in the social system with which he has associated himself in the college, the student must maintain a performance satisfactory to that social system, and standards of satisfaction are relatively high. He is less likely to find himself distracted by athletics and fraternity affairs because a liberal arts college, even in a metropolitan area, is a more insular institution than a university, which of necessity more greatly mirrors the outside world. In the college almost every aspect of the student's existence reflects and supports the college's teaching function and reinforces the motivation to be successful as a student. In at least one university with which I have been associated, for many students their classroom and learning activities were only incidentally associated with, and required for, their more important social activities.

It seems unlikely to me, then, that the liberal arts college will disappear from the context of American education. The better ones among them will remain and, in order to compete and survive, improve still more. It is probable that, because of their financial problems, they will become ever more restricted to the children of the affluent, unless, as seems possible, the state and federal governments undertake their partial support or the massive support of college students in general in something like the GI Bill. But the best of them will survive and it is certainly for the better that they do; many among them are truly excellent institutions of higher education and the civilization of the United States would be diminished without them.

THREE

A Nice Place to
Visit, But

Work and Mobility
in the College

Let us lay to rest some popular ideas about the academic labor market. There is, as has already been stated, no single market. Rather "the" market is highly balkanized into scores of labor exchanges oriented about the disciplines and specialties within them and to some extent about geographic areas and kinds of institutions and heavily influenced by professional and other forms of prestige. Some institutions, for example, seek faculty members largely from the religious denominations with which they are affiliated; others might look askance at anyone with (or without) a degree in the field of education. Thus, the classic economic model of a market where buyers and sellers of labor are fully informed about the state of supply and demand, where market price is determined by the equilibrium between supply and demand and subject to fluctuation as they vary, and where both buyers and sellers are economically rational, fits the labor market for academic men hardly at all. There are multiple markets; buyers and sellers have, in most instances, only fractional knowledge of who is available for what jobs; the price of labor tends to be fixed for the nation as a whole and does not vary as much either from region to region or among institutional types as it does among professional disciplines and specialties and in some instances is more influenced by nonacademic demand than by anything else. Finally, such a host of special preferences, conditions, and accidents influence choices by both buyers and sellers of academic labor that neither can be said to be economically rational in the traditional meaning of that term. Indeed, in many areas of academics it is considered bad taste for either party to bargain too strongly for "mere" monetary considerations, and in fact most academic men regard other matters as of more consequence than salary. This is not to say that professors are uninterested in salary. Quite the contrary, but they are interested in it under a highly circumscribed set of conditions: given a certain age, rank, professional specialty, and background, the professor may, when considering another position, bargain for all he can get within what he believes or knows to be reasonable for his status, but he will have in mind a scale of salaries he will be willing to accept if other matters are also to his liking. Such things as teaching load and specific classes, research time and funds, travel monies, library facilities, and so on may all be more important to him than salary in the sense that he is likely to be able to get more or less the same salary anywhere he can secure a position, and therefore the determination of what position he accepts, if any, will rest with advantages perceived in other areas.

For these reasons neither the simple supply of persons with doctorates available at any given time nor the demand for college teachers expressed as the total number of vacancies available in the country determines who will be hired nor where nor at what salary. "The" labor market for faculty is influenced by scores of factors—including academic convention—far more strongly than it is by simple supply and demand. It is true, of course, that the demand in recent years— largely from outside academics—for physicists and mathematicians has resulted in the raising of their salaries, on a national scale, rather above those of their academic colleagues in other fields. Economists are in a similar position. But a simple shortage in any field taught at the college level need not similarly elevate salaries. Physics, economics, and mathematics are fundamentals of any college program and must be offered in adequate measure. Although the relatively lower salary levels of artists are certainly in part a reflection of the abundant supply of teaching artists, it is difficult to believe that art is in such great demand in college teaching that a sudden shortage of artists would result in the kind of astronomical rise in salaries which mathematics has seen since 1945. Like many other areas conventionally included in the curriculum, art is simply less essential than mathematics and, therefore, it is less influenced by supply and demand. To put the matter another way, there is a constant level of demand for some fields created by the fact that they are conventional staples of curriculum which colleges must offer. Thus, any real (and not just local) shortage of persons available to teach them is likely to accelerate demand and, therefore, salary or "price." Many academic disciplines do not enjoy this conventional demand, however, and, unless they are popular for some other reason, or enjoy a truly critical shortage of practitioners (anthropology, for example), demand is unlikely to influence greatly the price of supply. The example of anthropology may be particularly instructive. A relatively new field of teaching endeavor, it claims only a few thousand Ph.D. practitioners in the entire nation. It is rarely, if ever, required toward a degree, and it is certainly not one of the conventional essentials such as freshman composition or college algebra. It is popular with students, however, and, with the advent of the post–World War II world cultural implosion, has begun to offer practical advantages to nonacademic enterprises, thus creating some small nonacademic demand as well. The result has been a truly acute shortage of anthropologists to man college departments, plus an acceleration in the creation of such departments, and salaries have begun to climb spectacularly. An equally acute shortage of logicians or teachers of Greek would probably not have a similar effect. With the warning to the reader, then, that academic culture and its values, rather than the conventional economist's models, must be the principal explanatory variables for understanding academic turnover, let us turn to the characteristics of the faculties of the eleven colleges here studied. What is it like to be a professor in such a college and what factors influence the conditions of work there?

Rank

Rank is one of the pervasive dimensions of academic stratification and a matter of significance to faculty members everywhere. There is a rather high association between advancing age and advancing rank. This is entirely to be expected. It has been noted earlier that advance in rank, at least among liberal arts personnel such as those we consider here, is to some degree a matter of sticking around long enough. Assistant professors—the lowest of the academic ranks considered in this research—were overwhelmingly (78 per cent) below the age of forty while full professors were even more overwhelmingly (87 per cent) age forty-one and over. Two-thirds of the entire group surveyed were between the ages of thirty-one and fifty and 86 per cent of associate professors were in this age group. Very few (11 per cent) were below thirty. This too is hardly surprising; few men receive the Ph.D. before the age of twenty-eight and few indeed would be assistant professors that young. In one sense, then, these figures elucidate the obvious, but their significance lies in their demonstration of the assertion that attainment of advanced rank is largely a matter of endurance and longevity. This generalization is, of course, an oversimplification, for we are dealing here, after all, with the population of survivors. Those who did not succeed in advancement and as a result quit the contest to do other things were not represented in the sample. Of those who remained in academics, however, most eventually received promotion.

Table 1 suggests that with advancing rank comes increasing financial security. Perhaps of greatest interest here are the marginal totals which inform us of the general conditions of financial affairs among small college teachers. The vast majority were in the salary range of $8,000 to $14,999, with only 7 per cent below those limits and only 9 per cent above them. It is apparent that riches are not likely to be the lot of the college teacher. (The highest salary reported among the interviewees—who were higher paid than most men in the colleges, as will be seen—was $18,000, and there were only four salaries of $16,000 or higher.) But equally important is the fact that over a fifth of small college teachers make between $12,000 and $15,000 a year in salary, and almost 10 per cent are even better rewarded. While these are not by any means high salaries in the United States at this time and hardly indicate sybaritic luxury for their earners, neither do they approximate the poverty which it is sometimes the academic man's wont to claim. The modal annual *family* income in the country in 1966–67, in fact, was about $7,500, and very few of the group (7

Table 1. RANK AND SALARY
(N = 303)[a]

Rank	Salary					Total	Total Sample[b]
	$7,999 or Under	$8,000–$9,999	$10,000–$11,999	$12,000–$14,999	$15,000 or Over		
	Per Cent						
Full professor	0	0	14	60	26	100	31
Associate professor	2	24	62	11	2	100	31
Assistant professor	17	71	11	0	0	100	38
Number	(22)	(105)	(84)	(66)	(26)	(303)	
Total sample	7	35	28	22	9	100	

[a] N will vary somewhat in the following tables due to incomplete information on specific items in some cases.

[b] In this and all tables following, percentages have been rounded to the nearest whole figure for ease of reading. The effect of this is sometimes to make per cent figures within a column or row add up to 99 per cent or to 101 per cent. Totals will always be rendered as 100 per cent, however, to indicate that all entries are accounted for. Differences, where found, are solely the result of rounding error.

per cent) earned less than that. When we consider the fact that these were *individual* salaries, for a work year of only nine months, we are led to the conclusion that, although relative to other occupations requiring similar formal preparation, academics may not be terribly competitive, neither is it an occupation to be pitied. (And university professors, remember, are, on the average, paid more.) Thus, considering that most men eventually achieve full professorships, we may conclude that financial security for the academic man at the small college is a matter of biding his time. If he sees the matter through, he will be promoted and rewarded, if not handsomely, at least satisfactorily, relative to other Americans. (He must, obviously, be performing his duties satisfactorily while seeing the matter through. Contrary to a great deal which is written about the professoriat, it has been my experience that there are few timeservers within it, although levels of competence certainly vary.)

The relationship between rank and academic preparation can be very simply indicated by listing the proportion in each rank holding the doctoral degree: of assistant professors, 51 per cent had doctorates; for associate professors the figure is 71 per cent; for full professors, 89 per cent. It is apparent that, although the doctoral degree is not absolutely required for advancement to the highest rank, it is for most men at least a necessary condition and perhaps a sufficient one. Worthy of note is the fact that only 4 per cent of the college teachers surveyed had no degrees beyond the bachelor's level, while 69 per cent of all ranks held the doctor's degree: Advanced training seems to be an almost absolute precondition of success in the occupation. Those without advanced training are almost exclusively in essentially nonacademic curricula, principally the performing arts. The fact that 69 per cent of those surveyed possessed an earned doctoral degree is also indicative of the general caliber of the eleven institutions sampled. There are many universities in the country which cannot boast so high a Ph.D. ratio on their faculties, and the national average for institutions of higher education is about 50 per cent.

Not only is simple possession of the doctor's degree of significance to success in the academic profession, but the source of such degrees, the nature and presumed quality of the granting institutions, is also important. Fifty-two per cent of all professors in our sample held doctorates from major universities, 13 per cent from minor universities, and 4 per cent from other institutions; 31 per cent did not have doctorates. For full professors the figures are 65 per cent from major universities, 15 per cent from minor universities, 8 per cent from other institutions; 11 per cent held no doctorates. Perhaps equally interesting is the fact that 43 per cent of our sample took their first degree at private colleges themselves, almost twice as many as completed undergraduate work at major universities (22 per cent), and more than twice as many as attended minor universities (20 per cent). This argues that, for many men, it is the experience of undergraduate education in the private college which sets their occupational direction for them. This may be of fundamental significance for college faculty recruiters, for it suggests either that the colleges are already recruiting heavily from persons with student experience in the private college, or that those with such experience are more likely to accept opportunities to teach in that environment, or both. There is no reason to suspect that men from the universities are poorer bets in terms of turnover, however, for proportions from the two sources remain remarkably stable. Once hired neither is more likely to depart than the other.

Table 2 shows something of the nature of the promotion system in the small college as it relates to the rank structure. In immediate evidence is the fact that over half of full professors had not received academic promotion in eight years or more, while almost half (44 per cent) of assistant professors had been promoted within three years. Neither of these circumstances is surprising. Full professor, the highest academic rank obtainable, once attained prevents any further promotion in rank no matter how long such rank is held. Assistant professor, on the contrary, is conventionally the rank to which an individual is appointed if he takes his first teaching job with the doctoral degree. For those who have not completed doctorates, promotion from instructor to assistant professor is often automatic on completion of the degree, sometimes being given even within an academic year, so significant is the change of status successful completion of the degree implies. Since almost half (49 per cent) of the assistant professors in the group studied did not yet possess doctoral degrees, however, we must assume that many of the promotions to that rank reported here represented rank increases from instructor made for some other reason, perhaps accompanying the award of tenure.

Table 2. Rank and Recency of Promotion
(N = 254)

Rank	Recency of Promotion						Total Sample
	Within 1 Year	2–3 Years	4–5 Years	6–7 Years	8 Years or More	Total	
	Per Cent						
Full professor	8	17	19	5	51	100	35
Associate professor	17	24	26	14	18	100	34
Assistant professor	27	44	16	6	6	100	30
Number	(43)	(70)	(52)	(22)	(67)	(254)	
Total sample	17	28	20	9	26		100

$\chi^2 = 62.3668 \qquad p < .001$

Seventy-one per cent of assistant professors had held that rank for only three years or less, while 16 per cent had been in it four or five years. This rather precipitous drop suggests that the modal length of service in the assistant professorship among private college teachers is probably three years. (In the universities, it is probably four, except in the natural sciences, particularly physics and mathematics, where market competition has lowered it.) Utilizing the same logic, the similar figure for associate professors is not more than five years, for less than a third had served in rank longer than that. These estimates roughly agree with the age distributions among the ranks discussed above if it is recalled that twenty-eight or thirty is about the youngest that most men can receive the doctoral degree and that many of those studied here (not solely full professors) were delayed in completing doctoral programs.

Perhaps the most important point made by Table 3 is that the differences in rank distribution among men of different departments

Table 3. DEPARTMENTAL AFFILIATION AND RANK
(N = 307)

Department	Full Professor	Associate Professor	Assistant Professor	Total	Total Sample
			Per Cent		
Natural science	26	35	38	100	29
Social science	27	34	39	100	21
Humanities and languages	36	22	42	100	23
Other	35	30	35	100	27
Number	(96)	(94)	(117)	(307)	
Total sample	31	31	38		100

(No chi square computed; differences statistically insignificant.)

were statistically indistinguishable from chance—no particular subject area was favored or retarded in the award of rank. This is important because it contradicts, for the colleges at least, the common belief that scientists, because of superior market opportunities, are favored in all academic perquisites, while humanists and artists in particular are discriminated against. (*Careers of Ph.D.'s, Academic Versus Nonacademic,* 1968, however, shows that, for the nation as a whole, scientists do advance most and humanists least rapidly.)

Departments and Disciplines

Departmental or disciplinary affiliation are of immense significance to academic men. Whether one is a chemist or a classicist, a geologist or a geographer, makes an immense difference in one's work and, in some respects, one's conditions of work. Table 4 explores an-

Table 4. Departmental Affiliation and Employment
Longevity
($N = 305$)

Department	Years Employed at Shadyside			Total	Total Sample
	4 Years or Fewer	5–8 Years	9 Years or More	Total	Total Sample
	Per Cent				
Natural science	32	18	50	100	29
Social science	44	22	34	100	21
Humanities and languages	36	16	48	100	23
Other	23	21	56	100	27
Number	(100)	(59)	(146)	(305)	
Total sample	33	19	48		100

$$\chi^2 = 9.734 \qquad p < .20 > .10$$

other academic myth about natural scientists—that they are more foot-loose than men in other fields, again, presumably, because of their supposedly greater market opportunities. As can be readily seen, nat-ural scientists are not by any means the least in proportionate longev-ity at the institutions where the study found them. Contrary to what might be expected, social scientists appear to be more footloose than men from other professional areas. They have both the highest pro-portion of recent appointments and the lowest of those of long dura-tion. The rather large proportion of new appointments is in part ex-plicable by the expansion in social science departments and offerings which has been going on at the private colleges, a reflection of the expansion in these fields which occurred after World War II. De-partments of sociology and anthropology, for example, are still being founded at a rather rapid rate in institutions which either had never taught the disciplines before or else had not had separate departments in these fields. Psychology departments in many institutions have dou-bled or even tripled in size since World War II as well, so some of the apparent brevity of the social scientists' stay at Shadyside is a function of the institution's belated recognition or expansion of their fields. Some, on the other hand, is undoubtedly also a reflection of greater occupational mobility, a phenomenon which the social scientist, being, presumably, a student of his own behavior, might perceive as natural while others would perceive it as hazardous.

Those with the greatest collective longevity and, therefore, the lowest mobility, are in the category "other." This group in the sample is dominated by artists of various kinds and otherwise consists of teach-ers of religion and a handful of professors of education and business administration. With the possible exception of the latter, these disci-plines are characterized by, even notorious for, their slow or low de-mand labor market, and the conditions of that market show clearly here. The situation of persons in the humanities and the languages conforms to common academic belief. Large proportions are recent arrivals, probably including numbers of language section men among whom turnover will be high. But another relatively large group are of long tenure at Shadyside, conforming to the perception that men in these areas do not move as much as others. These, of course, would be relatively older men, professors rather than section men.

Table 5 confirms one stereotype about social scientists: they

Table 5. DEPARTMENTAL AFFILIATION AND AGE
(N = 304)

Department	35 or Under	36 to 45	46 or Over	Total	Total Sample
			Per Cent		
Natural science	31	32	37	100	29
Social science	38	40	22	100	21
Humanities and languages	17	38	45	100	23
Other	16	34	50	100	27
Number	(76)	(108)	(120)	(304)	
Total sample	25	36	39		100
	$\chi^2 = 18.5817$		$p < .01$		

are, as a class, younger than their counterparts in other fields. The influence of the very late start men get in academic careers is visible in the fact that only 25 per cent of the faculties of the eleven institutions are thirty-five or younger. The relatively small proportion of young men in the humanities and languages probably reflects some tendency for training to be extended in those fields, in part by long degree programs and in part by time abroad as students immerse themselves in the cultures which are their study, thus delaying their entry into teaching and correspondingly advancing their age.

There is no statistically significant difference in remuneration for the different departmental areas. Sixty-three per cent of natural scientists, 50 per cent of social scientists, 58 per cent of humanists and linguists, and 56 per cent of other professors earn salaries of $10,000 or more ($\chi^2 = 2.6282$; $p < .50 > .30$). There are some differences among them, but they are not large. Natural scientists are somewhat better paid than men in other areas, presumably as a result of market competition for their services both within and from without academics, but the distinctions are not dramatic. Contrary to common belief, social scientists are least well rewarded among college teachers, although these figures are in part a reflection of the greater proportion of young men among them. One might leap to the conclusion that the apparent salary advantage enjoyed by natural scientists was a consequence of greater likelihood of completion of the doctoral degree among them, but this will not account for the matter. Among the academic disciplines virtually identical proportions of men possess the Ph.D. or other doctoral degree and, indeed, the proportions holding each degree are identical for the natural sciences and the humanities and language area, with the social scientists very similar. Artists do not, as a rule, go beyond the master's degree in their formal training, and this is visible in the much lower proportion of "others" who take the doctoral degree. There is little evidence of salary discrimination against members of "other" departments, however, which suggests that, if artists at the smaller colleges are in truth paid less because of their low marketability, the differences must be too small to appear in our rather gross categories of salary and department. Neither does the lack of doctoral degrees among the artists seem to influence salary.

Eighty per cent of natural scientists, 64 per cent of social scientists, 72 per cent of humanists and linguists, and 60 per cent of other professors hold doctorates from major universities. The predominance of the major university as a source of doctoral degrees in the natural sciences probably reflects the investments in program and equipment necessary to sustain doctoral studies in the sciences. Most doctoral programs in science are in the major universities because such institutions are the only ones which can afford the faculties and research equipment required to carry on teaching at that level. This would be least true for the arts, it is reasonable to suspect, and the proportion of major university degrees is, indeed, lowest among "others."

There were important differences between the fields in the rapidity with which men completed their doctoral programs. The most outstanding difference is that only 64 per cent of natural scientists took more than five years to complete their doctorates, compared to 82 per cent of social scientists, 74 per cent of humanists and linguists, and 94 per cent of other professors ($\chi^2 = 12.6347$; $p < .01$). The relatively shorter degree programs typical of the natural sciences, compared with humanities and languages, are also important. The probable explanation of these matters is that science degrees are more rapidly achievable for most men, perhaps because their objectives are capable of more precise limitation and their studies are more objective than work in humanities and languages, while artists, who make up the majority of the "other" category, may not seek doctoral degrees at all unless spurred by academic norms or institutional requirements.

Salary

The earlier discussion of rank concluded that both advanced rank and the increasing salary which was shown to accompany it are probably in large part functions of time for the private college professor; if he remains on the job and performs adequately he will receive both promotion and at least adequate salary in the passage of time. Table 6 supports this assertion. Of the faculties of the institutions surveyed, one-third of those who had served for more than fifteen years earned salaries of $15,000 or more, and two-thirds earned $12,000 or more. The tiny proportion (6 per cent) of men with service this long who earned less than $9000 may be assumed to be those judged by their institutions to be not only lacking proper credentials, but incompetent as well. Average annual advances in salary are impossible to compute from Table 6 because of its open-ended categories and the grouping of data. Nonetheless, if we examine its "line of central tendency," we can calculate that if we assume $7500 to be an average starting salary and $15,500 an average for those with long service, the average annual increment to be expected among faculty members at the institutions surveyed must be around $500. (Academic salaries do not, of course, usually advance by similar annual increments. Because of changes in professional status, budget restrictions or largess, and so on, even successful and highly desirable men may receive no raise some years, raises of as much as $2000 in other years, and positively absurd increments such as $464.27 in between. The logic of the academic budgeting process has not, to my knowledge, ever been studied. It should be. It is apparent, however, that decisions on individual salary items are often of a forced-choice nature; that is, they are the pragmatic results of the commitment of funds to other items first or of simple arithmetical division of funds remaining among men judged indistinguishable.)

There is considerable overlap between salary and service cate-

Table 6. Employment Longevity and Salary
(N = 308)

Longevity	Salary $8,999 or Less	$9,000– $11,999	$12,000– $14,999	$15,000 or More	Total	Total Sample
			Per Cent			
0–4 years	44	48	6	2	100	32
5–8 years	27	57	13	3	100	20
9–15 years	11	42	38	9	100	26
16 years or more	6	29	32	33	100	21
Number	(74)	(135)	(66)	(33)	(308)	
Total sample	24	44	21	11		100

gories—budget decisions are not made according to longevity. But longevity of appointment inevitably forces the hand of the budgeting officers (except in the case of the unfortunate 6 per cent) simply because salary has a peculiarly symbolic significance for academic men. It is imperative, in other words, that the president or the dean give frequent, even if small, raises to any man whom they are not actively trying to force out. Salary symbolizes appreciation and acceptance to faculty members, and reminders that a huge raise occurred three years ago are not considered adequate to explain a lack of any since. Raises and promotions are the only recurring empirical indicators a professor has of how he stands with his administration in the absence of the nonsalary perquisites and awards commonly available, for example, in the industrial and military world. And, since he is likely somewhat to mistrust administrative officers on principle, his occupational suspicion creates a paranoid projection-feedback circuit which only recurring pats on the back can effectively discharge.[1] Inevitably, then, even though longevity is not an explicit criterion for salary decisions, it becomes effectively a function of them.

There is a distinct relation between possession of the doctoral degree and access to the higher salary ranges. Of professors who earn $12,000 or more, 89 per cent have doctorates, compared to only 59 per cent of those who earn less than $12,000 ($\chi^2 = 27.7244$; p $<$ .001). It would be too simple to summarize these data by concluding that people with doctorates are paid more. Quite clearly, not all of them are. A trend in this direction is equally clear, but the variations are considerable. It is also overly simple to conclude that the doctoral degree is "just a union card." It is that, but it is more than that as well. For we must ask why we usually find associated with the possession of the doctoral degree such phenomena as higher pay, higher rank, variations by department, and so on. Are these, as the "union card" remark implies, just the results of the whims or prejudices of administra-

---

[1] I once remarked to a publisher that a chairman who was a mutual acquaintance was beginning to have difficulty with his department because his behavior suggested to his faculty that he did not love and appreciate them and that most faculty members needed these assurances perhaps above all others. The publisher was appalled, sure that I must be mistaken about such a collection of intelligent, hard-working, and, in some cases, eminent men. Two years later the department publicly blew up, fired the chairman without a dissenting vote, and experienced considerable outward mobility.

tors who seek to make their institutions look good by hiring and rewarding Ph.D.'s? They are not. That there is some desire on the part
of those charged with the administration of educational institutions to
upgrade their faculty by increasing its proportion of doctoral degree
holders is undeniable. But the pertinent question is not whether such
practices, and the differential rewards which accompany them, exist,
but why they do. And the answer to this query must, again, be found
in the social system of academics in America. Chapter Two described
the values of that system and how they came to be what they are. For
good or for ill, American academics are essentially discipline-oriented,
specialized, and research-centered. In most academic fields the doctoral degree is a research degree. Training for it is explicitly designed
to transmit the technical knowledge and skills of the field and to transmit the skills and mental capabilities required for the advancement of
knowledge in the field, that is, for research or scholarship. These values
and procedures are not, really, up for discussion in the United States.
The debate about them occurred in the last century and was resolved,
de facto if not de jure. The present value structure of the academic
profession is firmly fixed and, for those who work in it, can only be
accepted and used or, if resisted, resisted in knowledge of inevitable
consequence. This is not to say that there is not still debate about
teaching versus research, or that there should not be, perhaps, much
more debate than has occurred about the present nature of the multiversity, its general neglect of undergraduate instruction, the responsibility of professors for reaching out their understandings toward their
students instead of passively awaiting the approach of the students'
understandings to their own, and so on. (What responsibility the student has for his own education is also a matter worthy of attention;
teaching and learning are not separate processes, after all, but merely
obverse sides of the same process.) But the faculty member who objects to the nature of the present system because he believes it should
be different and therefore pretends that it *is* different is simply court-
ing irrelevance, not to mention difficulties in his own career. Whether
or not the Ph.D. is appropriate training for men who will invest the
major portion of their working energies in classroom teaching is a
question well worthy of debate and serious inquiry. That it is now
deemed appropriate is another matter, with the consequences for academic careers which we have seen and will continue to see. The failure

to make this distinction regarding many matters of academic custom and value structure is responsible for a great deal of wasted motion on the part of academics and their masters in the governing boards and state legislatures alike.

Table 7 describes another aspect of salary distribution. It con-

Table 7. SALARY AND AGE
(N = 307)

| | Age | | | | |
Salary	35 or Under	36 to 45	46 or Over	Total	Total Sample
	Per Cent				
$8,999 or less	*51*	25	24	100	23
$9,000–$11,999	26	*43*	31	100	45
$12,000–$14,999	1	39	*60*	100	22
$15,000 or more	10	20	*70*	100	10
Number	(77)	(109)	(121)	(307)	
Total sample	25	26	39		100

tains no surprises. We know already that rank and age are correlated with salary. This suggests that salary and age will also be associated, and, indeed, they are. The trend is clear: although almost a quarter of those receiving salaries of less than $9000 were over the age of forty-five, and 10 per cent of those receiving $15,000 or more were under thirty-six, it is apparent that for most men there is a positive correlation between advancing age and advance in salary. The apparent discrepancies are probably accounted for among those with low salaries by the 6 per cent of professors whose administrations apparently consider them incompetent and who are not rewarded with promotion either. The sudden apparent increase in young men at the highest salary level (from 1 per cent in the $12,000–$14,999 bracket to 10 per cent in the $15,000 and over bracket) is almost certainly due to the inclusion in that highest bracket of extraordinarily talented young men who must be very well paid in order to retain their services. Both these groups of individuals, however, are unrepresentative; the modal categories in the "line of central tendency" again tell the story: most of those least paid are among the youngest age group; most of those best paid are among the oldest, and the largest single group of those paid middle level salaries are also middle-aged.

Age and Academic Origins

We have alluded earlier to tensions between older and younger men and some of the sources of these. Not uncommon as a cause of friction or at least of suspicion on the part of the older scholars is the belief that younger men today are university-oriented and not very appreciative of the values of the liberal arts college. The facts show that younger scholars are not significantly different from the Old Guard in their educational origins. Table 8 shows source of first degree for men of varying lengths of institutional service. It is apparent that there have been few major changes over time in the origins of men who become private college faculty. Perhaps the general trend in the United States for students to attend publicly supported institutions, the universities in particular, is reflected in the somewhat declining proportions of young men who took degrees at private colleges, and what appears to be a slight increase in those earning bachelors' degrees at universities. The differences involved are not dramatic and may be random except in the private college figures where it appears to be quite real. It is not a cause for alarm among the colleges. As we have seen, almost half their faculties have experienced the private college as students, and it seems quite likely that it is that student experience which directs them back into the institution as faculty members. But, as reported in Chapter Two, the privately supported institutions are experiencing a serious net decline in the proportion of the college population which they matriculate, a decline which began shortly after the World War II veteran's boom ran out in 1949 and which has continued unabated since. In a nation where almost half the college age population does go on from high school to some form of further education, many students simply cannot afford the costs of private schooling. It is inevitable, then, that in time this decrease in proportions of students schooled in private institutions should be reflected in the academic labor supply. There seems no reason to believe that the declining proportions of faculty members initially schooled at private in-

Table 8. EMPLOYMENT LONGEVITY AND SOURCE OF FIRST DEGREE
(N = 305)

Employment Longevity	Source of First Degree						Total	Total Sample
	Major University	Minor University	Professional or Technical	Private College	Public College	Foreign		
	Per Cent							
4 years or fewer	25	25	5	35	6	4	100	32
5–8 years	20	20	0	49	8	3	100	20
9–15 years	17	17	6	46	11	13	100	26
16 years or more	28	17	5	50	0	0	100	21
Number	(69)	(62)	(13)	(134)	(20)	(7)	(305)	
Total sample	23	20	4	44	7	2		100

stitutions should have any effect on the colleges. Institutions of their academic quality do not need to rely on sentimental yearnings in order to assure an adequate labor supply, nor can student experience be assumed to somehow fit a man better for college teaching through letting him know what to expect. The smaller colleges are not that different from the universities.

How the Market Works

Before beginning a discussion of the similarities and differences between faculty members in the study who were or were not involved in the academic labor market during the study year, it may be useful to offer a brief parenthetical excursion concerning the way that market operates. For one thing, even among the sample of 125 market actives, there was not, actually, a great deal of mobility. Fully 58 per cent of the faculty members who reported themselves as having been involved in the market during the year also reported that, for one reason or another, nothing eventually came of the matter, and the proportion of the active sample who did accept positions at institutions other than those where the study found them was only 17 per cent. The first conclusion to be drawn about "the" academic labor market, at least for private college faculty and probably for everyone on it, is that a great deal of activity in it comes to naught. In many cases "market activity" consisted of nothing more than receiving some probe to the effect, "Would you be interested in a position at Fairlawn?" Such probes occur with varying degrees of formality, subtlety, and frequency for many men. Many originate with men without administrative authority to offer positions (friends), who then either do not follow up on the matter in their own institutions with the individuals who would have authority to do something about it or discover, when they follow up, that no appropriate positions are available. Some of these are casual barroom comradeships at professional meetings and are made without seriousness of purpose and accepted in that spirit. Others, a rather common category, are essentially shots in the dark aimed by inexpert marksmen at targets presumed desirable but fundamentally unlikely. ("No harm in asking even though we have no reason to believe he'd be interested.") A subdivision of this latter category is the blind letter, often sent to unknown individuals recommended by third parties and received by bemused addressees who have never heard of either the signer or his institution. It is not even particularly unusual for the recipient of such a blind probe not to know the third party suggesting his name to the sender of the letter. The marginal utility of this approach is very low indeed, and it is usually the hallmark of an institution or department of low prestige and in desperate straits for manpower.

Most of the "market activity" among a college faculty, then, is simply activity and nothing more. Academic men are a restless breed, and in a market as generally favorable as that which they have enjoyed for the past decade in most fields, a fair amount of stirring about is to be expected. But there are two other varieties of activity which come to naught, although they are more serious than the frequently meaningless probing and prying described above. In order for any serious market transaction to occur, the target faculty member must not only be approached or probed concerning his possible interest in shifting positions, he must also respond to the probe in ways of interest to its originator. There are, then, two opportunities for things to go awry. An individual seriously and hopefully approached by another institution often decides for a host of reasons and at various stages of the interaction with it (but before he is formally offered a contract) that he would prefer to remain where he is. An instance of this kind, even if it might have produced the legal proffer of a position if pursued, will fall into our "undeveloped" category because no proffer was made. Likewise, the proffering institution, even though dealing with a willing or even eager candidate, may decide at some stage of negotiation not to make him an offer after all. Such a decision need not reflect an adverse judgment about the candidate. A better man may appear, although the original was satisfactory enough, or the transaction may bring out the fact that the candidate would be too highly priced for the institution to afford, or not have exactly the specialty sought, or be too old or too young to be given the rank he would have to have without attracting intrainstitutional discord. And then finally, of course, an individual may be probed, interact with the proffering institution, be offered a position there, and decide to turn it down, sometimes because all he really wanted was an offer with which to boost his estimation at home, or for a variety of other reasons (including checking his own estimation of the job he already has), which are explored in Chapter Four. Approximately 26 per cent of the sample of market actives did receive such genuine proffers of other positions but decided in the end to remain where they were. Thus, of the original probing for interest with which a market interaction begins, only about 42 per cent of transactions develop further, and, of that proportion, men in our sample eventually elected to remain in place in a ratio of approximately three to two over those who elected to leave. And between the probings and the eventual decisions, whatever they may be, falls the shadow of a sometimes extended and always complicated social process conducted as a series of interactions between men and institutions and their representatives, each of which must be carried on in certain ways and come to certain outcomes in order for further stages of the interaction to occur. The process may be broken off at any point by either party for a variety of reasons and, as we have seen, the attrition rate is high.

Actives and Inactives

The total number of regular faculty members at the eleven institutions who were eligible for inclusion in the study was 710. I withdrew from this number those who reported themselves as having had some opportunity to engage in labor market activity during the year, 125 of these eventually being interviewed of 142 responding. (The remainder were ill, on leave, mistakenly self-reported, or absent at the time of interview.) A 50 per cent sample was taken from institutional records of 187 teaching faculty who reported no market activity of any kind. The data here reported, therefore, are based on two groups of men and women defined by self-report as having been active or inactive on the academic labor market during the academic year 1966–67. A third group was excluded from consideration entirely, those reporting that they had been probed about other positions without further action from the probing institution. To be classified as active the individual had to report that he had been asked to submit credentials or interview for the job in question, which is always at least a second stage in a transaction and is sometimes only the result of several probing or exploratory interactions. In one sense, then, this report understates the total volume of market activity since it excludes from report undeveloped probes.

Previous tables reported the characteristics of the total faculty group studied, both active and inactive. These 312 individuals represent 43.9 per cent of the total regular faculties in the academic disciplines of the eleven institutions, certainly a numerically adequate sample and one which I have no reason to feel is not thoroughly representative. Some of the differences discovered between faculty members active on the academic labor market during the year 1966–67 and those who reported no market activity for that period are statistically significant at very high levels. Had our question about market activity been asked concerning a longer time period, perhaps three years, such differences would undoubtedly have been even greater, for among the group inactive during 1966–67 there are unquestionably some persons who were on the market in years either immediately previous or immediately following. I assume, then, that any differences found to exist in any noticeable degree, whether statistically significant or not, are probably real. Where no differences are discovered, on the other hand, we must assume that none exist which would have been discernible by another differentiating technique.

The distribution of academic rank among the sample (actives) and control group (inactives) was virtually identical. In this sense, then, we are drawing from the same population. Whether this may also imply that in the matter of reward institutions do not differentiate between those who are active in the academic labor market and those who are not, however, is another matter. Evidence will be developed that they do make such distinctions among men, but rank, because of its considerable time component, is too gross a characteristic for them to appear.

When the same populations of market active and inactive faculty members are compared according to their departmental affiliations, apparent differences occur only among social scientists and "others," with actives and inactives occurring in almost identical proportions among natural scientists and humanists and linguists ($\chi^2 = 8.6599$; $p < .05$). "Others," who compose 27 per cent of the total group, make up only 21 per cent of the active group and 31 per cent of the inactive group. Since the "other" category includes a preponderance of artists of all kinds, these data may be taken to confirm their opinion that their market is slow. The degree of market activity displayed by the social scientists is also instructive. Although they make up a total of 21 per cent of the group, they represent only 16 per cent of inactives and 28 per cent of actives, suggesting that their development of market opportunities is disproportionate. Whether this is a result of a generally very good market for their services among the colleges or of self-conscious playing the market, there is no way to tell. Both may operate. Given that the category "other" is a residual one, we cannot account for their slow situation through any individualistic explanation based on the characteristics of one discipline, and we must assume it is a reflection of depressed marketability.

Table 9. SAMPLE AND CONTROL GROUPS BY SALARY
(N = 305)

	Salary					
	$7,999 or Less	$8,000– $9,999	$10,000– $11,999	$12,000– $14,999	$15,000 or More	Total
Sample (active)	3	41	24	26	7	100
Control (inactive)	10	31	31	19	10	100
Number	(22)	(106)	(85)	(66)	(26)	(305)
Total sample	7	35	28	22	9	100

The differences in salary for the active and inactive groups, shown in Table 9, are not startling. Indeed, no consistent trend may be apparent at first inspection. A statistically significant (5 per cent level) difference does occur, however, in favor of the market active faculty member. The differences are small, but they are discernible, and consistent. The market active group has less than its proportional share of members in the lower half of the pay scale (using $12,000 as a midpoint) and more than its share in the upper range, whereas the reverse is true for the inactive group—68 per cent of actives, compared to 72 per cent of inactives, have salaries below $12,000. Nor is this a function of differential rank distribution, for median and average salaries paid by rank are virtually identical in the two groups. This, of course, should not be unexpected. Chapter Two contended that the institutions must and do respond to market valuations set on men by their desirability to others. Men active on the market, then, are those with some salable characteristic, and the effect of possible sale is to drive their salaries up at home as their institutions bid against others to keep them. Actual mobility also has the same effect, for any institution wishing to hire a man must be willing to pay him more, as a rule, than he is receiving in place. If he really does not wish to move, typically, he lets his home school know what has been offered him in hope that they will match it. Since failure to do so might cause him to accept the proffered position, the employing institution will usually offer at least a token raise to reduce the disparity between his previous salary and that which he has been offered. The total effect of market activity, then, for the active class as a whole, is to raise their average salary over that of a group less active although in other ways similar.

But the actives and inactives in the eleven institution samples are not exactly similar in all other ways. A major distinction between them is in their educational preparation and certification as measured by highest earned degree. A much higher proportion of those active on the academic labor market have the Ph.D. or other doctoral degree (which also has something to do with salary, of course). Eighty-two per cent of actives hold the doctoral degree, compared to only 59 per cent of inactives. Only 2 per cent of actives hold no degree beyond the bachelor's, compared to 6 per cent of inactives. Again this should not be surprising: men without the standard credentials are perceived as less desirable and thus will have less frequent opportunity to act in the market. Since the chance that the association between the better certified and market activity is accidental is less than one in a thousand, we may conclude that despite what might be greater reason for the less certified to be unhappy in their positions, the market works in such ways as to reduce their opportunities to do much about it. Those without what is considered appropriate preparation have reduced chances to be mobile.[2] (The fact that the doctoral degree is not usually ob-

---

[2] It is not my purpose here to argue whether a doctoral degree is adequate preparation for college teaching and, thus, an appropriate requirement, or whether, for that matter, professional activity, publication, and so forth contribute to classroom effectiveness or much of anything else which undergraduate institutions may reasonably seek besides academic glamor. These considerations, while valid, are beside my point since the issues they raise have been effectively resolved in practice. This is the way in which market valuations are made, the way in which the academic social system works. Whether it ought to work that

tained by artists may have some impact on their lower mobility or marketability, for, while the master of fine arts is the terminal professional degree in a number of artistic fields, administrators who want to improve the ratio of Ph.D.'s on the faculty may be reluctant to hire persons without a doctoral degree, even if one is not conventional in a given area.)

Table 10 illustrates what may be a further aspect of respect-

Table 10. SAMPLE AND CONTROL GROUPS
BY SOURCE OF DOCTORATE
(N = 312)

	Source of Doctorate				
	Major University	Minor University	Other	No Doctorate	Total
	Per Cent				
Sample (active)	59	19	4	18	100
Control (inactive)	46	10	4	40	100
Number	(160)	(42)	(13)	(97)	(312)
Total sample	51	13	4	31	100

ability or desirability in academic credentials. The trend toward what would conventionally be considered better degrees among the active is consistent. We may conclude that while marketability is strongly related to the possession of the doctoral degree, among those with such degrees it is more desirable for them to have been taken at major universities than at minor ones. (Major universities were defined for this

way is a speculation perhaps entertaining although irrelevant since any changes in the way in which things are done are likely to be the result of hiring effectiveness rather than of logic or ethics. Faculty members, administrators, and students (loudly and endlessly) can debate the criteria for hiring and promotion, but in the long run individual market decisions (and, thus, vacancies and available replacements) are made with reference to what the individual wants and what the institution has to have.

study as those which had granted more than two thousand doctorates by 1962. All other institutions with graduate and professional curricula were considered minor. The second category, thus, is far more inclusive than the first and contains many quite dissimilar institutions.)

The data shown in the table do not permit us to make further distinctions, but it is probably true that hiring agents—chairmen, deans, and presidents—make distinctions among minor universities so that men with degrees from such institutions who are market active may often be judged to have better credentials than some of those similarly classified who are inactive. Connecticut Wesleyan and Ball State are really not in the same academic league, nor are the University of Oregon and Slippery Rock. These data may also be interpreted as reflecting different orientations toward professional activity among those differentially trained in different types of institution, for it may well be that one effect on an individual of taking his degree at a major university is to increase not only the likelihood that he will be probed for other positions, but that he will be doing the things that result in such probing.

Table 11 depicts what is clearly an extremely important factor in academic marketability. The association between the relative youth of the active group, as compared with the inactive, is marked. Par-

Table 11. SAMPLE AND CONTROL GROUPS BY AGE
(N = 307)

	30 and Under	31 to 40	41 to 50	51 and Over	Total
			Per Cent		
Sample (active)	18	44	33	5	100
Control (inactive)	6	31	30	34	100
Number	(33)	(111)	(94)	(69)	(307)
Total sample	11	36	31	22	100

ticularly significant, of course, is the final column which demonstrates the rapid reduction in mobility for men over fifty. Fully 33 per cent of actives are in the age category forty-one to fifty, but the proportion drops to 5 per cent for the older group although they compose 22 per cent of the total population studied. (Many, of course, are *far* over fifty, since in at least some of the institutions studied it is possible for men to teach as late in life as sixty-eight or seventy. This fact, that the other two major categories consist of decades while the last spans perhaps a decade and a half, accounts for some of the disparity, and we may safely assume that the 5 per cent of actives who fell into the oldest group were closer to fifty-one in age than to sixty-one. The dramatic drop in proportion active in the over fifty groups, however, is a result of market valuation, not a statistical artifact.) It is also interesting to note that although men below age thirty make up 11 per cent of the study population, only 6 per cent of the inactive group were in that age category which, however, includes 18 per cent of the actives. There are, of course, men of all ages in both groups; 37 per cent of inactives are forty or below, as are 62 per cent of actives. Thus, the decades below the middle years may be judged the most market active and younger men more likely to develop opportunities on the job market. This is likely to be true in most professions, but the disparate proportions in the two populations shown here raise the question of whether other phenomena may not also be operating—are those active and inactive likely to be different kinds of men?

Indeed they may. As Table 12 shows, more than twice as many of the active group took only five years or fewer to go from bachelor's to doctorate than did those in the inactive group. Somewhat larger proportions of the actives took six years or more to complete their degrees, but there are major differences between the two with regard to those who have not taken the doctorate. Among men with doctoral degrees only, a notably larger proportion of the control group than of the sample took more than six years to complete the degree—81 per cent and 70 per cent, respectively. Thus, whatever contributes to rapid completion of graduate work seems also to be related to market activity in professional life after graduate school. Although it is impossible to say what qualities or factors these may be, it is reasonable to guess that, on the whole, brighter and more professionally committed students might complete graduate work more rapidly than others. It is

Table 12.   Duration of Doctoral Programs
(N = 306)

	5 or Fewer Years	6 or More Years	No Doctorate	Total	Total Sample
			Per Cent		
Sample (active)	25	58	17	100	39
Control (inactive)	12	47	41	100	61
Number	(51)	(157)	(98)	(306)	
Total sample	17	51	32	100	

$$\chi^2 = 22.7087 \qquad p < .001$$

also possible that men who completed their degrees quickly attended graduate departments emphasizing attitudes and values which would lead both to speedy termination of work and to market activity later on. Our data do not permit us to make judgment on the matter, except to note that academic valuation is, generally, placed on rapid completion of degrees, and students who do so are judged well by graduate departments and are apt to be labeled as "comers," with all that this implies for their job placement in the future and its consequences. (Those highly evaluated are recommended to the best jobs the department has knowledge of. The better the job—as evaluated by professional or graduate school standards—the greater the valuation its context is likely to place on professional activity, including visibility, and the greater the consequent opportunity for further mobility. Academic reputations are difficult to change once established. Bright young men may go on being thought so well into middle age.)

Table 13 describes another aspect of time as it relates to the possibility of mobility or immobility: fully 41 per cent of actives were within their first four years of residence as opposed to only 27 per cent among inactives. The converse is also true; only 7 per cent of market actives had been in residence at the institutions where the study found them employed for as long as sixteen years as compared with 30 per

Table 13. SAMPLE AND CONTROL GROUPS
BY EMPLOYMENT LONGEVITY
(N = 308)

	Longevity at Employing Institution					Total Sample
	1 to 4 Years	5 to 8 Years	9 to 15 Years	16 Years or More	Total	
			Per Cent			
Sample (active)	41	23	29	7	100	40
Control (inactive)	27	18	24	30	100	60
Number	(100)	(62)	(81)	(65)	(308)	
Total sample	32	20	26	21	100	

$\chi^2 = 24.0593$ $p < .001$

cent of inactives. Again, these are not surprising findings if market active men are different in some way from men who do not become active on the academic labor market. If there are market active types, they would not be expected to remain in one place for as long at a time, on the average, as would inactive types. They would, as a class and at any institution, tend to have shorter longevity since they would move with greater frequency. More surprising, perhaps, is the fact that 29 per cent of actives had been in place for as long as nine to fifteen years, although we do not know whether their activity led them to eventual mobility. That the proportion active drops so drastically after sixteen years or more in place is hardly startling. In the first place, men build up strong emotional and capital investments (retirement programs, for example) in a position after so great a time, and, secondly, since most academic men do not complete their training until past the age of thirty, sixteen years on the job puts them very near fifty, which we have seen is the critical age for the decline of potential mobility.

Marginal totals may be of more interest in this table than individual cells. Administrators worried about continuing faculty turnover should take comfort from the fact that fully a fifth of college faculty members do remain in place for sixteen years or longer, and another quarter can be expected to be around for at least nine to fifteen years after recruitment. (And the fact that almost a third of the group had been in place for only four years or less is not necessarily an indication of excessive turnover. Because of the expansion of institutions during the sixties, many of these individuals held new positions rather than vacated ones.)

It would not have been unreasonable to suppose that market activity might be a function of dissatisfaction with promotion—that dissatisfied men might go on the market in order to secure promotion either elsewhere or by frightening their own institutions into it. Quite the contrary seems to be the case. As Table 14 shows, proportions in

Table 14. SAMPLE AND CONTROL GROUPS
BY RECENCY OF PROMOTION
(N = 255)

| | Recency of Promotion | | | | |
	Within 3 Years	4 to 7 Years	8 Years or More	Total	Total Sample
			Per Cent		
Sample (active)	52	33	15	100	49
Control (inactive)	37	25	37	100	51
Number	(113)	(74)	(68)	(255)	
Total sample	44	29	27	100	
	$\chi^2 = 15.9108$		p < .001		

the market active group show a linear decline as length of time in grade increases with only 15 per cent of those who had held their current ranks for eight years or longer being active and over half the actives having held their current ranks for three years or less. The control group, in contrast, shows no such trends in any direction, although one may be visible in the marginal totals for the faculties as a whole. This table may be interpreted as demonstrating that dissatisfaction with speed of promotion is not contributory to market activity as a general rule. If it were, we would expect the largest proportions of activity to fall in the four to seven years group, rather than among those with relatively recent promotions. Even allowing for the fact that the category of those who have served eight years or more since their last promotion must include many full professors who cannot be promoted any further, the fact that fully 27 per cent of all faculty members studied fall into that group although it comprises only 15 per cent of actives would seem to preclude any such explanation.

What is more likely the reason for this state of affairs is the nature of the promotion process as it interacts with the mechanics of the academic labor market. Chapter Two said that for any man with appropriate credentials and an even minimal record in the classroom and at institution chores, eventual promotion is probably assured. While this fact may be somewhat obscured, or even distorted, at the more competitive universities, it is reasonably well understood among liberal arts college faculty members, and that understanding may be presumed to reduce promotion anxieties among them as compared with their university brethren. But the decision of *when* to promote a man operates in similar fashion at both kinds of institution; the rules are pretty much the same although applied more liberally, and sometimes more humanely, in the college. Men are promoted as a reward for service. What constitutes this service is variously defined as contributions to one's discipline and its professional growth, good teaching, and service to the institution and its community or constituencies. But it is probable that professional activity weighs more heavily, and is more readily visible a reason for promotion at any given time rather than in the future than anything else. Thus, the faculty member who has been an assistant professor only three years but in that time has written a book which has received favorable reviews in professional journals and an article or two and has chaired sections at professional meetings is likely to be more seriously considered for promotion to associate professor than a man who has been assistant for five years but has managed to do less professionally in that time although he is known as a competent teacher and as someone whom the PTA can always call on to give an address. So the more professionally active faculty member is likely to be the one who experiences the most rapid promotion. In part, to be sure, this is to prevent his departure to another institution which will advance him. But the same activities which make him eligible for rapid promotion in place also act to draw him to the attention of other institutions; what makes him visible for promotion also makes him visible for recruitment, and the market is likely to come to him. Thus, we would expect that those most recently promoted, as a class, might also be those who would experience the greatest opportunity for market activity. Those who languish in a rank (full professors excepted) are likely to be less visible professionally and thus will come to the notice of recruiters least. In this way the facts become comprehensible. Market activity is inversely related to longevity in rank because there is not great dissatisfaction with speed of promotion in the smaller colleges since most men know they will eventually be promoted anyhow and because those activities which contribute to rapid promotion also contribute to market opportunities.

It appears, then, that market active faculty, although virtually indistinguishable from inactives in rank, are significantly different from them in that they are younger and better paid, they hold more doctorates, from better universities, and earned them more rapidly, they have been at their present institutions shorter times, and they have been promoted much faster than their inactive colleagues. They are also more likely to be social scientists than are inactives. Is this all a matter of "playing the game," a reflection of some cynical principle in academics that those who deliberately (and perhaps with malice aforethought) put themselves on the market are thereby better treated in some way? Or does the market reflect real differences among men? The data do not permit an absolute interpretation, but it is my opinion that market selection of persons with certain kinds of characteristics is quite real: the men who were active on the academic labor market in the academic year 1966–67 were a different type from those who were inactive, despite the inclusion among inactives of some persons who probably were active in preceding or later years. And the individuals the market selected for job transaction interactions with other institutions were, by professional standards, better men than those who were not so selected. They were better prepared, with better degrees; if speed of transit in graduate school is an adequate measure, they were better students; and the fact that they were paid more highly and promoted more rapidly suggests their institutions found their services more useful or, at least, more attractive.

There is, of course, some circularity of reasoning here, for, as suggested earlier, institutions judge their men in part according to their worth as attested by the interest of others in them. Furthermore, academic quality is not a clearly defined phenomenon. Men do make judgments about each other's qualifications, but they are apt to be made according to the criteria of the academic disciplines, which are more or less identical to the criteria of the academic labor market. Thus, the question, "Is a man really better and more valuable to an institution if he has the Ph.D. than if he does not, or if it is from Harvard instead of from Missouri State?" is unanswerable. We can only say that quality is presumed to be measured by academic convention and by the rules of the marketplace, by nature and source of degree, by professional activity, and so on. The doctoral degree, while not essential for the pursuit of college teaching, is necessary for a normal academic career in most fields. The source of this or another degree, however, is of significance only in the very early years of a man's professional career before he has had time to establish his status or competence through work, that is, through publication. When such professional activity takes place, it supersedes the source of the degree as a benchmark of his professional competence. In the absence of any further evidence of quality, source of degree may remain viable for perhaps ten years; after that time it seems to take on a distinctly double-edged quality in the minds of others. Thus, a fifty-year-old professor who has published nothing but took a degree from Harvard or Columbia in 1938 is likely to be regarded either as a man who did not live up to his promise or as one of the mistakes that even great departments occasionally make in licensing graduate students. Contrarily, a graduate of a lesser state university, of similar age and equally unpublished, who teaches at a smaller college, particularly if located in the same state as the university, has simply demonstrated the lack of worth implied by his unprestigious degree.

In general and without consideration of differences by field, the pecking order for graduate institutional prestige in the United States puts the great American universities (Harvard, Yale, Columbia, Berkeley) at the top; next come the great foreign universities (Oxford, Cambridge, the Sorbonne), then major universities (Big Ten, other large state or private universities), then minor universities (smaller state and private universities—Colorado, Duke, Wesleyan, Notre Dame, Nebraska, Temple), and, last, other places granting doctoral degrees (all the state colleges or universities that were recently state colleges; all colleges of education except, perhaps, Teachers College of Columbia; any Roman Catholic university except Notre Dame and Catholic University of America). The matter of institutional prestige will be explored further in Chapter Five. Many men, of course, are recognized as having great value to their institutions who either do not possess prestigious degrees or attain no recognition from their disciplines because of lack of professional contribution to them. And certainly few academics would argue that the competent classroom performance in undergraduate instruction sought in the liberal arts colleges cannot be expected of anyone without appropriate professional certification. The doctoral degree is typically a research degree, after all. Yet in general faculty members and institutional administrators tend to use the same criteria of judgment as those on which the market works. Indeed, market valuations are judgments of men's worth by other faculty members and administrators. In the relatively quick markets which most disciplines have enjoyed since World War II, an individual who receives absolutely no attention at all from other institutions is one who is totally unknown to anyone, with whatever that may imply, or is nearing retirement, or has been judged as of insufficient value to hire. It would of course be foolish to suggest that market activity be taken as an accurate estimate of an individual's contribution to his students, institution, and discipline. But it is equally foolish to pretend, as some small college administrators and faculty do, that market valuations, which are reflected in activity, are irrelevant. The market and the values it reflects are part of the academic social system, the institution of higher education in the United States, and the evidence of this study suggests that the market, and the behavior of the individuals in it, simply reflect other aspects of that institution and are in no way incongruous with them.

Concomitants of Decision

Let us now turn to the market decisions market active faculty made in 1966–67 and examine some of the reasons they made them and the characteristics associated with the makers. Table 15 illustrates the outcomes of market interactions experienced by our sample of 125 actives. Fifty-eight per cent of the interactions reported in interviews are classified as undeveloped, which means that explicit decisions about

Table 15. RANK AND OUTCOME OF MARKET TRANSACTION
(N = 125)

	Outcome					
Rank	Unde-veloped	Mobility	Fixed	In Process	Total	Total Sample
	Per Cent					
Full professor	61	17	14	8	100	29
Associate professor	54	5	22	19	100	33
Assistant professor	58	15	19	8	100	38
Number	(72)	(15)	(23)	(15)	(125)	
Total sample	58	12	18	12		100

$$\chi^2 = 6.3964 \qquad p > .50 > .30$$

accepting or rejecting offers occurred in only 42 per cent of the cases; for the rest, things either did not get or were not permitted to go that far. (In those cases, of course, some decision by the subject or recruiter was also obviously involved. It takes two to tango.) Two matters are immediately apparent from Table 15. First, as remarked above, most market activity does not result in the occurrence of an opportunity to move; it is dropped or turned off in earlier stages. Second, contrary to what might be expected, full professors were the most mobile of the three ranks, but were also the rank for which opportunities to be mobile were least developed. (Differences between rates for full and assistant professors, however, were trivial.) We can probably understand the relatively higher mobility of full professors by suggesting that, although opportunities to be mobile seem to come to assistant professors with about 10 per cent greater frequency, the full professor may be less likely to pursue them unless he is actually considering movement. The differences are neither great nor statistically significant, however. Assistant and full professors were the most mobile ranks and associate professor the least. As *The Academic Marketplace* (p. 42) remarked, "the associate professor is likely to define his best interests in staying put and getting promoted where he is." This interpretation is supported by the greater development of opportunities by associates compared with the other two ranks along with their much smaller tendency to become mobile. The high proportion of associates in process—double that of other ranks—may be presumed to be men with offers from other institutions who had taken them to their administrations and were waiting to see what would develop from that confrontation. This, too, supports the notion that they may prefer to better themselves where they are.

Perhaps the one really startling piece of information is how relatively little mobility there is. Mobility outcomes constituted 12 per cent of the market interactions reported by the members of our sample (all of whom, remember, were selected by reason of the fact that they had engaged in some sort of market activity in 1966–67). But those who elected to change their positions (fifteen persons) composed only 2.1 per cent of the total number in the professor ranks (710) on the faculties of the eleven institutions at the time of the study. Another 12 per cent of the sample interviewed (fifteen persons) had market interactions in process at the time of interview. If all these elected to accept new positions, the mobility rate would increase to 24 per cent of the total. If all rejected them, the rate of fixture would rise to over 30 per cent. Assuming that the ratio of mobility to fixture remained at two to three as it was at the time of interview, we can project the final outcomes as 57.6 per cent undeveloped, 16.8 per cent mobile, and 25.6 per cent fixed. This is close to the mobility rate of 14.9 per cent for college faculty reported by Ferriss (1966) from a United States Office of Education study of Spring, 1963, and seems a reasonable estimate which would give an overall rate for turnover due to mobility for the eleven institutions of 2.8 per cent of their total comparable faculties. (Total turnover, of course, would be higher due to deaths and retirements. And had instructors been included in the sample, it may be assumed that the proportion of mobiles would have been somewhat increased, since instructors traditionally have rather high rates of turnover, but in view of the very small mobility rate discovered, it is doubtful if the increase afforded by their inclusion would be significant.)

Table 16 compares salaries among men reporting different outcomes to their market interactions. There were no statistically significant differences among them, but we may nevertheless draw several rather interesting conclusions about the relationship between mobility and salary. The most important of these, of course, is that there is no significant relation between mobility and salary: Men do not develop market opportunities or leave their positions because their salaries are lower than those of their colleagues. Salary deprivation is not contributory to mobility. Market activity was relatively low among men with very high salaries ($15,000 and over) and, when it occurred, they tended to remain fixed about twice as frequently as they moved. This is not surprising; persons with very high salaries are probably priced out of the market for most positions available and are probably receiving, along with their salaries, as good a share of other perquisites as would be available elsewhere. Motivation for movement is thus not likely to be material betterment. It is also interesting to observe, however, that mobility is highest among higher salaried men (if we exclude the very highest salaries of $15,000 and over) and among those in the lowest salary category—27 per cent and 33 per cent respectively. Lack of development of market interaction is similar for men in most salary groups, while fixture in place is highest for men in the low to middle range of $10,000 to $11,000.

The relation between salary and mobility may be seen somewhat more clearly if we compare the upper third of the salary range reported by our respondents with the lower two-thirds and the salaries of mobiles with those of men reporting all other outcomes to their market experiences. Although the relationships do not begin to approach statistical significance, we have no reason to ignore the trend: although men with salaries of $12,000 or more constituted only 32 per cent of the total sample group, 40 per cent of mobiles had salaries falling in that range and only 31 per cent of nonmobiles did so ($\chi^2 = .5074$; $p < .50$). If there is any relation between salary and mobility, it seems to be that there is some tendency for mobility to be greater among men with relatively high salaries. This, of course, flies in the face of the con-

Table 16. OUTCOME BY SALARY
(N = 125)

Outcome	Salary							Total Sample
	$7,000–$8,999	$9,000–$9,999	$10,000–$11,999	$12,000–$14,999	$15,000 or More	Uncodable	Total	
	Per Cent							
Undeveloped	24	21	18	20	6	4	100	50
Mobility	27	20	13	33	7	0	100	12
Fixed	17	22	35	13	13	0	100	10
In process	13	27	40	20	0	0	100	12
Number	(27)	(27)	(29)	(31)	(8)	(3)	(125)	
Total sample	22	22	23	25	6	2	100	

ventional wisdom about motivations for mobility, but it is consistent with our earlier findings concerning salary relations between the sample group of market actives and the control group of market inactives and makes perfect sense in terms of what we know about the academic labor market as a social rather than as an economic phenomenon. The fact is that the more professionally attractive a person becomes, the more marketable he becomes and the more opportunities to move he receives; whether or not he elects to move at any given time, his salary increases as his own institution and others bid to secure or retain his services. To some degree, then, and within the general ranges of academic salary shared by all similar institutions (and, to a somewhat looser extent, by all institutions) in given disciplines, higher salaries and greater mobility will be positively correlated, as will lower salaries and reduced mobility. To put it another way, the sheer desire to move, for reasons of salary or not, is not sufficient to create a move; the opportunity to do so must also be present and available to an individual with the motivation. But, to some degree, opportunity is more readily available to those more academically attractive, which has the long-range effect of increasing their salaries and other perquisites, thus reducing motivations for mobility. To those that have shall be given.

There also seems to be a market for persons perhaps less academically attractive than average. More than a quarter (27 per cent) of those moving to other positions were men without the doctoral degree. As we have seen, it is not true, as the myth would have it, that the Ph.D. or other doctoral degree is a union card for college teaching careers in the sense that one cannot pursue the career without it: 18 per cent of the sample do not possess such a degree. But it is true that, in most fields (the arts are the notable exception), the doctoral degree is standard certification, and men cannot expect a successful career without one. College teaching as a career is open to persons without the doctorate, but as a rule they may expect to be second-class citizens of academia. In the present sample, 15 per cent of those with doctorates received salaries below $9000, compared to fully 63 per cent of those whose highest degree was a master's. Figures were closer in the $9000 to $11,999 salary range—45 per cent of those with doctorates and 37 per cent of those with only a master's. However, 40 per cent of those with doctorates received $12,000 or more, and none of those with only a master's received that much. I conclude from all these observations that the relationship between mobility and academic attractiveness is not linear but U-shaped. The market is more or less dominated by the search for the most attractive and competent as measured by conventional standards of certification and professional activity, but a subsection is concerned with the search more simply for men to fill classrooms or for replacements for vacancies at salaries so low that only less qualified persons are available to fill them.

Reflections of similar matters can be seen in Table 17, which

Table 17.   DURATION OF DOCTORAL PROGRAM AND OUTCOME
(N = 120)

	Years			
Outcome	5 or Fewer	6 or More	No Doctorate	Total Sample
	Per Cent			
Undeveloped	43	62	67	58
Mobility	23	4	19	12
Fixed	20	20	9	18
In process	13	13	5	12
Total	100	100	100	
Number	(30)	(69)	(21)	(120)
Total sample	25	58	18	100
	$\chi^2 = 18.8205$	p > .01 > .001		

relates duration of Ph.D. program to market outcomes for our sample of actives. It is based on the hypothesis that men who complete their doctoral degrees with dispatch may be more professionally motivated, or possibly even more competent, than those who take longer. This hypothesis suggests that there would be different market outcomes from their transactions, and the table suggests that these occur. Those who completed doctoral programs within five years of their baccalaureate degrees developed more of their market opportunities (57 per cent compared to 38 per cent for those taking six years or more and 33 per cent for those without the doctorate), and were 19 per cent more mobile than their colleagues who took longer. Those without the doctorate developed their opportunities—or had them develop—considerably less often, but were nearly as likely to be mobile when the chance occurred. Interestingly, both groups with the doctoral degree remained fixed in identical proportions, thus putting to rest the notion that being a graduate school prodigy inclines a man to loose feet in his professional life thereafter. (This rather common belief may be explained by the greater marketability and development of offers on the part of the rapid achievers, but they appear to stay put just as frequently as others. The lower mobility rate among the slow achievers, thus, is a function of lack of opportunity and lack of development of offers.) The low fixture rate on the part of those without doctorates may be presumed to indicate that they do not play the market as do people with more professional security; when activity occurs, it is deadly serious and with intentions for movement. It may also reflect lower bargaining power and professional attractiveness; an offer from another institution brought to the attention of one's own administration may result in a salary increase or promotion for men who are academically attractive. For those without conventional certification, on the other hand, it may result in a rebuff which makes it impossible for the individual not to leave in order to retain his self-respect. Academic poker is a losing game to play without winning cards; bluffing is difficult because the institution has little to lose by calling.

Promotion might also be presumed to have some effect on mobility to the degree that the individual faculty member can control his opportunities for promotion. It is reasonable to wonder if men who are dissatisfied with their rate of promotion are more mobile as they seek from other sources rewards they cannot secure at home. It was suggested by a previous finding (Table 14) that promotion dissatisfaction is not a relevant variable in mobility behavior, actives, in general, having histories of more rapid promotion than inactives. But Table 18 shows no relation between mobility or fixity (or, indeed, even development of opportunities, which might be thought useful for forcing promotion out of one's reluctant administration) and speed of promotion. It appears that dissatisfaction about promotion cannot account for mobility. Obviously, I have not discussed all the variables with which mobility and fixture are related in the academic context, nor

Table 18.   Recency of Promotion and Outcome

| | Recency of Promotion | | | |
Outcome	Within 3 Years	4 to 7 Years	8 Years or More	Total Sample
	Per Cent			
Undeveloped	56	61	53	57
Mobility	11	12	16	12
Fixed	17	20	21	19
In process	16	7	11	12
Total	100	100	100	100
Number	(64)	(41)	(19)	(124)

$$\chi^2 = 2.0866 \qquad p < .95 > .90$$

are the relations entirely clear between movement and variables discussed in this chapter. We can regard these facts simply as a demonstration that there is a sociology of the academic labor market as well as an economics of it and that the market is probably impossible to understand without at least familiarity with the social system in which it operates.

Institutions—Sacred and Secular

In addition to the personal characteristics which distinguish mobile and immobile employment patterns, institutional characteristics may affect mobility. Institutions were invited to participate in the study on the assurance that they would be kept anonymous and that no interinstitutional comparisons would be made. I shall not, consequently, describe the specific characteristics of mobility rates or faculty among the eleven colleges sampled. It is not a violation of confidentiality, however, to mark one characteristic which dichotomizes the institutions of the sample and looms large in the thinking of many academic men. One of the most evident distinctions among the colleges studied (although it is often unnoticeable on the campus) is that six are church-controlled or church-related while five are independent and, presumably, secular. Academics without experience in them are often wary of accepting positions in church-affiliated institutions on the assumption (perhaps a historical hangover) that their freedom in teaching or research may be curtailed by institutional adherence to denominational doctrine. That this fear was still not entirely unrealistic even in the late 1960s is shown by the turmoil over exactly these issues in a number of Roman Catholic colleges and universities, including the prestigious Catholic University of America, where the controversy over papal statements on birth control rent the institution in 1968, and by academic freedom cases reported by the AAUP in a handful of small, usually southern, fundamentalist colleges.

In the vast majority of Protestant-affiliated colleges, however, and in what may be at least a plurality of Catholic colleges, such fears are groundless. There is no indication of any kind—except for one respondent's admittedly speculative remarks about "the Lutherans" who control his school—that anything of the kind exists in any institution surveyed here. If such events did take place at any of the colleges here considered, they would have been likely to appear in the interviews of the research and to be reflected in market statistics. There were (with the single exception noted) no statements in interviews which indicated that church affiliation was regarded by respondents at church-affiliated schools as in any way affecting their employment and, hence, their market activity. However, even though development of market opportunities occurred with 5 per cent less frequency among the faculties of church-related institutions, faculty members in them were only half as likely to remain fixed when offers occurred (12 per cent remained fixed at church-related institutions compared with 23 per cent at others, with only a 2 per cent differential among those still in process). The faculty of the church-related institutions appear possibly to be more mobile than those in independent colleges, but the conclusion must be tentative due to the statistical insignificance of the relations shown ($p > .30 < .50$). It would be erroneous to conclude, however, that the purported lack of freedom at the church schools causes this phenomenon. There is an alternative explanation which seems to me more persuasive, although admittedly impressionistic: as a group, the church-related colleges in this study are probably of somewhat lower academic quality than the independent institutions with which they are compared. In the original ratings by academic administrators through which the sample was selected, no church-related institution was ranked in first, second, or third place among the group as a whole, and none was ranked as either first or second in its state. They are, typically, less well endowed, and a rank ordering by average faculty salary would find most of them toward the bottom. The somewhat greater mobility among their faculty, therefore, may be a reflection of professional and market phenomena rather than undesirability as determined by other criteria. (In fairness to them, it must also be remarked that all are schools of good quality, as compared with a national average, and that at least one of them has several academic departments of national, and, in one case, international, standing. Another, however, is in very serious financial straits.)

FOUR

Off to See the Wizard

Mobility Processes

Academic mobility is a social process: job opportunities do not, as a rule, come out of the blue to unsuspecting faculty members who then decide on the spot whether or not to accept them. Rather, the process is a series of more or less standard social interactions between agents of the proffering institution and the prospective recruit, often involving agents of the institution in which the recruit is employed as well. It usually follows a conventional sequence of steps: Step One is identification of the prospective recruit—the recruiting institution in some way fixes on an individual as a prospect. The faculty member himself occasionally initiates this identification through friends or casual acquaintances, or even by answering advertisements or written inquiry, but the initial location of individuals is more usually made by some agent of the institution seeking men—the proffering institution. Step One also frequently includes some initial screening, often vague, to ascertain that the potential recruit is at least generally suitable for the position, for example, that he does have a Ph.D. or that he has published. Location of potential recruits among the smaller colleges is somewhat haphazard. Members of the proffering departments write their friends inquiring either about their own availability or for their nominations; the department advertises its vacancies in professional journals; deans and presidents make recruiting trips actively seeking candidates in the field; universities either nearby or prestigious are asked to nominate candidates.

Step Two is the first probe of the prospective recruit—the individual located in Step One and identified as of possible desirability is in some way approached to determine his availability as a candidate. If he has responded to an advertisement or in some other way identified himself as a potential recruit, this step is, of course, omitted. For most prospects, however, this probe is the first indication they receive of the proffering department's interest in them. Probing, too, is highly generalized and sometimes vague, running the gamut from quite straightforward letters or personal inquiries to extremely casual overtures in unlikely places and ways.

> Well, it was through my wife. I don't know whether this fits into your questionnaire, but the whole problem arises from the fact that my wife is also a Ph.D. candidate, and she wants a job for a couple of years from now. The probe was not for this year particularly, although they were willing to consider it for this year. But I first heard about it through one of her professors, so it operated through her, actually.

Step Three is the first response of the prospective recruit; it may be positive, negative, or ambiguous. At this point, the process becomes more various. Depending on a host of more or less random factors—including the relative prestiges of the potential recruit and the proffering department, the desperation of the department, and the desirability of the job—positive or ambiguous responses may be met with further probing of several varieties; even a negative response may not be accepted as final if the proffering institution really wants a particular individual. However, positive responses usually, but by no means always, result in Step Four, the identification of the potential recruit as an active candidate. Probing is likely to be carried on in ways that permit graceful refusal on the candidate's part without implying strong rejection of the proffering persons or institution. Candidates understand this and usually respond politely even if negatively.

> My reply was that I was interested but I planned to stay here another year. And I tried to suggest that perhaps the year after next they might contact me again.

Once a positive response has been elicited, however, the institution may drop its pose of diffident circumspection and describe specifically the position it has to offer and ask the candidate frankly for a statement of his qualifications for it. These actions are usually followed by Step Five, the period of mutual inspection, a time in which the proffering department or institution (and hiring at small colleges is, as we have noted, more commonly institutional than departmental) reviews the professional biographies of all the candidates and, not infrequently, invites the best prospects to the campus for a visit and mutual look-over.

> I did have an interview . . . and previous to the interview I had had some other information about the college, and there were other external things which came into it which probably shouldn't influence whether a person will take a particular job or not. But they do condition you. It was, well, my family; I'm not quite sure they wanted me to go to that place, and I wasn't really that encouraged by the school. I know it sounds terribly, terribly snobbish, but the quality of the school I didn't feel was of the standard I had expected of the students here.

> It was a very nice visit. They were very hospitable, we talked, and they introduced me to all of the people who would like to look me over, and they didn't make me feel like a horse that you look at his teeth. So it was thoroughly enjoyable.

It is not uncommon, at the conclusion of these site visits, for Step Six, negotiations, to occur, although candidates do not always realize that they are being negotiated with, for the discussions may be informal, conducted with more than one party, and never couched in specific terms of salary, teaching load, and responsibilities. The site visit which may conclude the period of mutual inspection (if the candidate is not hired without a visit or in effect dropped in favor of others more attractive by not being asked to visit) is often concluded by Step Seven, the offer, although that may follow by letter either immediately after the visit or after a period of time in which other candidates are looked over. Candidates for whom this period is too long may be well advised to reconsider their decisions before accepting, for it means the institution is settling for them when it could find no one it wanted more, although it tried. Institutions, likewise, are well advised to rank candidates for desirability, asking the best first, or they may lose to someone else the man they really want. It is not uncommon for candidates to be given verbal offers, either at the time of the site visit or afterward by telephone, and then receive a letter confirming the terms proposed or agreed on.

The offer, usually quite rapidly, must then be subject to Step Eight, decision—acceptance, rejection, or haggling. There were no instances of haggling in the handful of mobility cases in the sample, and it is relatively unusual for haggling to occur here rather than in Step Six (negotiations) where it belongs. In cases where candidates have not had it made clear to them that they are being negotiated with, however, they may attempt to do so at the time they finally—and for the first time—receive a clear statement of the terms of the position they are being asked to take. Haggling at this stage is seldom very productive. In the first place, if an institution makes its decisions about what to offer a man without consulting him through negotiation, it is unlikely to change its terms much. In the second place, if the individual has not already made it his business to find out exactly what the institution had in mind, it seems reasonable to suppose that he was not overly concerned with details and thus will either accept or reject what is offered without qualification. Some disappointment and unhappiness, however, undoubtedly accompanies such tactics, and they probably result in fewer appointments being made than would be made under other strategies.

Institutional agents, such as deans, are usually better negotiators than faculty members. They have more experience, and they do not suffer from the typical faculty member's hesitation to flatter himself by setting a high price on his services. There are no connotations of self-advertisement or lack of humility in a dean's driving a hard bargain as an agent for the institution, which is incapable of being embarrassed by its own tenacity anyway. Individuals bargaining for themselves, on the contrary, are likely to be foolishly hesitant about asking for what they really want. This seems to be particularly true of financial matters, but similar hesitations may occur even in bargaining for working conditions.

Acceptance or rejection of the offer is often not the final stage in the market transaction. In the case of acceptances, Step Nine, last contacts, of course, involves continuing communications, usually mutually pleasurable and mutually congratulatory, leading to the appearance of the recruit on his new campus at some later time. Rejections, however, are also subject to last contacts. These may be mere polite expressions of regret from both parties, but they may also consist of offers for another time, offers of summer employment, requests for nominations of other candidates, and so on. The market transaction may be over, in other words, but still lead to continuing interactions.

Probes

One of the expectations with which the *Janus* study was begun was that most mobility among men of the private colleges would be among institutions of similar kind, that is, that there would be a small college market within which the majority of transactions would take place. The results of the pilot study, however, gave reason to doubt this assumption, and the data of the principal work confirm that suspicion. More than one-third (36 per cent) of the probes reported by the sample of market active faculty members came from institutions classified as minor universities, with only 29 per cent originating in small private colleges. The significance of this for the colleges and for their Janus character is clear: they are in competition for faculty with institutions which are usually larger, often better supported, and more apt to be committed to highly professionalized values. Under the circumstances it may be surprising that their mobility rate was as low as it was, but we will see later that it is, indeed, the most highly professionalized faculty members who do become mobile. Small colleges, both public and private, however, accounted for 43 per cent of the activity and all sizes of universities for 43 per cent. Probing was dominated by institutions of low and middle levels of academic prestige; major universities[1] accounted for only 7 per cent of probes reported and nonteaching or even nonacademic professional opportunities together accounted for only 6 per cent (8 per cent of responses were uncodable). The absence of even a single report of a nonprofessional

---

[1] The use of the terms *major league, minor league,* and *bush league* to describe institutional prestige levels or strata simply conforms to common academic practice. Some invidious comparison is probably implied, especially as a result of the cultural value assigned to the term *bush league,* but it is in the common usage, not the personal values of the writer. There are a number of academically superb small institutions which are, nonetheless, bush league as regards national standing.

probe was undoubtedly the result of the failure of respondents to define nonacademic and nonprofessional positions as opportunities rather than a reflection of an absence of chances to obtain work at something different. Once finished with graduate study and employed on a regular basis in an academic institution, few faculty members ever even seriously fantasy about doing anything else for a living. However, in many academic disciplines, employment opportunities do exist on the general labor market, some of which would even permit exercise of professional skills, and there is certainly no lack of respectable white-collar employment available in industry and commerce. Such positions are not socially visible, however, for men whose lives are committed to academics, and so, although the evening paper may report positions available for which professors might be qualified, it does not occur even to an individual unhappy in the teaching position he holds that he might investigate the nonacademic labor market.

Probes of an academic and professional nature, however, came from all over. Eighty-six per cent of those reported were for teaching positions in universities and colleges, and another 2 per cent concerned academic work of a nonteaching nature. Some impression of the variety of sources from which probes originated may be gained from the replies of social scientists at one of the eleven colleges to the question "When I contacted you earlier, you indicated that you had had an opportunity to take another job this year. Where was that?" The answers included the University of Pittsburgh, Resources for Tomorrow, the University of Nebraska, Beloit College, Indiana University, the University of California at Santa Cruz, William and Mary, the University of Wisconsin, Colorado Woman's College at Denver, and the University of Minnesota. This list suggests the range of opportunities available and something of the great demand for academic services as well. It is unrepresentative of the small college labor market as this study found it, however, in an overrepresentation of universities and an underrepresentation of other small colleges both public and private. This is, of course, accidental, although it may be related to the high quality of the institution from which the replies were drawn. One thing is very clear, however: the view rather common in the multiversities that the good small college is a Siberian wasteland from which there can be no return under any circumstances is false. It is, apparently, rather difficult to draw the attention of a major university to oneself if one is located in a private college (and we have seen in Chapter Two that there is reason to believe that most teachers in small colleges do not define their jobs as consistent with the values of the multiversity). But that one need be stuck in any particular institution because of an inability to leave is, for the members of our sample at least, not true. It should be recalled, however, that the persons eligible for inclusion in the sample were more mobile than those in the control group. For men who are professionally inactive, the market is much less quick. The "to him that hath shall be given" nature of the market is also indicated by many respondents' replies. The more professionally active a man is, the more visible he becomes and the more likely he is to receive probes.

> Well, it is tough to say exactly from where . . . there are a couple of places. I was on leave of absence from the college last year, and I had a research grant from Resources for Tomorrow, and there's been a continuing interest at Resources to hire me to do research. [Interviewer: Oh, on a permanent basis?] Right. And I was interviewed by the University of Michigan a couple of weeks ago, and at Christmas time I talked to the University of California at Santa Barbara.

> Well, I actually had two this year that were quite serious, from the other end at least, I thought. One was back in the fall at Westmount College, in Santa Barbara, and the other was, it must have been March sometime, was Macalester College up in St. Paul.

> Well, there are four indications of interest as far as . . . all of them for dean of the faculty.

The data of this study, being based on recipients, do not permit exploration of the processes in the proffering institutions which select Professor X as the target of a probe instead of Professor Y, but we do have respondents' descriptions of how the inquiries came to them and their guesses as to the process of origination. Table 19 describes the nature of the probing process from recipients' perspectives. Differences among ranks are not statistically significant, but those which do occur make sense. The largest category of probes, 25 per cent, were direct— that is, made directly to the recipient—and unforeseen. These were frequently referred to as "bolts from the blue" or as coming "out of a clear blue sky."

Table 19.   RANK AND NATURE OF FIRST CONTACT
(N = 125)

Nature of Contact	Rank			Total Sample
	Assistant Professor	Associate Professor	Full Professor	
	Per Cent			
"Blue sky" probe, direct and unforeseen	23	34	17	25
Occurred in the course of some professional interaction	10	12	19	14
Occurred in the course of some social interaction	2	2	8	4
Inquiry from acquaintance	13	17	17	15
Unsolicited application by respondent	10	12	11	11
Former employment at proffering institution	4	7	8	6
Former study at proffering institution	6	2	6	5
Indirect, through intermediary	31	12	14	20
Total	100	100	100	100
Number	(48)	(41)	(36)	(125)

The president wrote me and said, "I understand you might be interested." It came as a bolt out of the blue, as a matter of fact, and I have been trying to canvas my mind as to how the man got my name.

This type of probe seems to be least common among full professors. The second most frequent type of probe was indirect, carried on through intermediaries.

I got a letter from my thesis chairman who had a letter from Indiana, from the chairman of the department there. And he [the thesis chairman] told me that they were interested in a person, and that if I were interested in a job to send my credentials on. And I did, and they got in touch with me.

It was from a colleague here whose brother-in-law is on the staff there. Chairman of the department of history, whose brother-in-law called and said, "We're looking for candidates. Do you have anyone at Shadyside that we might be interested in?" And he checked with me and I was interested, and so he referred to me.

Assistant professors seem to be the favorite target for indirect probing of this type. This is not inexplicable, nor is the fact that the principal means by which senior men were probed were inquiries made during the course of professional interaction aimed at some other end, for example, during attendance at professional meetings or through inquiries from acquaintances. Indirect approaches are usually of the variety suggested by the quotations above, that is, essentially unaimed at particular individuals, and thus would be chiefly devised for persons of junior rank where the variety of persons who might fit a position is presumed to be somewhat broad. Indirect approaches also occur, however, in cases aimed very specifically at particular men when the proffering institution employs someone who knows the target well to sound him out before exposing its interest in him through a direct contact. The logic of this tactic is that if he is approached directly by representatives unknown to him of an institution unknown to him he is likely to refuse them before interest can be aroused, but an intimate contact may be able to do some advance publicity. Senior men, being better known and often more professionally visible, have more opportunities for probes to occur during the course of other kinds of interactions and often have a wider professional acquaintance in their fields, so that a direct approach is facilitated by the opportunities to get together afforded by professional meetings and other interactions. Nor is it surprising that assistant professors were least likely to be probed through inquiries from acquaintances. Being junior, they had had less time to develop networks of professional acquaintances, and what friends they may have had in the disciplines were unlikely to be involved in departmental or institutional hiring processes.

One interesting feature of a minority of respondents' reports is the cross-disciplinary probing activity indicated in the "brother-in-law" quotation above. Since the institution is a far more important referent to small college teachers than it is to university men, often more significant than the department, it would not be terribly unusual for a sociologist, let us say, at Fairlawn, acting as an informal agent for the chemistry department there, to contact a professional acquaintance at Shadyside, asking the second sociologist if he would inquire among his friends in chemistry to see if any of them would be interested in moving. (Because of the larger departmental sizes and the nature of departmental commitments at multiversities, such events are less likely to occur among them and may be treated with suspicion when they do.) Inquiries from acquaintances, then, play a part (15 per cent) in the probing process. Informal friendship networks and grapevines of this nature are a well-known characteristic of academics and, since job information is of vital importance in any occupational system and the transmission of it is very badly institutionalized or regulated in academics, it is not surprising that informal systems play a role in transmitting it.

One feature of Table 19 is important because of the light it casts on a difference of conventions between universities and colleges: 11 per cent of the probes reported by respondents were self-initiated in some way. These were mostly of two types—direct and unsolicited approach by the individual to an institution in which he has some interest (often for reasons of location or climate) and initiation of himself as a prospect by answering institutional broadsides directed at anyone who may be interested in applying or by maintaining an active file with a professional or institutional placement agency.

> [Direct approach] I wrote to an individual at that particular institution. [Friend of yours?] An acquaintance. A man who is director of education in my field. I wrote him because I realized that this was a good liberal arts college and they were going to have graduate students there. There really isn't too much that I can accomplish in a setting like this that I haven't already accomplished, if you follow me. That is, if I was to look forward to another twenty-five or thirty years of doing the same sort of thing I'm doing now, it becomes clearly a matter of opportunity.

> [Response to institutional broadside] One of the members of the faculty here received a form letter from Fairlawn. . . . The position they wanted filled was chairman of their zoology department, and the kind of person that they were looking for, that is,

the one . . . the age and experience and background seemed to fit my qualifications. So I replied. [The person who got the letter here gave it to you, or informed you of it?] That's right, yes. Well, informed all the staff. We do this if we get either personal or circular letters in regard to either student or faculty opportunities. We inform each other, we circulate them.

[Use of institutional placement service] My name is on the books with the placement bureau at Wisconsin, and they sent me a notice that Fairlawn was looking for people in German, and then I heard from the chairman there a couple of weeks later [in response to the respondent's submission of credentials].

[Use of commercial placement service] Well, this came through, I believe, a notice from the Lutton Agency, a private placement agency in Chicago. [Did you then apply directly to Fairlawn University, or did you respond to the agency?] They ask that you do that and I did. You send a notice to the agency and they send your credentials. *My credentials are always on file at Lutton; they always have been.* [They specialize in musicians, don't they?] Yes, they do. I have two more positions here, one from the University of Colorado that I would love to look into, but I'm not going to do it for various reasons. [Did Fairlawn ever reply directly to you?] Yes, I received an initial acknowledgment of the receipt of the credentials probably, oh, just shortly after I sent them. Then I received a notice the last week in April that they had filled the position. [Emphasis added.]

What is significant about these forms of self-initiation of candidacy among the faculties of private colleges is that there seems to be no stigma attached to the practice. There were no indications in interviews that respondents who initiated employment contacts felt that they were in any way engaging in nonprofessional or socially disapproved behavior nor that their initiation of their own candidacies would be held against them by Fairlawn. Nor, in the occasional discussion of hiring by men who had engaged in it for Shadyside, was there any indication that they regarded self-initiation as stigmatizing for the candidate. (There was one chairman who remarked, perhaps patronizingly, "Of course you know the quality of person who usually does this kind of thing," referring to self-initiation. Even this respondent indicated, however, that he did review the letters or credentials of self-initiated candidates.) Quite the contrary is true at the multiversities, where there is a distinct convention that persons who initiate

their own candidacies for vacant positions either through direct contact or through the use of placement agencies must be of inferior
professional quality or they would not have to resort to such devices
(Caplow and McGee, 1958, pp. 111, 120–121). The logic of this convention is that self-initiation cannot carry the guarantees of disciplinary
respectability which, for the multiversity, are essential requirements for
the consideration of a candidate in order to prevent the department
from making a foolish selection (which is also the reason that initiation by someone from another discipline is frowned upon). The taboo
does not seem to exist in small colleges, perhaps because of the relative
absence in them of the more esoteric features of the disciplinary prestige system.

Table 19 showed that in 26 per cent of cases the nature of the
first probe was such as to indicate some prior contact between the
candidate and the proffering institution (acquaintance or prior presence as a student or faculty member). Although in only 11 per cent
of the cases did the recipient of a probe report that he had been a
student or faculty member at Fairlawn in the past, fully 69 per cent
of all respondents reported themselves known to persons at the proffering institution, and in 32 per cent of instances a fairly close relation
existed with at least one individual in the proffering department:
14 per cent reported indirect acquaintance (that is, acquaintance
with persons elsewhere who had acquaintances at the proffering institution), 11 per cent had direct acquaintances in the institution but
not in the proffering department, 12 per cent had slight acquaintance
in the department, 5 per cent had a close acquaintance in the department, 14 per cent had a good friend in the department, and 13
per cent were known to several members of the department.

The reason for this situation is to be found in the nature of
information transmission in the academic profession. It is perhaps
natural that when a department has a position to fill its members
should seek to interest in it persons with whom they are familiar and
congenial. It is also necessary that they do so, for there are no other
effective means of communication between institutions and departments. The key word is, of course, *effective*. Means of communication
other than the informal and interpersonal grapevine do exist in academics. In recruiting faculty, advertisement in professional journals

and listings with academic and commercial placement agencies are certainly means of communication, as are letters and recruiting visits to potential sources of candidates. But, in the small colleges little less than in the multiversities, the kinds of information about potential colleagues which are of greatest concern to academic men cannot be communicated by these means. Formally, the information most needed by a hiring institution concerns the candidate's teaching ability and research potential (if the latter is at issue at all). Informally, and of greater concern at least to department members, is his compatibility and (sometimes, in the colleges) his potential for adding luster to the departmental image through disciplinary prestige.

All these phenomena are fuzzy, subjective, and subject to the problem that appraisals of them are no better than one's knowledge of the appraiser. For this reason, the kinds of information that can be elicited by formal means, means open to all candidates, are relatively useless in the hiring process. What departments really need to know about potential candidates can be known best only about persons with whom the hiring agents are already acquainted or, at the last useful remove, only through persons whose judgments the agents are capable of evaluating, that is, through friends or acquaintances who know the candidate. Thus, in the absence of institutionalized means of transmitting the information which it is most necessary for hiring agents to possess, informal and unofficial channels of communication develop to serve the need, and most candidates for probes are those of whom something is already known by the proffering department. Multitudes of quotations from interviews illuminate the point.

> [How closely would you say you were acquainted with this individual, the now dean?] Quite—friends. And colleagues, but friends first, I guess. [Was he your chairman at your previous school?] He was at Dakota when I was working on my master's. Then he went to Omaha, and I went to Omaha and then I came here.

> There was one man . . . whom I corresponded with in connection with an anthology I was editing . . . and then there was another man that I taught with at Smith.

> [How closely acquainted with this man were you?] Very. He's a close friend. We've gone through high school and college and graduate school together.

One of the faculty members there used to be on the staff here and we were pretty good friends. [Do you think he nominated you for the position?] I know he did.

There's one faculty member there who was from here, but he had nothing to do with this connection. We did go to visit them while we were there, but he wasn't involved in the offer.

The last statement is particularly interesting. There was frequent insistence in interviews that "he wasn't involved in the offer," that is, that the respondent's acquaintance at the proffering institution had not instigated the offer or probe, particularly when the acquaintance was across disciplinary lines. Such claims are almost undoubtedly true, but instigation and involvement are not the same thing. Offers or probes may only be officially initiated by the department, the dean, or another executive, but the nomination of potential candidates to departments known to be seeking them very frequently comes on the initiative of a prospective candidate's acquaintances on the proffering faculty, who then remain otherwise uninvolved in any further transaction. It is extremely unlikely that the proportion of prior acquaintance described was only a function of the candidates' wide acquaintance in the profession. The profession at large is too large and the circles of many small college professors too restricted relative to the total number of persons in college teaching. The degree to which prior acquaintance operates in hiring transactions can also be estimated from respondents' reports of how the probes which they received originated in the proffering institution. In only 20 per cent of instances was ignorance professed, while self-initiation for the position in question accounted for another 14 per cent. But in 45 per cent of all transactions studied the subjects of the interaction reported that they were nominated as candidates by acquaintances at the proffering institution.

Institutions seeking recruits tend to cast about among persons already known to them in one way or another. This does not reveal, however, why particular men are selected as targets for probes. Most professors have a variety of acquaintances, after all; why should A be selected as an appropriate candidate instead of B? Our data, based on the opinions of recipients, cannot definitively answer this question, but the respondents' answers do reveal the reasons they think they were selected as targets for probes which, in turn, illuminates both what the proffering departments told them and their own value systems regarding the characteristics desirable in academic men in their disciplines. Seven per cent of respondents believed they were selected as candidates because of their professional reputations, 22 per cent because of their research and publications, 5 per cent because of other professional activity, 27 per cent because of the quality of their teaching or because of their teaching specialties, 11 per cent because of their service to their current institutions, and 2 per cent for personality variables. Two per cent had no idea why they were selected, and 10 per cent of responses were uncodable.

Although we have noted that some prior acquaintance in the proffering institution was reported to have existed in 69 per cent of the probes studied and 45 per cent were reportedly initiated by acquaintances at the proffering institution, friendship or professional contacts were seen as the actual reason for their selection as candidates by only 13 per cent of the respondents. These may be quite accurate estimates, of course, but they may be an unreasonably low projection in the light of the high rates of "nepotism" found. It seems more likely that the principal reason many men receive probes is simply that they are quantities known to the probers and thus preferable to quantities unknown. To a degree impossible in most other large organizations, academic men have to live together amicably for them to prosper in their work. Thus, hiring is fraught with danger when the men being considered are strangers, and getting to know the candidates is always a major aim of site visits. Under these circumstances it is neither surprising nor pathological that acquaintance should play so large a part in candidate selection.

The reports respondents made concerning the reasons for their own selection as candidates for a probe suggest that their reasoning is essentially after the fact. Many times they did not know exactly why they were chosen and thus, when asked, had to guess about the matter from what they know of themselves, the job, and the nature of the academic labor market. That they *were* guessing is sometimes explicitly recognized.

> There's only one letter that is the contact at all, and I don't recall precisely what they did say. I think they wanted someone in

American history. I don't think, though, that they cared about
. . . so far as I know . . . there was nothing said about rank
or age.

[They were looking specifically for an English historian?] Uh huh.
[Were there any other specifications about the kind of man they
wanted?] Well, I think they wanted someone who had had some
experience in the field. That is, they presumably didn't want a
young man, someone just out of graduate school.

This was a chairmanship. [French or modern languages?] I believe it's modern languages there. Romance languages, I believe
it is. [Were they looking for anything more specific?] No, I believe
the chairmanship. [You didn't have to be a Spanish scholar, or
in French literature or something like that?] No. I don't believe
so. You know, the usual requirements: must be a scholar and
have the Ph.D., and so forth.

They never really spelled it out to me. They didn't seem to care
what your area specialization was. So I think they were simply
looking for a good administrator who could handle a rather large
department, who had some standing as a scholar, who would
continue to publish significantly. That was about it. And later on,
the crucial qualification turned out to be experience in directing
graduate programs. [How well do you fit the description you just
gave?] I'm not trying to be evasive when I say that's a hard question.

Not all probes, of course, result in proffers of employment or
even in further discussion of specific positions. A probe, by definition,
may be as vague as "Do you think you might ever have any interest
in a position at Fairlawn?" When probing is this indefinite—and it
not uncommonly is—for the transaction to proceed further there must
come some point at which the proffering institution begins to talk with
the candidate about a specific position to which duties attach, and at
that point, if they have not done so earlier, candidates must react.

Reactions

Respondents were asked how they had reacted to the probes
they received. Seven per cent received these probes enthusiastically
as a good way out of an impossible situation at the employing institution. Fifty-four per cent received them with interest as offering poten-

tially better situations elsewhere. One per cent perceived them as a chance to effect changes in their personal situations while remaining in place. The principal feature of these data may be their revelation of the non-Machiavellian nature of the typical faculty member's response; among small college faculty, at least, a nonmanipulative reaction seems to be the rule, contrary to popular belief. It does seem to be true, as we remarked in *Marketplace,* that a great many faculty members are passively on the market all the time, as indicated by the "received with interest" category, but that only one man perceived his probe as offering the possibility of manipulation is highly instructive. An additional 11 per cent of the respondents had reported problems of some kind in their institutions but did not, apparently, see either mobility or manipulation of the probe as offering any solution to them; 25 per cent reported themselves as having no employment problems and so would not be expected to react to probing with interest.

These figures provide an additional measure of the general satisfaction with their positions which we have previously remarked among the men of the private colleges. Only 7 per cent of respondents received their probes enthusiastically as a way out of an intolerable situation and, although 54 per cent are classified as having received them with interest as offering a potentially better situation elsewhere, much of this interest must have been generic, really a form of curiosity, for, as we know, few men actually completed the market interaction and left their jobs. If asked, they might reply that they were on the market all the time in the sense of being open to information about positions and at least willing in principle to consider moving to another job if it promised to be markedly superior to the one they had. Most of those "receiving with interest," however, were not particularly dissatisfied and did not take seriously the probes which come their way.

[Would it be correct for me to infer, since you are registered with this placement agency and you responded to their notice, that you are actively seeking to leave Shadyside?] Oh, not actively. As is the case with most people who have almost twenty years' experience in college teaching, and some of it on different levels. . . . I've taught graduate—graduate students at the University of Kansas for two, three, summers; private colleges. . . . I've taught in two church-related colleges. . . . I'm in my fifteenth year here and I've been registered with an agency most of the time. I first registered nineteen years ago. I think that this is more a way to keep tabs on the market than necessarily getting out of a private college. I'm not necessarily looking to get away from a small school. In fact, I'm not so sure that I'm really looking to change unless something comes along that is really much better.

[Would it be fair for me to infer from the fact that you have received several offers this year and are at least very seriously thinking about taking this one, that you are planning to leave Shadyside?] You know, it's a strange thing, but I'm not. I mean these have all come to me. I'm very happy at Shadyside. I'm not disaffected at all, and Shadyside has given me opportunities for growth that have been unparalleled both in my discipline and in the kinds of experience that would lead toward [administrative positions] . . . I'd be perfectly happy to stay at Shadyside for the rest of my academic career. But I also . . . my philosophy has been that I like to be where I feel that I'm extending myself to a full potential and, while I'm happy here, I really think that there are some horizons yet to cross.

Another reaction to probing which may be of some significance in understanding labor market phenomena is disclosure: once the probe has been received, whom, if anyone, does the recipient tell about the matter? Disclosure is theoretically interesting because patterns of information transmission within an organization can be used to diagnoses informal social structures, the folkways of the system, friendship cliques, and battle lines. Indeed, it had been one of the expectations with which this research commenced that it would be possible to predict mobility or immobility simply from knowledge of disclosure patterns and the relative prestiges of the individuals and institutions involved in market transactions. When respondents were asked whom they first told about the probe, 24 per cent replied that they told no one, 19 per cent told their wives, 17 per cent told a departmental colleague, 7 per cent told a colleague in the institution but in another department, 14 per cent told their chairmen, and 12 per cent told the dean or other administrator. None confided in a nonacademic friend. (Seven per cent of responses were uncodable.)

Despite occasional complaints at some schools about "paper-wavers" (men who seek to increase their local prestige by informing others of the probes they receive), the modal response to the receipt of a probe seems to be to tell no one about it. Indeed, in some respondents' remarks it was apparent that disclosure is considered bad taste. It is also of note that many men do not seem to consider that informing their wives of such matters constitutes telling anyone. But word sometimes gets out anyway.

[Question: Did you tell anyone about this at the time? Who? How? Where did the conversation take place? How did he or they respond?]

No. That's one of the things I feel is an indiscretion and that is something that is a black mark on a person . . . can become a black mark. And some of the colleagues have had it happen that way here. They have boasted of having received the offer from someone else or some other institution, and then the institution has turned them down and, well, and just simply lowered their stock in the eyes of the college people around.

No, I didn't, because I wanted to think about it. I didn't say anything here until September. [Did you talk it over with your wife?] Oh, of course.

No. Because it was completely . . . I wasn't really sure. I had turned it down before and so, you know, I wasn't about to say anything unless I had really made up my mind. [Did you talk it over with your wife?] Yes. [What did she say, do you remember?] No, I don't. I think she was, well, noncommittal.

No, but I dare say, the town being the way it is—small—when I did go to get airline tickets to fly to California—for personal reasons, not for this job—everybody in town knew it. That is to say, everybody who had anything to do with the college because it was . . . there were people at the agency, not the lady behind the counter, but people who were also there on their own travel affairs, noticed that I was getting a ticket to go to California, and the word got out that I was going, so the suspicion is that I didn't just pick up to go on a vacation but that I'll be looking for something, but they don't know where.

No. You mean informally? [Yes.] I don't even think that I did informally, really. Certainly not any . . . I might have mentioned that I got the letter, but I certainly didn't go to anybody and talk.

The last respondent's remarks are a classic illustration both of the academic man's dilemma concerning the uses of probes and of his solution to it. It is dangerous to bring to the attention of one's administration any hint that one may be thinking of leaving for another institution, not because they will be punitive, but because they may not care. Since this would be an intolerable affront to an individual's self-esteem, he is unlikely to run the risk unless he is ready to leave anyway and has the offer to do so in his pocket or unless he already knows that he will receive support and encouragement to stay, that is, administrative acknowledgment of his value to the institution. One way of getting around the dilemma is to bifurcate the perception of "telling anyone" into formal and informal "telling," where only a formal presentation of possibilities to an administrator counts as telling. It is also possible to "mention that I got the letter" as long as it is done in a context such that persons other than the one informed will hear of it only indirectly, and thus a confrontation—which might turn out badly—will be avoided. Probes, of course, are not offers of employment, and thus are wisely suppressed in formal disclosure, but it is probable that many explanations of failure to disclose as fear of punitive reaction may really be expressions of fears of indifference.

Spouses are the persons most likely to be first informed of probes received if anyone is, but we have already noted that many men do not count spouses as "anyone" in response to the query, so it is probable that, in fact, wives are far more commonly first informed than our figures indicate, which points to a curious matter. One of the assumptions with which the study was begun was that wives might be far more important in the mobility process than has been previously recognized in considerations of the academic labor market. They turn out to be almost totally unimportant as gauged by respondent's reports of conferral with them. No one said that he left it up to his wife (although such self-abnegation is hardly to be expected, either), but, more importantly, wives were simply mentioned very rarely in men's accounts of their decision-making processes. From the few remarks which were made, and from the handful of interviews conducted with wives, it is possible to conclude that in job acceptance or rejection the wife acts as a vetoing agent but not as a positive influence on decisions where she has no acceptable reason to exercise a veto. Acceptable reasons for veto seem largely to involve climate, local culture, and effects of moves or new locations on children.

[During this discussion, did you indicate either to your husband or the dean what your feelings about the matter were?] No. [Did you have any at the time?] Oh, mixed, I guess. [What if a final offer does come; would you have any feeling that you should either encourage or discourage the acceptance of it?] No, I think that if he came to me now and said, "What do you think of it?" I would say, "We've already discussed it." I mean that *he knows how I feel and I have tried to be fair and honest and see that there are more than two sides to each question. And he knows how I feel; he knows what we want for the family,* and if he decided that he wanted to go to Fairlawn, that it was something he had to do, then we would go to Fairlawn. [And you would not feel that you should play any more part in the process?] No, absolutely not. As a matter of fact I feel that, *outside of aims for the family,* professionally I shouldn't, *except to question his true aim, to help him decide what it is he wants to do and why he's going.* [Emphasis added.]

It is easy to see, in this quotation and in others like it, how wives who do not perceive themselves as actively participating in the decision-making process, and whose husbands do not see them as doing so either, may yet have significant, although hidden, impacts on decision. In the quotation above the situation may have been exactly as the wife described it or, as the added emphasis implies, her husband's knowledge of her feelings may have been very important. The role of the wife as subtle vetoer is even more clear in the following conversation (exactly as taped with emphasis added):

[Did he mention this to you when it came in?] Yes. [Do you recall what your response was?] Oh, no! [Meaning what, please?] I can't face it. [What was it you couldn't face?] Another move right now. You know, just gotten sort of settled and dug in. [Was it Fairlawn, or Cleveland, or just the idea of moving?] Just the idea of moving. Because it hit me, I don't know about John, but that was my reaction. [No matter where it was, you would have reacted the same way?] Exactly. [I see. Did he, at the time you were discussing this, indicate any interest in it at all?] Yes. [Oh, he did? (Husband said that he had never been interested.)] Do you think that it was your response that. . . . He never replied to this, did he?] Oh, I didn't respond in this way to him. It was an inner feeling. [May I ask, what did you say to him?] Well, "What do you think?" I can't remember except that I just asked him, you know, what he thought about it, and he said that it seemed to be a little more money and I said, *"Yes, but it isn't enough money to make it worth while."* [But you did not then indicate to him that the idea of moving just tore you up?] Well, I did *after I could see that he wasn't really interested.* [How would you see your role or define your rights in the decision whether to move or not?] None. [None whatsoever?] Where he goes, I go. And I . . . *the only thing I would do is to carefully examine with him the pros and cons.* [Do you feel that you have the right to express reservations or to indicate that you would rather not do something like this?] *Well, I think that I probably would, as a question.* Certainly not as a demand . . . I think that probably what I would say was, "It'll be awfully expensive, and another shakeup, and you'll have to begin at the bottom again and start all that churning, is it worth it to you?"

Disclosure seems to follow patterns associated with rank. About the same proportions of men in each rank reported that they informed no one of probes received, but full professors reported wives as first informed almost twice as frequently as did men in other ranks, while others were more likely to discuss the matter with colleagues but less likely to mention them to administrators. These patterns illustrate the probe as dilemma-creating. Being probed by another institution conveys some status; it marks the recipient as one who is both desirable and visible to others. The status it conveys is a function of the prestige of the proffering institution and of the nature of the job. Younger men, who are less well established than full professors, thus disclose their probes to colleagues in attempts to improve local prestige but do not mention the matter to administrators for fear of having the incident taken formally and being rejected. Senior professors have less prestige conferred by probes from inferior institutions and do not mention them for this reason, and, already having status among other faculty, either pridefully inform their wives or casually mention it to administrators in an attempt to prove their worth in their superior's eyes. Being senior, however, they do not have to fear administrative rejection—they have already had their status validated by promotion to full professor.

The pattern of disclosure by rank may also reflect experience and stage in the life cycle. The first probes received by a young professor just beginning his career are exciting events; they represent signs that he will have a career and need not be forever stuck in the location in which he has begun. Thus, he is more likely to talk about them than the senior man for whom the reception of inquiries has become more or less routine. Senior men may be more likely to report probes or opportunities to their wives first simply because their families are older and thus would be more affected by a move. For a junior man to move his children at preschool ages probably has little effect on them, and certainly the children—and perhaps the mother who in some ways represents their interests—need not be first consulted. But for older persons with children established in networks of school and friendship, such decisions have great impact on family members and may, thus, be first reported to them.

When coders classified the reported reactions to probes of chairmen and deans, it became apparent that most men do not choose ever to inform their administrative superiors of probes received. Respondents did not inform their chairmen of probes in 41 per cent of cases and failed to tell their deans about 62 per cent of the time—which is not to say the dean does not learn about the matter anyway. The reasons for nondisclosure to administrators are related to the matter of formalization described earlier. Looking at another position is a serious matter. Most men, therefore, do not enter into it lightly. It is a serious matter because in the consideration of another position there must always be comparison of the proffered job with one's own, with the possibility that the latter will be found lacking. This possibility of invidious comparison raises questions both in the mind of others to whom the matter is disclosed (Will he reject us by going elsewhere?) and in the mind of the candidate, for the reception of a clearly superior offer necessarily suggests that one has not been adequately treated by one's employing institution (If others think that well of me, why doesn't my own department or college, or if they do, why have they not shown it in salary, rank, and duties?). Furthermore, disclosure, once formalized by informing the chairman or the dean, becomes official notice that an individual considers himself on the market, with the risk, for assistant and associate professors, that at the same time they are reassessing their positions to determine whether they wish to keep them, the administrators may be reassessing them. These are unsettling thoughts, and thus many men prefer not to open "that can of worms," as one respondent put it. If they are reasonably satisfied where they are, they either reject most probes out of hand or else examine them only deeply enough to assure themselves that they are not by accident ignoring Utopia. And finally, of course, most probes come to naught. They are often only semiofficial and it is embarrassing to have revealed that one is being considered and then discover later that another was selected for the position with the implication that he was found superior.

The reactions of chairmen and deans in cases where they were informed of probes were rather similar, although one interesting difference appeared. Deans largely seem to react positively, perhaps defining their positions as requiring the provision of emotional support and possibly also recognizing that failure to react positively might be interpreted as an invitation for the recipient to pursue the matter. Chairmen, on the other hand, are more likely only to indicate polite interest or even, in two cases in this study, to react negatively to the candidate for letting the situation occur. It is probably safe to assume that the more varied reactions of chairmen are the consequence of a more intimate knowledge of their colleagues so that they do not feel required to role-play in the ways in which deans may.

In general, then, the typical reaction to the reception of a probe is to keep the matter quiet on any formal or official level while disclosing it in some way to friends or spouses. Reactions of those told seem to be largely supportive, so that failure to disclose is a result either of misapprehension on the candidate's part as to what reactions may be or, more commonly, a reluctance to engage in the subjective strains which may accompany market activity. Respondents were asked if there was anyone from whom they had deliberately kept knowledge of a probe. Fully 43 per cent kept it from general knowledge but not from anyone in particular. This confirms our previous discussion of the reasons, including feelings that disclosure is bad form, that faculty do not disclose probes. Two per cent tried to keep the knowledge from their chairmen in particular, and three per cent from the dean or other administrative officer. (This is not contradictory to our earlier discussion: men do not care if the dean finds out unofficially. It is only official notification that is avoided.) Six per cent tried to keep the matter from a particular departmental colleague; none tried to keep it from an extradepartmental colleague. Twenty-five per cent made no specific efforts to keep it from anyone, and 17 per cent were not asked or gave uncodable replies.

Only 2 per cent made deliberate efforts to keep the matter secret from everyone, which is revealing, for it is evidence that the better small colleges are nonpunitive in their social systems. This refutes another academic myth, that small schools are necessarily parochial and regard market activity as disloyal. The myth has some roots in fact, of course, and undoubtedly some of the horror stories with which academic men regale themselves about the miserable conditions elsewhere are true. But, as is often the case with academic myth, this one appears to be overgeneralized. I suspect that, had the same men whose reports of their own activity appear here been asked whether, as a general rule, they felt it wise to keep market transactions secret from everyone for fear of punitive retaliation, considerably larger proportions would have reported that they felt so than did, in fact, do so. This doing of one set of realities while believing another is certainly not peculiar to academics but is, equally certainly, prevalent there despite the commitment of the profession to the exploration of truth.

Formal Offers

Previous pages have spoken of probes about the possibility of an individual's taking another position as "opportunities." This may be a misusage for, in a pragmatic sense, a possibility does not become an actual opportunity until a choice between real alternatives is presented. It is one thing, for both the candidate and the proffering institution, to discuss the possibility that he might be offered a position and might wish to accept it; the choice does not become real, however (that is, the candidate does not have to make a choice), until the job is actually offered him. Nonetheless, as noted earlier, it is rare for offers of contracts to come out of the blue. Preliminary discussion is the rule so that the proffering institution can explore the candidate's suitability for the position and vice versa. When speaking informally with friends about their market experiences, professors do not always observe the distinction between probe and offer. (It enhances their prestige with their acquaintances not to do so.) But it is a vital one, for obvious reasons, and when professors speak for the record or in more formal ways it is almost universally observed.

One occasionally hears of men who either did not recognize the distinction between a probe and an offer or who chose for manipulative reasons to ignore it in order to bluff in negotiating with their chairman or dean for an improvement in their working conditions. While, again, some of this is probably mythological, it is significant that the tales are told of persons for whom the tactic did not work— they are always, in the story, caught at it with unfortunate results. The significance of the repetition of the tale, of course, is that it emphasizes the distinction, thus implying wide recognition of its importance. Another important distinction, which is also widely accepted, is that between disclosing probes before they have been responded to and making one's chairman or dean aware of them after they have been rejected. The latter is considered perfectly proper and it is expected, in fact, that the administrator will take note of the event and of one's loyalty and respond favorably. This convention may well have something to do with maintaining the rather common reverse belief that "thinking about" probes will be construed as disloyal.

The most marked relationship between probes and offers for our sample was that 66 per cent of probes did not result in formal offers or profferment of contracts. There is, in other words, a great deal of market activity which goes nowhere in the sense that it does not create a decision-making situation for the faculty member. Of course this does not mean that both he and the proffering institution may not have already made the decisions that lead to the lack of an offer; it requires decision either for an individual to reject a probe or for an institution to decide not to continue one.

No, because I didn't follow through. I wrote back and told them that I felt that I did not have the type of experience that I thought I should have. I did not follow through on it.

No, for they would not pay moving expenses.

We wandered back and forth on offers but could never get together on a price. What it boiled down to was my salary here was at least what they were planning on paying, maybe in excess of what they were paying, plus they had the added complication that here I have research money, grants. And there was some question on whether the position was going to be twelve months, whether I could keep my research grants, and salary, and so on and on.

Forty persons did receive offers; they were made verbally for 25 per cent, by telephone for 12 per cent, by letter for 18 per cent, and in discussion followed up by letter for 45 per cent. The typical procedure is for the candidate and institutional representatives to discuss the terms of the offer while he makes his site visit in order to determine whether agreement can be reached. If mutually satisfactory terms are found, they are put in the form of a contract (or a letter which serves that function) which then follows up the visit. Such discussions are probably usually successful, for they are unlikely to occur in problematic situations—one party or the other will avoid the discussion if it seems likely to have no useful, that is, successful, result.)

> After dinner, another session with the dean of the graduate school, and an offer was made at that time. [Describes terms.] [Was this a verbal offer made to you while you were there?] While I was there, with the statement that I didn't have to answer at that point, but it would be put on paper and sent to me. I could mull it over while returning home, and then when it was down on paper I could mull it over again and see what I wanted to do. [Did you give them any reply at that time?] No. I said, "Of course I am interested," but I would want to talk it over at home and I left it at that.

Wives may be more important in the market decision-making process than respondents recognize. Fully 60 per cent of respondents stated that their wives were the first persons told of the reception of the offer, but it seems likely that even some of those who reported informing institutional figures first may not have been counting their wives. Twenty per cent informed the dean or other administrator first, 10 per cent informed their chairmen, 7 per cent informed departmental colleagues, and 3 per cent informed extradepartmental colleagues. There are slight variations by rank which may have some significance. Only assistant professors reported first informing colleagues (excluding chairmen). This may reflect the greater importance of offers for younger men, their inexperience in receiving them, and their greater needs for esteem. Thirty per cent of full professors reported first informing the dean or other administrator, as opposed to 13 per cent and 17 per cent of associate and assistant professors. Chairmen were informed first by similar proportions of all ranks (about 10 per cent). The significance of the dean (and the recognition of it shown by full professors) is that in the smaller colleges he is typically the only one who can do anything in response to a challenge from another institution—grant a raise or promotion and so on. The persons informed of the offer, however, reacted in various ways.

> Which, the contract? Showed it to my wife, I guess. [How did she respond?] Well, her response was "That's a lot of money and maybe we should think about it." And we did do a lot of thinking about it, and we discussed it with several friends, and I also went in and talked to the President about it. [Oh, you did? How did he react?] Well, he was fairly noncommittal.

> I had told the dean informally that I wouldn't be back. [Did he make any attempt to dissuade you?] No, there was no "thank you," or "we'd like you to stay."

> At some time in talking with the dean I did tell him what the terms would be. And that was the time when the dean said, "Be sure that you know what the future will be in terms of fringe benefits, and so forth." [Did he offer to meet any figure they came up with?] No, he couldn't. He told me what the raises would be for next year and pointed out to me in various ways that this wasn't a big raise that I would be getting. [The salary at the proffering institution.]

The emotional insecurity of academic men, particularly those below the rank of full professor, has been remarked previously, as have the misconceptions about their profession which these insecurities create. A certain mild paranoid resignation to being taken advantage of (which these data consistently show to be unrealistic) seems to be characteristic. In the matter of offers from other institutions these insecurities are manifested in the general feeling that one is not adequately appreciated by one's administration, will not be promoted as rapidly as one has a right to expect, and is probably being underpaid. These fears are in part a function of ignorance, of course, which accounts for their greater prevalence among junior men (who know less about the way the profession actually works and who are less likely to be involved in promotion and salary recommendations). But they are also in part a function of the ambiguity of the standards by which men are estimated, which means that there is always the possibility that those doing the estimating may misapply them in one's own particular case. Thus, even men who have good reason to suppose that they are valued by their institutions and are well-regarded by the dean may bring him offers from other places only with great anxiety that he will not respond adequately thus forcing them, in pride, to leave a position with which they are otherwise completely satisfied. This fact may account for the relatively large proportion of offers which, although entirely genuine, are not reported in any official way. It would be specious to decide that grown men should have more sense, as more than one nonacademic with whom I have discussed the matter has concluded. The structure of the profession, with its immense uncertainties and ambiguities, is responsible for the phenomenon. It is also possible that persons who elect to become academics, perhaps particularly at the smaller colleges, are less aggressive and sure of themselves than men who go into business or other high risk activities.

Perhaps more important still—since men often inform administrators of offers received in hopes of securing some compensatory reward from Shadyside if they elect to remain there—are the material responses which their announcements may eventually receive. Indeed, the decision whether to heed the call to Fairlawn or to remain at Shadyside not infrequently hinges on the nature of the dean's response, material as well as affective. Thirty-six per cent of chairmen and 44 per cent of deans were not informed of offers. In cases where the dean was informed of the offer, some favorable adjustment in rank, salary, or working conditions was often made in response. Chairmen made little response, but that is not a reflection on them: they usually have no authority to do so. In some instances they were reported to have responded materially, but it is likely that either the informant was mistaken about the source of the response or the chairman elected to take credit for an action which was, in fact, the dean's. In some of these instances, of course, it may have been strong affirmative action on the chairman's part, known to the respondent, which resulted in the dean's action. Of the cases actually reported to deans, however, 42 per cent received favorable response and 16 per cent more received some overwhelming material reaction. (For coding purposes, an overwhelming material response was defined as a raise of more than $1000 or more than 10 per cent of the previous year's salary, whichever was larger, a jump in ranks (as from assistant professor to full professor), a reduction in teaching load by more than one course, and so on. In practice, all responses coded as overwhelming were massive salary raises, sometimes accompanied by other rewards.)

> [Did he (the dean) offer, for example, to pay you more?] Oh, yes, everything, everything! All the courses I always wanted to teach suddenly were available; the money was available; everything, just overnight.

It is worthy of note that, although eight cases (42 per cent of those reported to deans) were met with no material response, there were no reports of any kind of punitive reactions (threats of future nonpromotion, loss of perquisites, and so on), as rumor sometimes alleges. Occasionally, of course, the offer is inferior to the candidate's situation in place, in which case, presumably, the dean's attention would not be invited. Certainly in some instances the dean's failure to react favorably is his way of telling the candidate he does not care whether he leaves or not—and it is probably the fear of this reaction which inhibits some official disclosure. But some deans, apparently, simply do not like disclosure and regard it as an attempt on the part of the faculty member to blackmail his way into reward that is not rightfully his. Such deans may be supposed to be intensely local and in time will probably cost the institution most of the really professionalized faculty it has. A generalized toughness is a dubious virtue in an administrator except in very special situations, such as with a faculty which is in intellectual bankruptcy. So, too, is unresponsiveness.

> I told the Dean to the extent that I was going to Fairlawn to discuss the music program. And that's all I said. [Do you think he guessed that it was an interview?] Well, he could hardly help but be aware of it, yeah. [What was his reaction to this?] Oh, he wrote and said, "You may go," and that was all. [What was his reaction when he discovered that you had accepted an offer there?] At first they [dean and president] said, "We are surprised. We knew you were at Fairlawn, and we're sorry you're leaving." But that was before they found out what a hassle there was going to be [to find a replacement for the subject, who was chairman]. Now they're really sorry I'm leaving.

This comment points to a matter which makes it even more odd that institutions sometimes are not more responsive to men who may go elsewhere unless their emotional and material needs are met. It is, of course, a difficult problem, for the very reception of an offer can create needs for institutional response in the mind of a faculty member where they had not existed before, because it constitutes a change in his status which he may feel requires institutional recognition. Nonetheless, unless the dean would really prefer to get rid of someone through the device of unresponsiveness—and it often has that effect, if not with the offer in question then with the next attractive one which comes along—lack of response may actually penalize him as a result of the difficulties he will have in finding a replacement. This is particularly true of the departmental chairman. At one time chairmanships were much sought after by faculty members as positions of prestige and sometimes of power. This is no longer true and seems to be becoming less so almost yearly. To run the risk of losing even a rather mediocre chairman is to invite serious difficulty in replacing him, for too often the only people who will want the job will be types whom the dean will not (or should not) want in it. Replacement in a seller's market with some serious shortages is not to be undertaken lightly, and if institutions counted the real costs of the process, those which have that tendency might be less blase about unresponsiveness to outside offers.

That there was a seller's market at the time of interview is manifest in many things respondents said as well as in their replies to a direct question as to whether the event concerning which they were included in the study had been the only probe received during the study year. In a majority of cases, it had not: the same characteristics which made men visible and desirable to one institution had the same effect on other institutions.

[Question: Have you had any offers or probes this year other than the one we have been discussing?]

I think I've received three or four less direct than this. People have written to my adviser saying, "Can you suggest anyone?" He's given them my name and they've written to me saying, "Dr. —— says that you might be looking for a position; if you are, we'd be happy to hear from you." [Where were these from?] Well, let's see, one was from a small girl's school on Long Island; one was from . . . it was in the panhandle area of Texas. As a matter of fact, when I was looking for this job, I'd corresponded with Austin College at Sherman, Texas.

Small colleges here or there, liberal arts colleges, none of them very interesting or outstanding.

Well, yes, from this placement directory, I've had several.

Well, you know, the usual form letters sort of thing that you get all the time, like, "We have a position at so and so open," you must get, what, maybe twenty or thirty of these a year.

Well, sort of a probe, yeah. I went to the economics convention, which is the market, in December, and as a result of another Shadyside faculty member who was talking with a friend of his, who was chairman of the department at Queens College, in New York, was interested in hiring people. He invited me to apply.

[And then you mentioned there was a probe from Fairlawn?] Right. This is the chairman, or the dean, actually, who'd been chairman of the history department here before he left to become dean there. And he knew me and simply called to see if I would be interested in taking on the chairmanship of the department in my field at Fairlawn.

Most of these other probes did not become formal offers, probably for the same reason that most of the probes reported here did not—many are called but few are chosen. Others failed to become offers because they came after some other market transaction (often the one reported here) had been undertaken, and the respondent had resolved to his own satisfaction that he either did or did not wish to leave Shadyside at that time. In either event, the probe would be refused. During the course of the academic year 1966–67, 62 per cent of the men sampled received probes other than the one about which they were interviewed, and 13 per cent of those other probes actually resulted in formal offers of positions being made to them. For a significant majority of the sample, then, the opportunity to change jobs is not something which occurs occasionally; it might be called almost a routine part of their academic experience. At least 3 per cent of the respondents actually received two or more offers in addition to the offers about which they were interviewed, which is also a measure of the activity of the market, although we may presume that these were individuals with considerable professional visibility. (And the proportion of other probes actually eventuating in offers is probably underrepresented by this tabulation because the question was not phrased as to distinguish between other probes and those which eventually became offers. The count here is thus of those responses where it was possible for the coder to make the distinction. If this could not be done, the response was coded "not asked" for the enumeration of other probes which became offers, thus accounting for a very large proportion (41 per cent) in this category. Needless to say, some of those which were nothing more than probes probably could have been turned into offers if the recipients had desired to continue the interactions to that point.)

Evaluation

The labor market transaction as described thus far shows numerous evidences of its processual nature: probes are made, originating in a variety of ways and directed at candidates selected in manners equally various; they are responded to in similarly diverse ways, with the nature of the response depending on or being influenced by another host of variables. Some probes eventually become formal offers which, in turn, produce yet another set of diversified responses and reactions from the candidates and from other persons involved. Although a market transaction is often viewed by the participant as a peculiarly private and individualistic matter, it is apparent that others participate in it as well, sometimes with determining effect (for example, the Dean). At this stage in the process, however, there must occur an event which is apt to be private, subjective, and often idiosyncratic: making the decision whether to accept the offer or to spurn it. Others may be involved in the decision, as persons whose advice is sought or, as in the case of wives, who must be considered, but the act of making it, and the judgments which must be made about various factors in order to do so, are subjective events in which only the candidate participates. Nor is this decision-making entirely a rational matter; the decisions made are usually rational, certainly, and may be explained after the fact by the actor as the rational outcome of rational judgments concerning a number of empirical matters. The actor's emotional response to the offer, the proffering institution, and the men there in relation to their counterparts where he is, however, decidedly affect his feelings about it, and this feeling about a job or place or certain people greatly colors his judgments of them.

[But even a $7000 salary increase wasn't enough to make you send in your credentials?] No, I guess not. No, it wasn't, period. If I would become dissatisfied with [my chairman] or the department or the school, I would move tomorrow. I'm not an individual to stay someplace where I'm unhappy.

Well, basically their philosophy toward teaching undergraduate geology is different from mine. Not that it's any worse or any better, but I just don't agree with this, so why leap into something of this nature?

To be honest, I was . . . well . . . I didn't really . . . well I took their offer seriously, but there was no stage in which I saw myself going to Carolina and starting a physics department from scratch. Never really thought I would do it.

It's very difficult to pin this down. I think that I was predisposed to take the offer until about forty-eight hours before I had to make a definite decision. And it was . . . it was hanging very close in some respects, a last minute decision to stay. [Well, something must have happened, then, to change your mind?] Well, it's hard to . . . hard to pin down. I don't think there was any one big thing that happened. The dean had made the situation here clear right away: I had known for at least a week what Shadyside's position was and my immediate reaction upon hearing this was, "Well, I should probably go anyway." But I guess that it was the kind of gnawing concerns I had had all along that loomed larger and larger the closer I got to making the particular decision.

One factor that clearly affects decision-making a great deal is the terms of the offer itself, relative to the conditions of the position which the individual holds at the time he receives it. Proffers of salaries $7000 higher for essentially the same work, related by the first respondent above, are extremely rare. (So, probably, are respondents who would reject them.) But obviously men will rarely move to positions where salary and other working conditions are inferior to those they already enjoy or endure. Thus, a raw acceptance-rejection rate for formal offers does not fully explain the vitality of the labor market. Some institutions might experience considerable turnover from a given set of proffers to their faculty because their working conditions were inferior to those generally available on the market. Others, better situated, might experience relatively little disturbance from the same set of proffers. This is not to say that rational balancing of the conditions available fully explains acceptance or rejection of offers, but simply that the relative superiority or inferiority of proffered conditions may set boundaries on the decision-making process. Offers of distinctly inferior conditions would probably always be rejected except by persons caught in the grip of some overpowering irrationality (perhaps a fit of rage against a dean or chairman), while offers of extremely superior conditions for essentially the same work would be accepted with some alacrity by most people. Within these limits, however, other factors seem to operate more determinatively. When the offers received by respondents and the jobs they already held are compared in terms of salary, rank, and other specific working conditions such as teaching load and leave policies, 62 per cent of offers appear distinctly superior, 13 per cent slightly superior, 15 per cent essentially similar, 8 per cent slightly inferior. None were distinctly inferior; in 2 per cent of cases it was impossible to make a comparison. Even allowing for the undeniable fact that men's memories may inflate the terms of the positions offered them, these facts do reveal a very important phenomenon: although 62 per cent of the offers received were distinctly superior to the reported terms of respondents' employment, few men were lured away from Shadyside by the blandishments of Fairlawn. Better salaries and working conditions are not sufficient to account for mobility. This is significant because it flatly refutes the very widespread academic belief that men move for money. Potential moves may usually be expected to yield more money (or better terms in other matters), which may account for the prevalence of the belief that faculty members change jobs *for* better salaries (or the conclusions of Marshall, 1964, discussed above in Chapter One), but the low mobility rates among these same individuals clearly show that other phenomena are the determining factors in academic mobility. Those who move may expect to receive better terms—the advantage in working conditions may be a necessary condition for the move, a reward for mobility—but they are insufficient, in themselves, to motivate men to move.

What some of these other factors may be is explored in Tables 20 and 21. Table 20 compares aspects of the employing and proffering institutions which seemed to respondents to constitute either reasons to accept the positions they were proffered or reasons not to accept them, whether they did so in fact or not. It involves, thus, a simul-

Table 20. MOTIVES FOR MOBILITY AND IMMOBILITY[a]
(N = 125)

Institutional Feature	Motives for Accepting Offer		Motives for Rejecting Offer	
	Shadyside	Fairlawn	Shadyside	Fairlawn
	Per Cent			
Disciplinary professional, prestige, or research matters	18	25	9	11
Curricular or instructional matters, students	14	18	17	14
Institutional matters other than prestige, research, or instruction	13	10	6	14
Geographic phenomena, location	8	14	8	16
Idiosyncratic and personal matters	6	5	18	7
Personalities present	8	0	4	3
Financial matters	10	12	9	9
No compelling reason	19	14	26	20
Do not know, no answer, uncodable	3	3	4	6
Total	100	100	100	100
Number	(125)	(125)	(125)	(125)

[a] Respondents were not asked for direct comparisons. The table is constructed from coders' classifications of the items mentioned by respondents when asked the questions, "What did you decide to do? Why? What factors did you consider? What were the specific attractions and negative features both about taking that position or staying on in this one?"

taneous comparison of the two positions and institutions relevant for each individual. One way of interpreting this rather complicated tabulation is to regard the first two columns, "Motives for Accepting Offer," as describing what the respondents saw as reasons for leaving their positions at Shadyside for new ones at Fairlawn. Some of the reasons were things of which they were critical or with which they were dissatisfied at Shadyside; others were things they found attractive about Fairlawn. The last two columns, "Motives for Rejecting Offer," describe reasons the respondents saw for remaining at Shadyside. Again, some of these reasons consist of things with which they were dissatisfied, this time at Fairlawn, and some of the ways in which they found Shadyside superior to the proffering institution. Reading the table in this way, we can see, for example, that dissatisfaction with the condition of disciplinary professional, prestige, or research matters at Shadyside was cited twice as frequently as a reason to leave it as satisfaction with such matters was cited as a reason for staying. Similarly, the attractiveness of such matters at Fairlawn was cited more than twice as frequently as a reason to go there than was their attractiveness at Shadyside seen as a reason to remain. Matters concerning curriculum, instruction, or students (typically student quality) seem to balance out—they were as frequently causes for satisfaction with or attraction to either institution as they were for dissatisfaction with either.

"Institutional matters other than prestige, research, or instruction" include administrative policy and personalities, promotion policies, operation, and so on. Some small measure of disaffection with Shadyside is shown by the fact that twice as many men perceived such phenomena at their employing institutions as a reason to leave as cited them as a reason to remain. When the same matters at Fairlawn were considered, however, more faculty members cited them as a reason not to accept the offer than as a reason for doing so. Matters of geography, climate, and locale appeared with almost equal frequency as reasons to go and reasons to remain. Escape from or cleaving to particular persons, friends or enemies, seems not to be a major motive for either mobility or immobility, although a desire to leave enemies was mentioned twice as often as one to remain with friends, while idiosyncratic or personal reasons loomed large only as causes for remaining in place, suggesting that ties of friendship and familiarity (and unquestionably of family, for family considerations are frequent in interview reports) may account for more decisions than direct reference indicates.

Interestingly enough, from about a fifth to a quarter of all respondents mentioned nothing as being of particular consequence to them as a motive for either mobility or immobility. Only 14 per cent failed to find something quite attractive about the proffered position, while 26 per cent failed to mention anything particularly binding them to the job they had, at least to the point that it provided a reason for rejecting the one they were offered. However, 20 per cent saw no particular reason in the unattractiveness of the proffering institution to reject the offer they received, while 19 per cent could or did mention nothing about their own positions which motivated them to leave. Financial matters, again, did not loom at all large. Ten per cent of respondents were sufficiently dissatisfied with their financial arrangements that these became a reason to move, but only 12 per cent saw the reward at Fairlawn as reason to go there. Nine per cent each were either sufficiently satisfied with their pay as to see that as a reason for remaining at Shadyside or sufficiently unimpressed with what Fairlawn had to offer so that they did not wish to move.

Another way of assessing the relative significance of the various motives for mobility or immobility is computation of the rank order of importance for each. Table 21, which is simply an average of the frequency of the two entries in each column of Table 20, shows the result of this operation. While this summary operation obscures some subtleties (such as the distinction between dissatisfaction where one is and attraction to where one might be as different motives for migration), it makes much clearer the role of the various factors in men's deliberations. Perhaps most significant is that substantial proportions of the respondents were essentially unmoved by either the offers they received or the conditions of their existing positions. They either took their own institutions so completely for granted that when asked to specify elements of their positions in them which might keep them in place they could think of nothing, or else a significant and somewhat similar proportion of positions offered them appeared either inferior or so similar to those they had as to offer nothing to catch their notice. Thus, "nothing compelling mentioned" was the most frequent reason for rejecting an offer and was also second most frequent as a motivation for movement.

As might be expected from the general level of professionalization which characterized the sample of market active faculty, the primary reasons for movement fell into the disciplinary professional category. When men think about moving, they think of the professional reasons for doing so and are attracted only to those positions which

Table 21. REASONS FOR ACCEPTING OR REJECTING
POSITIONS—RANK ORDERED

Motives for Accepting Offer	Per Cent	Motives for Rejecting Offer	Per Cent
Disciplinary professional, prestige, or research matters	21.5	No compelling reason	23.0
No compelling reason	16.5	Curricular or instructional matters, students	15.5
Curricular or instructional matters, students	16.0	Geographic phenomena, location	12.0
Institutional matters other than prestige, research, or instruction	11.5	Disciplinary professional, prestige, or research matters	10.0
Financial matters	11.0	Institutional matters other than prestige, research, or instruction	10.0
Geographic phenomena, location	11.0	Financial matters	9.0
Idiosyncratic and personal matters	5.5	Idiosyncratic and personal matters	7.5
Personalities present	4.0	Do not know, no answer, uncodable	5.0
Do not know, no answer, uncodable	3.0	Personalities present	3.5

offer professional possibilities. When they reject opportunities to move, however, they seem more likely to do so either in terms of the quality of curricular and instructional matters where they are or the lack of such quality in the places to which they have been invited to go, while matters pertaining to the locale also play a fairly frequent part in decisions to reject the possibility of movement. These apparent inconsistencies are not as paradoxical as they may at first appear. If we remember that the reports we are dealing with are those of a generally competent and satisfied group of faculty members, many of whom have already attained success in their professions and institutions, who have many opportunities to change positions if they become dissatisfied, and who are professionally dedicated to the kind of teaching they do (for curricular and instructional matters were the third ranking reason for accepting offers), the disparity between motivations for movement and those for remaining fixed becomes clearer.

When men with these characteristics think about movement, they look to matters which will make it worth the trouble to them; the work and professional opportunity must be significantly better or it is not worth their while to go. In many cases it does not appear to be better, and then the more local reasons for staying in place become important—the nature of the teaching and the students with whom they interact, the character of the locale which has become home for them. It is probably especially important, too, to emphasize the lack of significance of financial matters, although we have seen that offers received were mostly distinctly superior to jobs held in salary and in other ways. Financial features took only fifth place out of eight as motives for movement and ranked sixth as motives for fixture. Thus, despite the impression given by much of their conversation that academics are obsessed with pay, it appears that in making job decisions it is not an important matter; what men do about things is probably a better measure of their significance to them than what they say about them.

It is also worth noting the relatively low position on both orderings of institutional matters other than prestige, research, and instruction, where dissatisfactions with or references to administrative personnel would be classified (fourth place as a movement motive, fourth as a fixture motive), and the even lower place (next to last and last, respectively) of personalities. If discontent, feuding, and discord were prominent features of the small colleges and were as significant a motive for migration as mythology would have it (see McCarthy, 1951), these categories would undoubtedly occupy higher places on the scales than they do. In fact, the data of this research consistently demonstrate that the faculties of the better liberal arts colleges, if our respondents were representative of them, are remarkably contented with their lot considering the disputatious nature of their calling and public reputation.

In keeping with the study's policy of not phrasing questions in such a way as to suggest answers to respondents, subjects were not specifically asked if there were matters at Shadyside with which they were dissatisfied. However, a number of queries offered opportunities to air complaints, and many came out in the course of unsolicited monologues about other matters. Twenty per cent of respondents were dissatisfied with conditions of personal work, such as class size, teaching load, equipment, and student relations; 14 per cent were dissatisfied with salary, rank, or prospects of promotion. Thirteen per cent were dissatisfied with institutional or administrative philosophy or educational policy, for example, excessive emphasis on classroom teaching, excessive emphasis on service to the institution, or curricular goals; 9 per cent were dissatisfied with administrators or administrative relations or methods. Nine per cent were dissatisfied with the locale, including not only climate and geography but also isolation from metropolitan centers or centers of professional activity such as libraries and provincialism of the surrounding community. Seven per cent had personal or idiosyncratic dissatisfactions, 2 per cent were unhappy with the quality of students, none with the quality of faculty colleagues. Twenty-five per cent expressed no dissatisfaction. One per cent of responses were uncodable. (Since no question to the effect "tell me your complaints here" was directly asked, it may be, of course, that the 25 per cent would have responded with complaints if so queried. On the other hand, the fact that 74 per cent of respondents did have something to say which was codable as an expression of problems or dissatisfaction suggests that the opportunity for such expression was offered.)

Although dissatisfaction with one's institution may certainly become a motive for migration, the above figures actually are a clear demonstration of the general degree of satisfaction which respondents found in their positions: the modal response, of fully a quarter of respondents, was of no dissatisfactions. This means, of course, that nearly three-quarters were classified by coders as having reported some sort of dissatisfaction with their positions, but it would probably be erroneous to interpret this fact as an expression of overwhelming disaffection. In the first place, of course, although expressing dissatisfactions of various sorts, the respondents were persons who had the opportunity to change positions or to develop such opportunities, and the large majority chose not to do so. Their complaints, therefore, do not seem to have been grave. In the second place it must be remembered that any persons as deeply involved in the operations of an organizational social system as are faculty members at a small college are likely to be aware of any defects in it, and faculty members, because of the role definition of their job, may be more likely than other workers to demand perfection of their work organizations. Defects in the operation of the system, therefore, are less likely to be accepted as just being in the nature of things and more likely to be noticed and criticized.

This state of affairs seems to be quite visible in the pattern of problems which received the most attention from the respondents. All three categories of complaint made by more than 10 per cent of respondents are deeply involved in college operation, and two of the three (conditions of personal work and institutional philosophy or policy) have to do directly with the nature of the professor's work and its outcomes. It is undoubtedly significant that the single greatest subject of complaints was conditions of personal work. Faculty members are work-oriented. For many, indeed, work is probably the single most important value in their lives, and thus anything which is perceived as getting in the way of the best possible performance of work is frustrating. That complaints about reward are no more frequent than they are is also instructive. The popular press and some academic and student critics of the professoriat like to depict academic men as largely concerned with feathering their own nests and the search for personal reward. There is little evidence of such orientation in these data. Complaints about administrative or institutional policy are as frequent as those about reward or its prospects and are more frequent than complaints concerning specific administrators or administrative methods, which seems to shatter another myth, that of the endless antagonism between faculty and administrative personnel. The plurality of complaints, in other words (33 per cent), can be viewed as essentially altruistic: men want their own conditions of work improved so as to do better at it, and they are concerned with the directions in which their institutions move when policy does not seem to them to be aiming at the goals they deem important.

> This is another problem . . . the liberal arts colleges' desperate search for identity: "Where are we? What's our purpose?" In what way the system of the specialty of your field fits into liberal education, whatever that may be, and, by God, there are so many

definitions! There I see another danger which may eventually chase people who are professionally committed, chase them away from this kind of school. Because in the terms of liberal education there may be a pressure exercised. I don't mean specifically styled, structured, from those administration buildings, from the president's office or the dean's office and so on. But indirectly, from the climate around the college because all these colleges are fighting for some kind of survival situation. I don't mean financially and so on, but in a sense of identifying what it is we are doing differently from the liberal arts program at the university, for instance. So they integrate the liberal arts studies and so on. Now this tendency, "let us redefine ourselves," may result in a pressure which may threaten your professional identity. And there lies a real crucial issue, when suddenly you may eventually say, "By God, I *will not* become a teacher of a reduced social science, period." . . . So this can develop into a tension situation or a conflict situation in almost any liberal arts college. . . . Your research orientation . . . may create your internal pressure where you have to cut off your relation to the college on account of you could not possibly be really satisfied and truthful and live with yourself, you know, while bypassing a certain opportunity or call that you believe is yours.

Dissatisfaction with conditions of work is clearly an element in the process of decision-making which may become manifest when an individual receives an opportunity to move to another position, but, for the men here reported, it does not appear to be an important one. It may well be that among the relatively few individuals in the sample who actually accepted new positions, dissatisfaction with their old ones played an important part, but for the total sample of market active men, it does not appear to have been decisive. Respondents were asked how their minds were made up when they had to respond to a definite offer and whether there was a definite turning point in their considerations. About half the respondents who actually received offers apparently went into the market transaction with their minds largely made up as to what they were going to do. They had made their decisions on first receipt of the initial probe or even beforehand: 27 per cent intended to leave their positions from the beginning; 24 per cent apparently knew from the beginning that they would not leave but were willing to play the situation out from curiosity, desire to receive an offer for bargaining purposes at home, or some similar motive.

The remaining 49 per cent of individuals receiving offers apparently entered the transactions which resulted in them with no clear idea of where the interaction might lead. Five per cent of those who decided to accept offers and 8 per cent of those who stayed where they were said that their decisions were based on minor details which added up during negotiations. Eight per cent of those who accepted offers and 14 per cent of those who stayed cited a critical incident or discovery during negotiations which decided the issue. Finally, 3 per cent of decisions to leave and 11 per cent of decisions to stay simply evolved, with the subject becoming aware that he had already reached a decision only after the fact. Thus, men who entered market transactions undecided as to what they would do were twice as likely to decide eventually to reject the offer as they were to accept it. This accords with what is already known of academic job decision-making. *The Academic Marketplace* noted that there always seemed to be a push out of academic positions as well as a pull toward new ones in instances of turnover; and these data, particularly when interpreted in the light of the previously reported fact that 75 per cent of offers were considered superior to existing jobs, fully support that hypothesis. Even when the new positions offered are distinctly superior, men who are contented where they are will be unlikely to accept them; pull toward a job is not enough. But if the push of some dissatisfaction or discontent is also present, then in a sizable proportion of cases all the market negotiation does is to settle what institution the individual will leave his position for and on what terms.

It is certainly important that in at least 22 per cent of cases the transaction convinced the subject that he did not want to accept the position he was eventually proffered. Either minor details added up in his mind until he was convinced he should not accept it or during the course of negotiation some discovery about the proffering institution or the job convinced him that it was not the place for him: faculty members are not the only ones who need to fear the revelations of a market interaction; institutions sometimes have feet of clay as well. In an additional 11 per cent of cases the process whereby the offer became insufficiently attractive, or the candidate became aware of his lack of motivation to leave, was so subtle as to be really evolutionary: he discovered his own state of mind only after all the evidence was in and the decision, in essence, was already made. (Market negotiations, because they signify so very much for candidates, sometimes demanding readjustment of one's whole life style, are often extremely upsetting to men. They may be entered into only with reluctance and it has been my observation that they are sometimes unconsciously sabotaged by the reluctance of the candidate. In one instance in my own experience, I really wanted the offer but did not, emotionally at any rate, want the job, and I behaved in such a way, it turned out, that I received neither. After having been asked by the dean what my desires for the position were, and having had explained to me why a number were impossible to meet, I managed to repeat them all in different ways as absolute conditions for my acceptance.)

Most people, it seems, enter a market transaction either set to accept an offer if one is forthcoming or set to reject it if it comes. Those ready to accept are apparently seriously dissatisfied where they are and explore only those possibilities which seem to offer the chance of a satisfactory outcome, rebuffing in early stages probes which do not meet their requirements. Those who enter negotiations prepared to reject offers probably do so from one of two, or a mixture of both, motives: they are curious, and perhaps anxious, about their own professional standing or marketability and enter the market in order to find out where they stand in relation to their own institutions and their attractiveness to others, or they want an offer as a bargaining lever. In the latter endeavor they may sometimes be encouraged by their colleagues, or even chairmen, who see getting an outside offer as a way to validate an internal status apparently unrecognized by the institution's administration. More often, however, such a maneuver is a response to the (usually unfounded) rumor that "the only way to get a promotion here is to get an offer." In any event, of those receiving offers, over half (57 per cent) rejected them, electing, finally, to remain where they were, sometimes, to be sure, because the conditions offered them were met, or bettered, by their home institutions.

> Yes, I would not accept an offer without talking to the president here. And I called him up . . . and said there were a couple of points I wanted to clarify about my situation here. First, my salary, just to make a comparative estimate, and secondly, what about my administrative load here. [What did the President say?] Well, he said he thought he could reduce my administrative load, and in terms of salary, as I suspected, my salary here will be

more than they offered me anyway, so there's not much point in going. He'd already made out a salary for me, and it was more than they were offering.

Well, I talked to the dean and the chairman here. . . . They indicated very strong hope that I would remain, and as to the terms of my appointment, they . . . I was assured that . . . I was assured immediately that I could count on being promoted. The dean did not wish to name a salary figure, but he said he would get back to me after discussing this with the president and well before I had to make a decision about Duke. So they responded with a very, with what I felt was a very favorable counterproposition. So I decided to stay. [Do you think that the salary you will have next year will be higher than it would otherwise have been?] I think so. I think so. I can't be certain, but it was an increase of seventeen or eighteen per cent, which is quite a bit larger than any increase I have had. [Who fixes salary at Shadyside?] The dean and the president.

All in all it appears that institutions need not fear activity in the labor market from their faculty and certainly should not discourage it. As we have seen, the majority of such squirming and prying comes to naught in the first place; it is probing and nothing more. But even of those relatively few men who do carry the process to the point of formal offer, over half elect to remain where they are—and they are probably better off for it, for in the process they learn more about themselves as well as about the conditions of the market; apparently a significant proportion find out they are better off where they are. Indeed, in one of the institutions sampled it is the practice of president and dean actively to encourage men to investigate other opportunities on exactly this rationale. By all reports from that college, from faculty as well as administration, the policy works well; it is probably the happiest faculty in the group. Perhaps not fortuitously, the institution is also one of the best of the eleven studied.

Acceptance and Rejection

A market transaction does not end with the profferment of a contract and the candidate's decision to accept or reject it, although certainly the emotional peak toward which the candidate is oriented throughout the preceding steps is reached at that point. But once a decision has been made it must be communicated, often to several persons—the agent of the proffering institution, friends and family at the employing institution and sometimes other figures there, and so on. In the case of negative decisions, last exchanges must be made between candidate and proffering institution. Even these events may not exhaust the total social process, however, for after the last actual interaction between candidate and recruiter, events may occur at the employing institution which were occasioned by the interaction, such as promotions or raises. And there are, at the end, the candidate's reflections upon what has occurred which may, if they are of a certain kind ("I was robbed!"), constitute the stimulus for yet another cycle of transaction which this time might have a different result.

The first step in the postdecision sequence is normally the communication of that decision to others. Interviews indicated that the persons actually first informed of the candidate's decision were almost always colleagues and friends at his own institution. (Wives may be presumed to be really the first to know, but again they did not seem to our informants to count as people told.) The first official communication is normally to the proffering institution, which may receive notification of acceptance or rejection before the dean of the employing school is informed. As in the case of the formal offer, this notification takes place in a variety of ways. The modal behavior was the letter of acceptance or regret (38 per cent), with the telephone the second most commonly used vehicle (29 per cent). A surprising proportion of offers were responded to in face-to-face interaction (15 per cent). These occurred when the offer was made and accepted or rejected during a site visit to Fairlawn or in the occasional instance where a recruiting agent returned to Shadyside to receive a candidate's decision.

The form in which the decision is communicated to the recruiting institution seems to have no particular significance. It seems normal, however, for recruiting institutions to make some kind of reply to the candidate's decision, even in cases of refusal. It appears that recruiting agents do not, as a rule, accept a candidate's negative decision without making some effort to change his mind (46 per cent of cases) and occasionally they even promise to come back to him in the future in another attempt to recruit him (13 per cent). How much of this is mere civility it is impossible to say—probably more than candidates believe, because institutions typically recruit for positions vacant at a particular time and thus cannot promise to have another in an uncertain future. Dissuasion, of course, may be very real, for if a candidate has not absolutely rejected a position, or shows some signs of weakness in his resolve, it is certainly in the interests of the recruiter to attempt to change his mind before abandoning him and beginning the process over again with another recruit, who may still have to be located. The reverse of this phenomenon can be seen in the ways in which institutions are reported to have greeted affirmative decisions: wholehearted expressions of delight appear to outnumber mere satisfaction three to one. A small number of recruiters (8 per cent) were so crass (or so put out) that they did not respond at all to a candidate's negative decision, but none were so disturbed by his refusal as to scold him for it.

It is very important to note the processual nature of market transactions. A recruiting attempt, even if unsuccessful, either initiates or further implements a social relation between the members of a recruiting institution and the candidate. Thirty-nine per cent of respondents accepted offers made to them. For another 31 per cent, the last contact with the proffering institution was the respondent's negative reply; for 5 per cent the institution's reaction to a negative reply was the last contact. But in 14 per cent of cases the institution initiated continuing contact related to future attempts to hire, and in 6 per cent of cases it initiated contact unrelated to hiring. Three per cent of respondents initiated continuing contact related to hiring, and 3 per cent initiated contact unrelated to hiring. Thus, in 26 per cent of all cases, interaction continued between candidate and recruiter, usually initiated by the recruiting institution. (If only cases where formal offers were rejected are considered, the proportion rises to 50 per cent.) A negative decision, then, is not necessarily the end of all contact between the individual and the proffering institution. Once an offer of membership in the recruiting organization is made, the recruit's status is not only changed where he has elected to remain, it is also changed where he was asked to go: for a time, at least, he becomes a quasi member of the other institution, and he continues to interact with it. Furthermore, no respondent reported any instance of later accidental contact with the proffering department; what contacts occurred were deliberate. For a quarter of those who received offers, a negative reply was not terminal, and in only 6 per cent of cases was the continuing interaction initiated by the respondent; the recruiting institution, once having selected its man, does not want to let go.

The nature of the continuing contacts between candidates and the institution they have rejected is various. It often takes the form of keeping in touch with the candidate in case he becomes available at a later date. In some cases offers of summer employment or research collaboration are made. In others, acquaintances made during the transaction become professional friendships and may endure for years. This continuing interaction is probably not a threat, in most instances, to the tenure of the individual at his employing college. Occasionally, an offer repeated two or three or four times will finally bear fruit, apparently because the candidate sometimes feels he can no longer continue to reject his friends at the suitor institution. Usually, however, once having made his decision between Shadyside and Fairlawn, the candidate does not rethink it: he came, he saw, he said no, and the reasons, whatever they were, remain valid. The decision, once made, becomes self-confirming, and with every offer he rejects, the roots are made deeper and firmer.

From the perspective of the candidate, the final stage of the entire process of labor market activity is probably his reflection on the matter once it is over, for what he concludes from the experience may have influential effects on what he does in the future, either in binding him more closely to Shadyside or in determining that the next time he will behave differently and leave. Respondents for whom transactions were over were asked about their considered reactions to the whole affair, what they thought about the outcomes after some time to reflect upon them. Seven per cent were euphoric, enthusiastically happy it turned out as it did. Eighteen per cent were glad things worked out the way they did and really would not have preferred a different outcome. Twenty-six per cent felt indifference or calm acceptance of the outcome. Eight per cent were mildly sorry about the outcome and would have preferred a different one. None felt anger or despair. Six per cent were uncertain about the outcome, did not know how to evaluate it, or were ambivalent. Thirty-four per cent could give no reaction because the interaction was still in process. All the euphorics and perhaps half of those who were happy about the outcomes were men who accepted opportunities to change positions or who had wanted to receive offers in order to improve their positions at home and did so, while all those who reported sorrow were individuals who wanted offers (for whatever reason) but failed to receive them. Most of those who reported themselves indifferent were men whose probes did not result in offers but who did not care about it because they had no intention of leaving anyway. The ambivalent individuals, by and large, were men whose experiences with the labor market were not satisfying to them and who were anxious about their reception at home. In the typical case the dean's reaction was so vague or ambiguous that it left them wondering where they stood with him even though they did not receive or accept an offer.

Perhaps the outstanding fact is that no respondent reported anger or despair at the failure of his hopes on the market. Of those for whom transactions were over (eighty-three men), 37 per cent were happy about them and another 40 per cent were at least indifferent or accepting of the outcome. Since only fifteen (18 per cent) of these individuals actually were changing jobs, we must read this as an indication, again, of the satisfaction of the rest with what they have. This suggests that those who really want to move are able to do so (and are happy with the outcome), while the activity of the rest either has an effect pleasing to them at home or is of little consequence to them. Thus, again, these data suggest that activity on the market is probably a healthy thing for a faculty: the dissidents are drained away, hopefully to positions in which they will be happier, while the preponderant majority of the remaining market activists find out for themselves that, if things are not better where they are, at least they can live with them contentedly.

FIVE

Who Is the Fairest
of Them All?

Institutional Reputation,
Personal Prestige

⋙⋙⋙⋙⋙⋙⋙⋙⋙⋙⋙⋙⋘⋘⋘⋘⋘⋘⋘⋘⋘⋘⋘⋘

Matters of professional and institutional standing or reputation are of considerable importance to faculty members, at least to the more professionalized or cosmopolitan among them. So important, in fact, are these phenomena that it is impossible to understand academic mobility and academic labor market behavior without an awareness of the various academic prestige systems. Chapter Four discussed some elements of decision which operate in the determination of whether to pursue a probe and to accept or reject offers once developed, and there were hints in those data of matters pertaining to personal or professional and to institutional prestige. There are two separate, although related, systems of academic prestige or standing, that by which individuals are rated in their fields of work and that by which institutions are rated. These systems are obviously logically separate in that they rank entirely different kinds of phenomena, but they are related empirically in that to some degree ratings of individuals are influenced by the rating of the institutions with which they are identified. Thus, just being at Harvard or Berkeley (as a member of the regular faculties; visiting or other temporary appointments do not count) adds to the reputation of individuals because it is assumed they must be especially competent or they would not be there, an assumption not necessarily made concerning the faculties of Michigan State or Purdue and rarely considered regarding faculty members at any liberal arts college except the three or four of highest perceived quality. In this chapter, we will refer to ratings of institutions as their "reputations" and to the ratings of individuals as their personal or professional "prestige." (The words are often used interchangeably and will be differentiated here only for clarity and convenience.)

When we consider the matter of individual prestige and institutional reputation in the light of academic labor market decisions, however, it soon becomes apparent that the two rating systems are applied to three different rating phenomena: the individual's self-rating for professional prestige and his ratings of the institution where he is employed and that where he has the opportunity to work. The matter is further complicated in that academic departments also have professional reputations which, again, are somewhat although not entirely separate from the reputations of the institutions which house them. And finally, the variables used in making all these different ratings are numerous, given different weightings by different individuals, and not by any means without ambiguity or obscurity. The reader may, at this point, be tempted to throw up his hands and feel that no practice so tentative can possibly have any serious impact on decision-making in comparison with such concrete phenomena as salary and teaching load. Quite the contrary is true, however, and the workings of the individual and institutional rating systems permeate the labor market and its activities.

The ordering of American academic institutions according to the perceptions of faculty members in them is probably that institutions are divided into a series of types based essentially on their size and degree of national influence and student drawing power. The scheme is dominated by the esteem in which the larger universities are held and is essentially oriented to graduate and professional education as the most prestigious of academic pursuits. (And the most influential, not only on academics but on the nation.) If we make an analogy to sports, the place of the liberal arts college is, in general, in the bush league and little league, although some of the best known and most prestigious (such as Swarthmore or Antioch) might be considered sufficiently important in American higher education to be accorded minor league standing by faculty raters. No *colleges* could ever be considered major league. Lacking graduate and professional faculties and students, their influence on higher education is simply too limited.

Contrary to what might be expected from a system so loose, most academic men probably agree rather closely on the rankings of institutions with which they were familiar. Thus, there might be some quarrel concerning whether Wisconsin, Columbia, Chicago, or Yale should be rated as the third greatest institution in the country (Harvard and Berkeley would clearly be first and second, in either order) but there would be very little disagreement that all were great universities. And while there might be dispute as to whether Tennessee or Rice is really major league (most academics would say no), there would be little question that either is superior in academic status to Texas A & M or Brigham Young. One reason for the rather general degree of unanimity in ratings is that most are based on poor information, hearsay, familiarity with the name (which may result from football prowess or from simple proximity of an institution to New York, the base of so many of the mass media), or information vaguely remembered from graduate school to the effect that the University of such and so had a dominating department in one's own field. Thus the more vague and ambiguous the information about an institution a man possesses, the more he will base his ratings of it on general knowledge and the more greatly halo effect will operate, thus producing similarity in ratings among numbers of equally ignorant raters. We will explore later some of the variables which our respondents in this study actually did use in rating their own institutions and those proffering them probes or offers of employment, but it is clear that the more national the scale of the rating asked, the more vague become the bases on which the ratings are made, although they may continue to show surprising unanimity of opinion.

Ratings of *departmental* reputations by academic men are, in general, based on better information, and thus are less unanimous than ratings of institutional reputations. The reason for this, of course, is that men do not usually rate departments other than those in their own fields, about which they are apt both to know more and to be better qualified to judge. Furthermore, departmental reputations, far more than institutional ones, are based on the presence (or one-time presence)[1] of individual faculty members with high standing in their fields, so that the rating of the department becomes very much a function of what one thinks of the work of the individuals with whom it is associated. More specifically, departmental ratings among natural scientists and mathematicians probably show considerable degrees of unanimity; there is little quarrel among men in these fields either as to what the fields themselves are about or concerning the ways in which study in them is to be conducted. This enables them to agree fairly readily that the work of a given individual is or is not of superior quality; rating departments composed of known individuals is relatively easy. However, in the social sciences the nature of the fields themselves is still debated among their practitioners, as are the utilities of their methods of study. And unanimity in rating of departments may be all but impossible in many of the humanities and language areas, where there may even be disagreement on what a man does as well as on whether or not it is really art or criticism or what have you. In general, however, the ratings of departments by the respondents in this study either were admittedly done in ignorance or were of departments with which the rater had some working familiarity and thus competence to judge. And again, having had access to the rating process, we know some of the variables they used in judgment.

There are probably two ratings of individual prestige or standing in their fields for faculty members with any degree of professionalization—their own self-rating and the ratings others make of them. That the former might look better than the latter probably goes without saying. For our purposes, since we are exploring the academic labor market from the perspective of the job candidate, we are concerned only with his own assessment of his professional standing. (Clearly the assessment which the proffering department makes has something to do with his selection in the first place, and it is possible that in a case where the individual's self-esteem considerably overshadowed the proffering department's rating of him, no bargain might be struck, but if we assume that hiring departments find the best men

---

[1] For both departmental and institutional reputations are very slow to change, once established. This is particularly true of institutional rating, of course, precisely because it *is* based on vague information.

available, there is some evidence that the assessments of the departments and those of the candidates tend to coincide.)

The norm for self-assessment is the disciplinary professional model. When they can point to scholarly publications in print or papers offered at professional meetings as measures of their standing, men do so. In the absence of these bench marks or of other professional activities such as officerships in professional societies and consultantships (which rate below scholarly publication as measures of a man's worth according to general professional norms), they may speak of their teaching, internal services to the institution, activity in state teaching associations, and so forth. And it is apparent in much they say that the reference group some men use as the judging body whose approval they seek is a function of where approval may be available to them. No one enjoys feeling like a failure. When men know that they do not measure up to disciplinary professional standards for research productivity, they are likely, instead of assessing themselves as failures, to find some group by the standards of which they can feel that their performance has been at least adequate. These may be the student body of the college ("I was voted Teacher of the Year last year"), their colleagues on the faculty ("I was elected to the Faculty Steering Committee which, since it is an important committee in the college, shows something of what my colleagues think of me"), or even some extra-academy body entirely ("I am continually asked by the local Businessman's Association to give them speeches on the nature of the economic system").

The reason these rating systems are important is that they influence the outcomes of transactions on the academic labor market. When an individual receives a probe from Fairlawn one of his first reactions is to assess the proffering institution. In universities this assessment would usually be a double one, of the institution itself and of the proffering department. In private colleges, where the department is less important and the institution correspondingly more so, concern at this stage will probably be limited to the institution. But in either case the assessment made will reflect not just what has been heard or is known of the institution but also what its standing is relative to the candidate's own professional prestige and the reputation of the institution where he is currently employed. If his decision is that either his own prestige or the reputation of Shadyside is superior to the reputation of Fairlawn, or that both are, he will be uninterested in the probe and will reject it forthwith. (In this case, the probe is not even useful as a merit badge for local esteem and would certainly not be brought to the attention of the dean for, being inferior, it would compromise the professor's local status and the dean would not take it seriously, thus calling his bluff.) If the individual regards Fairlawn's reputation as superior to that of Shadyside, he may very well pursue the probe, at least to the point of turning it into an offer, for if his self-assessment is that his prestige is superior to that of either place, this would at least be a step in the right direction; if he thinks himself too good for Shadyside but appropriate to, or even not good enough for, Fairlawn, a very good exchange indeed is in the offing. (For Fairlawn's misjudgment of his standing is their problem, not his!) The basic rule operating here is what Caplow has called the principle of the conservation of status: gains in status will usually, although not invariably, be sought; loss of status will invariably be resisted (Caplow and McGee, 1958, pp. 74–76).

Once the probe becomes an offer, the calculation of prestige increases in its importance, and one of the things with which the candidate busies himself during the period between initial probe and formal offer is locating and assessing the variables with which to make it. "I went to the library and got out all of these guides to colleges and looked up everything I could find about them."

To the small college faculty member, the site visit is extremely important in the recruiting process because, unless he happens to know the place, it affords him what may be his only opportunity to assess departmental factors. He already knows or can discover what it is important to know, for rating purposes, about the institution itself, but the relative insignificance of departmental organization in most colleges is such that, except for departments in his field at colleges in his immediate locality, he may know nothing of those at other colleges. His concern with the department, then, will not be directed toward its professional reputation, for few college departments have one, but rather toward whether he can live and work within the confines of the department, for if he comes to Fairlawn, it will be the institutional reputation which will reflect on his own, not that of the department. (That is why it is more permissible for men to leave major league universities for teaching posts at prestigious liberal arts colleges than for them to go to the minor leagues. Minor league departments are known quantities, and joining one affects one's professional prestige. The colleges are known as colleges, however, not as outposts of the professional disciplines, so from the standpoint of professional prestige it is better to go to a good college with an unknown department in one's field than to a minor university with only a mediocre department.)

The commentary above implies that it is possible to devise an "algebra" of prestige ratings which will predict whether or not an individual will accept or reject a particular offer, given knowledge of his assessments of his own professional prestige and the reputation of the proffering department and institution. (This hypothesis also implies the possibility of calculating which individuals would be sought by recruiting departments, given knowledge of recruiting agents' assessments of their own departmental and institutional reputations and of candidates' prestiges.) I have made no attempt, given the small numbers of men involved and the unclearness of some of their ratings, to make such a computation for the individuals who received offers reported in this work. However, as we will see, the kinds of differences in ratings which such an algebra would produce do distinguish mobile faculty members from fixed faculty among this group, that is, different calculations of relative prestige are associated with different outcomes to market transactions. It would be a mistake to believe the prestige algebra represents anything invariable or to perceive this statement of it as an attempt at universal generalization. The data reported here support the claim that tendencies for the algebra to operate in the manner described are discernible in the comparison of mobile and fixed faculty, and this result in itself is startling: if prestige is a variable sufficiently important to show striking association with mobility or immobility with nothing else considered (rank, salary, work load, and so on), it is clearly one of major import.

With this introduction to the nature of academic rating systems and their operation in the labor market, let us now examine the kinds of ratings which respondents made of themselves and the various organizations involved in their market experience (employing and proffering departments and institutions), and also examine the bases on which the ratings were made. The bases of ratings are important in revealing what matters faculty members consider important, what they look for in a position, and how they evaluate its presence or absence. This information in turn expands our knowledge not just of the academic labor market but of the social structure of the whole profession.

Table 22 shows respondents' ratings of their own colleges and

Table 22. RESPONDENTS' RATINGS OF INSTITUTIONAL STANDINGS
(N = 125)

Rating	Employing Institution	Proffering Institution
	Per Cent	
One of the very best of its kind in the nation or the world	18	7
Good, but not among the top schools of its kind	38	19
Fair; mediocre	6	10
Rather weak in most ways	2	4
Unqualifiedly poor	0	1
Impossible to rate totally; some strengths, some weaknesses	2	2
Multiple ratings given on noncomparable scales	2	2
Not an academic job or institution	0	1
Do not know or not asked	6	26
Uncodable reply	26	28
Total	100	100
Number	(125)	(125)

of the institutions which probed them or made formal offers of employment. Given our previous finding that about half the probes or offers came from universities, most of which rank above most colleges on the professional scales of institutional rankings, it is fair to say that

Aggrandizement Effect is visible: Shadyside was rated good or superior by 56 per cent of respondents while only 26 per cent thought as highly of Fairlawn. (The ratings, as asked, however, were not comparative.) Correlatively, only 8 per cent rated their own colleges fair or weak while 15 per cent rated the proffering institutions fair to poor. Another phenomenon visible in the table is the *willingness* to rate on the respondents' parts. Sixty-four per cent were able to make a rating of their own institutions which fitted into the quality categories of the table, and similar ratings were made for 41 per cent of the proffering institutions. In only 4 per cent of either group were ratings made which indicated some sophistication in the methodology of assessing institutional quality (the impossible and multiple entries), while another 26 and 28 per cent of interviewees gave replies which were impossible to classify under the scheme used here. All this suggests that rating is an accepted activity in the academic world; it is used and everyone understands its uses. That as many as 26 per cent of the subjects were unable to give a rating of Fairlawn is not surprising; many had never heard of the proffering institutions before the probe arrived, and a significant number rejected the probe without bothering to make inquiries.

In general, respondents thought well of their own colleges and somewhat less well of the places offering them employment, although about a quarter of the sample professed not to know anything about the standings of the institutions probing them. Table 23 describes the bases on which their ratings of the two institutions were made.

Well, I think it's probably among the top forty liberal arts colleges in the country. [This is *your* judgment?] I've heard this figure. Now I think it's . . . in my personal opinion, I think, well, let's see . . . if I could put a grade to it, I would say B. B or A to B. [On what basis do you make this grading?] Well, probably just based on the type of students that we get here and comparing them with colleges that I consider A, Carleton or Oberlin or some of the Eastern schools, Swarthmore. . . . [Is Shadyside less selective than these schools would be?] Oh, I should imagine so. I mean, we don't have enough applicants that have 650 to 700, 750 board scores that we can say, "Well, that's all we're going to take," like, I would guess, colleges of that nature would be able to do,

Table 23. VARIABLE EMPHASIZED IN RATING
INSTITUTIONAL REPUTATION
$(N = 125)$

Variable	Employing Institution	Proffering Institution
	Per Cent	
General reputation, tradition, and so on	24	19
Reputation as research institution or graduate school (in the arts, performance)	0	6
Student quality or aptitudes	26	16
Curriculum, teaching, administration, aspects of operation	9	2
Location, climate, geography	0	0
Specific publicity of some kind (for example, athletics)	6	6
Faculty reputation or quality	16	10
Finances	1	2
Do not know or not asked	10	22
Uncodable	9	17
Total	100	100
Number	(125)	(125)

For both sets of ratings, the members of the sample tended to use an institution's general reputation as the basis on which their ratings were made, together with its reputation for the quality of its students.

> Oh, jeez, I don't know. I would think it would be in the top twenty, but I can't tell you. [You're not sure why you think so?] Well, I have vague memories. . . . I looked at the last American A.C.E. thing that came out . . . but I can't really remember much about it. . . . I really don't know much about one university as opposed to another university.

Most men really do not know a great deal about other institutions and make their ratings on the basis of hearsay or folklore. That student quality should be important to faculty members of liberal arts colleges is to be expected. The members of the sample were, with few exceptions, primarily teachers, and the quality of student to be taught was very important to them because it so deeply influenced what they could do in the classroom and the kinds of satisfactions they could receive from teaching. (Neither is it surprising that in both cases more men elected these matters as the basis for rating their own institutions than for the other; they knew more about it.) Another reason students are important is that they provide the only possible quantitative or objective measure of institutional quality. Student success in postgraduate work and on national standardized examinations such as the Graduate Record (GRE) provides a bench mark with which institutions can be compared on "product." No other phenomenon does. (Ratio of Ph.D.'s on the faculty, for example, is commonly used, but it is subject to considerable ambiguity in interpretation and, indeed, in real meaning. But if an institution consistently has graduates admitted to advanced study at Harvard, or if its graduates consistently score well on the GRE, it can claim that it must be doing something right. What it is doing right, of course, may be the selectiveness of its admissions policy.) Quality of faculty ranks third on both lists. Nothing else seems to matter very much in rating institutions, but it is worthy of note that, although they were factors in decision-making, climate, location, and geography received no mention from any respondent. These variables, in other words, may have some importance in determining whether one wants to go or stay somewhere, but they are recognized as having no significance in estimating the quality of an institution. The failure to make this distinction is responsible for some confusion in journalistic discussion of labor market matters.

Some of the more sophisticated comments on ratings, both in praise of particular institutions or in criticism of them, appear in Table 23 as uncodable because they did not fit the categories into which the table places responses. These often had to do with what could be called the atmosphere or feel of a college.

It's very difficult. We have to use certain criteria. If we use the criteria of students going on to excellent graduate schools, we are doing excellently. *I* think the education is lousy here. [Oh, really? Why?] We are supposed to be dedicated to a humanistic education, but we're not doing it at all. Overly specializing. We don't give the students time to digest, to meditate, to draw conclusions, tentative hypotheses, and so on. We just pile books on them and say, "Here, get the facts and spit them back at the final exam," and I see this just because I usually give essay exams and, you know, the ignorance is appalling. The students are dissatisfied with their own lack of overall knowledge.

I would have to do this within the framework of a far more comprehensive generalization. I have the general opinion that Shadyside and [the two other institutions in the state with best public reputations] are not as educationally sound as they are cracked up to be. I think there is a tendency in all three of them to substitute talk for action. They claim, it seems to me, academic distinction beyond their actual achievements. [What is the basis for your feeling on this?] It's a matter of dynamism, that's what makes a college distinctive. Whether you have a dynamic, driving, highly ambitious, and productive faculty. The Shadyside faculty, as a group, does not. There's a great deal of talk about the great teaching that goes on here, but in my opinion it's not taking place. I think it's a fallacy that one can be a great teacher without expanding one's horizons, studying, keeping up with your field. I don't think you can be a great teacher and just take it all out of the textbook. There's no unmitigated pursuit of excellence here because nonexcellence is safer. I've said all this to the dean many times. [How does he react to statements like this?] He simply accepts it as being healthy disagreement and praises me for my scholarly productivity.

It's an excellent teaching faculty. And I suspect that this community that exists here has a lot to do with the excellence of the teaching. I think that there's less pettiness, less backbiting, less of the kind of scrabbling over each other for position, this sort of thing, than most educational institutions that I'm familiar with. And I think that the students are beneficiaries in this kind of interaction. [What accounts for the existence of this sense of community among the faculty here?] Oh, a few individuals, I suspect, and I think the president has mainly most to do with it. . . . Negative history has something to do with it, the kind of college it's *been.*

Ratings of departmental quality tended to follow the same patterns as those for institutions: men seemed to feel their own departments were superior to those which proffered them probes or offers by a ratio of approximately two to one, and large proportions were unable to make a rating of proffering departments because of lack of information concerning them. Table 24 shows respondents' ratings of departmental standings. As with institutional ratings, the Aggrandizement

Table 24. RESPONDENTS' RATINGS OF DEPARTMENTAL
REPUTATION
($N = 125$)

Rating	Employing Department	Proffering Department
	Per Cent	
One of the very best of its kind in the nation or the world	12	7
Good, but not among the top group of its kind	30	14
Fair; mediocre	3	9
Rather weak in most ways	3	6
Unqualifiedly poor	2	2
Impossible to rate totally; some strengths, some weaknesses	4	1
Multiple ratings given on noncomparable scales	2	2
Not an academic job or institution	0	1
Do not know or not asked	11	40
Uncodable reply	32	19
Total	100	100
Number	(125)	(125)

Effect is plainly visible. It is possible that 12 per cent of the departments in which men were interviewed for this study were among the very best of their kind in the nation or the world, but it is unlikely. Among the eleven institutions surveyed there is only one which might hope to be rated among the great liberal arts colleges of the United

States and, although certainly others of the eleven have some fine departments, it seems doubtful that 12 per cent of the total are of this quality. It seems rather doubtful, furthermore, that an additional 30 per cent of departments ought to be rated as "good." There were a number of two and three man departments represented (some where only one of the two or three faculty members held the doctorate), and when departments are this small it is doubtful that their professional quality can be good regardless of the devotion or competence of the teachers in them. It is probable that ratings of proffering departments are more realistic than those of employing departments.

As with institutional ratings, the basis on which departmental ratings were made reveals the academic value system. Table 25 shows that the most important aspect of departmental ratings is personnel: reputation or quality of faculty was mentioned twice as frequently as any other variable as the basis on which departmental reputations were assessed, although scholarly performance and internal harmony and operations played a secondary part in the evaluation of the departments where respondents worked and a lesser role in evaluating other departments.

> Competent people, very affable, very cooperative with each other, each quite good in his own field. [Would the department be known to the profession?] No—lack of publication, I would say.

> Excellent. Absolutely first-rate, in just about every respect. We're not a flock of huge publishers, scholars, but I think we've published more than any other department [in the college] man for man. I think so; at least as much. And I think that just in general competence and awareness, it's a very good department indeed. It's certainly the best department I've ever been a teacher in. And it may be the best department I've had close contact with. I'm trying to compare it against the best previous one, which would be the Williams department that I went to as an undergraduate. And I think there are no more excellent people here, but I think there are fewer meatheads. All in all it's an excellent department, which is one of my chief sources of pleasure in teaching.

> I think it's good. I'm not sure it's as good on the graduate level as this school is on the undergraduate level. [What do you look at to make such a judgment?] Faculty, standards, performance, quality of the students we've had here, quality of the students

Table 25. Variable Emphasized in Rating
Departmental Reputation
(N = 125)

Variable	Employing Department	Proffering Department
	Per Cent	
Size	7	4
Research or performance accomplished or possible there	19	5
Reputation or quality of faculty	30	42
Quality of students	13	1
Curriculum, teaching, administration, operation	15	10
Students formerly graduated from there[a]	1	0
Personal qualities of faculty or chairman	0	1
Finances	0	0
Do not know or not asked	9	32
Uncodable reply	6	6
Total	100	100
Number	(125)	(125)

[a] That is, claims to departmental fame because of famous persons who were formerly students. Claims for fame based on postgraduate success of students in general fell, depending on phrasing, into "quality of students" or "curriculum, teaching. . . ."

they graduate, kinds of jobs the students get, the books and publications that come out, the whole bit.

That quality of students and research or performance possible should have greater significance in the evaluation of the departments where men were than for those proffering them positions is understandable: they knew much more of these matters where their own departments are concerned. It is undoubtedly significant that nearly a third of responses concerning other departments were "do not know," the second most frequent response category. If men have heard of other departments at all, or can find out anything about them, what they are apt to learn is who is in them and what they have done; this, in other words, is what is important about another department when one has the chance to join it. It is also what is important, apparently, about one's own, but in estimating one's own, other things also come into play—the work that can be done (which there is no way of ascertaining at second hand about another department), the nature of the teaching and other operation, and the quality of the students.

> [Did you say you were suspicious of the quality of the department there?] Well, it didn't seem to have . . . I looked over the course offerings, and I wasn't really interested in the kinds of things that they were offering compared with other places. The people I didn't know. The structure of the department seemed a little bit hit or miss. This would be a kind of systematic rationale behind the people in it in terms of their interests and kind of in the courses.

> It's very good. The ranking members of the department, for instance, are all Ph.D.'s and all from prestige schools, Harvard, Yale, Princeton, the University of Chicago. [Do you send many students on to graduate school?] Very few. Oh, I doubt if there's one or two a year. [Is that a function of Shadyside and its student body or of the department, do you think?] I think it's essentially Shadyside and the student body. Most of the students who major in English, with a few exceptions, are girls going into secondary school teaching.

A twist on the "we're good because we can place our students" theme is the rare situation where a faculty member says his department's reputation is high because other institutions try to place their graduates on his faculty, a rating scheme which would more commonly be found among university departments.

> I would say that it was considered to be a very competent department. Good men, you know. But it's hard to judge . . . all of the students we've graduated as music majors and who have pursued music have done very well in graduate school. [Would Curtis or Juilliard know of Shadyside as a source of students?] Yes. They would in the sense that every opening we've ever had we've been besieged by Juilliard and Curtis . . . to hire one of

their men. They know the college is an excellent college as such, and so the assumption is that the music department could not be less so, because the college being what it is, they could not tolerate an inferior department, you see.

Men, then, are the basis on which departmental reputations are built—men and women—for what happens to the students after graduation is a frequent source of judgment for departmental ratings.

I have to judge it by saying that we can send our kids out. . . . We have, right now, three kids at Harvard doing graduate work and successfully. . . . We have one at the University of North Carolina. We have three at Indiana University which is strong in [one of our specialties]. We have two at the University of Chicago and one at Stanford; these are all right now in the works, doing their graduate work for the Ph.D. So it means that whatever our preparation, however conservative-oriented . . . our products have met the test of graduate school competition, so I would rate it as a solid, good quality [department] . . . which fits them for what the best institutions expect to be the level of competency in graduate work.

But if departmental reputations are built on men, how are men judged? In assessing others, men tend to use scholarly productivity as an almost exclusive criterion. Men who write are known to other men; therefore, they have professional reputations. Men who do not write, however, are known only to themselves and to their immediate colleagues, and they find other ways of ranking themselves. The study did not investigate the process of rating others, but Table 26 describes respondents' self-ratings, by rank because there were some obvious differences among the ranks in how men rated themselves. It is impossible, of course, to give an unequivocal assessment of the accuracy or realism of a set of ratings of this kind. For the group as a whole, they do not appear unrealistic. Only 3 per cent rated themselves in such ways as to be classified as widely known, while 43 per cent gave ratings which permitted coders to classify them as relatively or totally unknown in their fields. (It is also interesting that a maximum of 19 per cent indicated that they did not know their own relative rankings or gave answers which could not be coded: men are used to assessing themselves and tend to use similar criteria.) The apparent realism of self-rating is probably in part a function of the more clearly defined criteria

Table 26. Respondents' Self-rating on
Professional Reputation
(N = 125)

Self-ratings	Assistant Professor	Associate Professor	Full Professor	Total Sample	Number
			Per Cent		
Widely known nationally or internationally	0	5	6	3	(4)
Some national reputation	0	10	28	11	(14)
Known in a specialty but not in his field as a whole	15	15	19	16	(20)
Known regionally but not nationally	6	15	11	10	(13)
Relatively unknown in his field	23	27	14	22	(27)
Totally unknown in his field	42	10	6	21	(26)
Do not know or not asked	6	5	14	8	(10)
Uncodable reply	8	14	3	9	(11)
Total	100	100	100	100	(125)

which are used in rating individuals; men are judged professionally, by and large, by their written work, and there was little tendency among the respondents to evade that judgment. The inescapable comparison between the modesty of self-ratings and the somewhat florid conceptions which the same men hold of their departments is explained by this same phenomenon: The criteria for the assessment of individuals are clear and specific; those for judging departmental quality are less clear and more various, thus permitting individuals of modest accomplishment to gain reflected glory from claimed organizational superiority. For men, publication is the criterion.

> Well, I haven't written anything, so I would say that I just don't have any [professional reputation]. I haven't either written anything nor have I given any talks. So the people who know me are the people here in the department. [Would this be the sole basis for a professional reputation in your field?] Well, a local reputation could be made in terms of teaching, of the teacher, but I think this kind of thing tends to spread out rather slowly.

> In the profession? Oh, I've published maybe three or four papers and I've got these two textbooky things that are coming out, so I'd say that some people know about me, but that's just about all.

> I've only published three articles and I've got a book underway and until that gets out . . . as you know, that's the way one gets known, and so: very limited indeed. Simply within my circle of acquaintances.

> It's undistinguished. I have not published . . . I have had considerable success as a teacher, but that doesn't make one a professional reputation.

> My own reputation? Probably virtually nonexistent. I haven't really published anything of significance.

The nearly unanimous agreement that scholarly publication is what counts in the matter of professional reputation is matched, by those who mention the matter, in agreement concerning what does not count. What does not count, and there is no evidence that respondents' assessments are inaccurate, is teaching, training teachers, editing, and local organizational work, even for essentially professional activities.

> Oh, negative . . . yeah, because I'm from a small school, a school that is frowned upon because it prizes teaching and stu-

dent contact rather than publication, a school that's in a rural area instead of a cosmopolitan, big city, civilizing, commuting, all the things, country club, IBM; we don't even have a computer on campus, and stuff like this. We're really old hat, terribly backward.

I really think that as far as a general reputation, I have a pretty lousy reputation nationally, as a guy in the field. I have not produced any epoch-making new studies nor revived the teaching and study of comparative literature nor have I, in linguistics, done anything but train in summer school three hundred practicing teachers of language in public and private high schools throughout the country and in some way or other, affected their students, but this . . . once again, you're teaching teachers, and you know what Education means as far as the general evaluation of the liberal arts and the basic research environment.

That's easy, my total publication is in textbooks. . . . Actually, I'm an editor, but no one looks on editing in the same class of effort with being a book-publishing scholar. The book-publishing scholar is what the university celebrates, and deservedly so.

Oh, it's almost nonexistent except on a local level. And even then back-scenes. In state organizations, for example, I've been a kind of quiet but founding member of various kinds of organizations like the State Council of Teachers of my subject and a couple of other groups. . . . There have been some significant changes made. But I'm nobody. That's not modesty. I'm nobody.

The degree of unanimity our respondents accorded the publication basis of professional prestige in academics was considerable. Research and writing were mentioned by 34 per cent as the variables on which they based their self-estimates. No other factor attained any appreciable significance, and only 15 per cent gave other responses—4 per cent mentioned activity in professional societies; 4 per cent mentioned other professional activity, such as consulting; 3 per cent mentioned teaching and student opinion; 2 per cent named personal qualities or social relationships; 1 per cent named administrative or other institutional activity; and 1 per cent named professional relationships or acquaintance. (Fifty per cent rated themselves as relatively or totally unknown, giving no indication of basis, and 1 per cent gave no answer or uncodable answers.) If only the respondents who rated themselves as having prestige are computed (that is, if those rating themselves unknown or giving uncodable replies are excluded from the calculation) then 71 per cent indicated that research or writing was the basis of their estimate of their professional standing. This is not unanimous agreement, of course, but it is persuasive, especially since the respondents were liberal arts college teachers, not multiversity professors: the disciplinary professional norms of achievement have been adopted by the men of the private colleges.

Respondents not only were aware of the various academic rating systems and their bases but also used them themselves. They recognized that the halos of superior institutions may rub off on their faculty members, but it was opportunity for increased research or writing activity which was most prominently seen as enhancing reputation. The presumed significance of research and writing for professional prestige can be seen clearly in Table 27 when they are contrasted with Table 22. Only 26 per cent of respondents rated Fairlawn as good or among the best, yet 38 per cent saw a move there as enhancing their professional standings, most of them because of the better opportunity they would have at Fairlawn for professional activity. Interestingly enough, since so many respondents rated Fairlawn as inferior to Shadyside, only 6 per cent felt they would lose professional status by going there, but of these, again, twice as many saw the reasons for it in professional opportunity. It is apparent that although institutional affiliation was perceived as having some effect on the assessments which other men made of them, the faculty members interviewed felt quite strongly that the dominating influence was their own professional activity, which we have seen means almost exclusively research and writing. In this perception they are probably entirely correct. We will see later that these assessments seem to have had very definite effects on men's market decisions.

Implicit in all that has been said is the notion that the academic rating system makes a difference, that it is important to men and that they act on it, but that latter implication has not yet been demonstrated. The following tables show that ratings do make a difference in the market behavior of the faculty members studied. Because of the relatively small numbers of men involved, the differences found are not statistically significant, but if the patterns of mobility and fixture which seem to be associated with the different ratings were maintained in larger groups, statistical significance would result. Table 28 shows

Table 27. Perceived Effect on Professional Reputation
of Acceptance of Offer[a]
(N = 125)

Effect	Per Cent	
Acceptance would enhance reputation		38
As a result of institutional "halo"[b]	12	
As a result of departmental "halo"	5	
As a result of increased opportunity for research and/or professional activity	21	
Acceptance would detract from reputation		6
As a result of institutional "halo"	2	
As a result of departmental "halo"	0	
As a result of decreased opportunity for research and/or professional activity	4	
Effects of acceptance would be ambiguous as a result of special features of the particular situation		11
Acceptance would have no particular effect on reputation		22
Do not know, or not asked		17
Uncodable		6
Total		100

[a] Respondents who had accepted new positions were asked the effect of the acceptance upon their professional reputations. Respondents who had not been made offers or who had rejected them were asked what effect an acceptance would have had.
[b] Halo effect is defined as the tendency to judge specific qualities or characteristics of an event or individual according to a prior general impression. Thus, going to Harvard might be expected to increase an individual's reputation. The "halo" of the institution would also brighten him.

Table 28. OUTCOME AND RATED INSTITUTIONAL STANDINGS
(N = 125)

	Outcome									
	Undeveloped		Mobility		Fixed		In Process		Total Sample	
Rating	Shady-side	Fair-lawn	Shady-side	Fair-lawn	Shady-side	Fair-lawn	Shady-side	Fair-lawn	Shady-side	Fair-lawn
	Per Cent									
One of the very best of its kind in the nation or the world	17	4	7	13	35	13	7	7	18	7
Good, but not among the top schools of its kind	35	18	47	27	39	22	46	13	38	19
Fair, mediocre	7	13	0	13	4	6	7	7	6	10
Rather weak in most ways	1	6	7	0	0	4	0	0	2	4
Unqualifiedly poor	0	1	0	0	0	0	0	0	0	1
Multiple ratings given on noncomparable scales[a]	3	5	13	7	0	0	7	13	4	6
Do not know or not asked	1	21	20	27	13	39	7	27	6	25
Uncodable reply	36	32	7	13	9	22	27	33	26	28
Total	100		100		100		100		100	
Number	(72)		(15)		(23)		(15)		(125)	
Total sample	58		12		18		12		100	

[a] Includes the one instance of a nonacademic job offer.

the outcomes of respondents' market interactions according to their ratings of their own institutions and of those proffering them probes or offers. It is not as complicated as it looks. The meaning of this table may be seen at a glance by comparing the ratings of Shadyside and Fairlawn given by men who received and accepted offers (the mobility outcome) with those of men who received but rejected them (the fixed outcome). Only 54 per cent of those who elected to leave Shadyside in favor of Fairlawn rated Shadyside as either good or among the very best, compared to 74 per cent of those who elected to remain at Shadyside, *and of the former group, only 7 per cent rated their own college as among the best, compared to 35 per cent of the fixed faculty members;* another 7 per cent of the mobiles rated it as weak. To put it simply, the best ratings were given to their own school five times as often by those who elected to remain there when they had a chance to leave as by those who elected to depart. That push out of a position makes a difference is very visible here as well: the same proportions of mobile and fixed faculty members gave Fairlawn the best rating and only a few more mobiles than fixed rated it as good. To both groups, then, in similar proportions, Fairlawn appeared quite attractive. The principal difference between the two groups is not how highly they esteem the proffering institution, but what they think of their own. Those who already think their own the best seem to be far less likely to leave it, while even among men who think relatively well of the institution where they are employed mobility is most likely to result if they receive an offer from one they esteem more highly. (We may assume, furthermore, that some of the good ratings given Shadyside by mobile men were a function of ego protection and, perhaps, of noblesse oblige once they knew they were leaving.)

Another pattern visible in the table which may be significant is the comparison between faculty members whose opportunities were undeveloped (that is, did not eventuate in offers) and those whose interactions were still in process at the time of the interview. The rating pattern of the undeveloped group is not unlike that of the fixed, which is not really surprising for, in any given case, lack of development is at least as likely to result from the candidate's foreclosure of the transaction as from the recruiter's. We would, therefore, expect the undeveloped category to resemble the fixed since it probably includes a significant proportion of individuals who made essentially the same market decision although at different stages of the process. The group whose interactions were still in process, however, shows a rating pattern very similar to that of the mobiles—almost identical proportional ratings of Shadyside and similar proportions (one to two) of best and good ratings of Fairlawn. We would, therefore, expect that most of these individuals would eventually elect to accept offers if they were forthcoming. To test that expectation, in early 1969 inquiries were mailed to the fifteen faculty members whose transactions had been in process in the spring of 1967 when they were interviewed for the study.[1] Of the fifteen, six (40 per cent) had accepted another position since 1967, eight (53 per cent) remained in the position held in 1967, and one did not reply to the inquiry.

This distribution seems to offer some support for the hypothesis that mobility can be predicted in a general way for grouped data from the prestige algebra. The ratings made by men in process in 1967 much more closely resembled those made by mobile than fixed faculty members, and mobility among men in process turns out to have been more than twice as high as it was in the sample as a whole. The final pattern of outcomes for the market active faculty group interviewed now appear as undeveloped, 58 per cent, mobility, 17 per cent, fixed, 25 per cent, and unknown, 1 per cent. (These figures are not entirely accurate since they are, in effect, based on data from a two-and-one-half–year period. Figures for undeveloped outcomes are from 1967 while the corrections made for fixed and mobility outcomes result from the parceling out of those in process in 1967. But since new mobility may have occurred in the academic years 1967–68 or 1968–69 for persons undeveloped or fixed in 1966–67, and some of the new mobility shown did occur in those years for men in process in 1966–67, the tabulation does not refer to 1967 outcomes only. For this reason the remainder of this chapter continues to refer to the original [1966–67] data only.)

The relationship between self-rating and the outcomes of market transactions is shown in Table 29. It is apparent that mobiles have higher self-assessments than others. While none rated themselves as

---

[1] The text to this point was written before the inquiry described was made, that is, without the author's knowing what the outcome of the market transactions coded as in process were. That the prediction made here turned out as accurately as it did is an indication of the significance of prestige ratings in the market process.

Table 29. OUTCOME AND SELF-RATING
(N = 125)

Self-rating	Unde-veloped	Mobility	Fixed	In Process	Total Sample
			Per Cent		
Widely known nation-ally or internation-ally	4	0	4	0	3
Some national reputa-tion	11	27	9	0	11
Known in a specialty but not in his field as a whole	18	7	9	27	16
Known regionally but not nationally	11	13	0	20	10
Relatively unknown to his field	24	7	35	7	22
Totally unknown to his field	17	27	26	27	21
Do not know or not asked, uncodable re-ply	15	20	17	20	17
Total	100	100	100	100	100
Number	(72)	(15)	(23)	(15)	(125)

widely known nationally or internationally, 27 per cent claimed some national reputation as opposed to 15 per cent and 13 per cent of un-developed and fixed faculty members who made either claim. Once again there is a very strong similarity between mobile faculty members' ratings and the self-assessments of those in process. As noted earlier, it is difficult to appraise self-assessment, and we must expect some infla-tion from what an objective measure might show if such a measure existed. Working professionals should have some reasonable idea of their own standings in their fields, however, and if there is any bias in self-assessment, we might expect that it would operate across the board. This last assumption may not be true, however. As noted earlier, the reception of an offer changes a man's status. Thus, if he were reasonably objective, his self-assessment would also change. What is visible here, in the difference between mobile and in process respondents, may be a set of reasonably accurate self-assessments which, in the one case, have just been changed upward by the acceptance of an offer and the concomitants of the market transaction which led to it, and, in the other, have not yet been adjusted upward by the completion of the process. For self-assessment is apt to be improved by a successful market transaction whether or not it results in the acceptance of an agreeable offer. (More than a third of the offers received, remember, were at best only slightly superior to the positions the respondents held, and about a quarter of the sample went into the transaction with no intention of accepting offers. Thus, some fixed faculty would not experience this increase in self-esteem if their offers came from institutions they deemed inferior or if they had had no intention of departing.) During the course of the transaction the recruiting institution must demonstrate to the candidate that they appreciate his good qualities, think well of him, want him to join them, and so on. Otherwise he is not apt to come. The effect of this attention may be to cause him to revise upward a previously modest self-assessment.

But another phenomenon is also operating here: we have seen that men in all categories think well of the institutions with which they are dealing, but that mobiles and those in process seem to think less well than others of the institutions and departments where they are. Table 29 showed that they have higher self-assessments than other men as well (only 34 per cent rated themselves unknown in one way or another as opposed to 41 per cent and 61 per cent). Self-ratings of a certain kind, along with departmental and institutional rating patterns, are associated with the tendency to be mobile. The men who were moving perceived themselves as making gains of status not only by movement to a better place but also as a result of leaving one which was inferior both departmentally and institutionally, and they saw an already developed individual prestige as involved in the move. Table 30 shows this motivation on the part of the mobiles very clearly indeed. Sixty-seven per cent saw their professional prestige as being enhanced by the move they were about to make, while a high of only 40 per cent of men in other categories expected enhancement as a result of the move if they had made or did make it. None of the mobiles expected

Table 30. OUTCOME AND PERCEIVED EFFECT
ON PROFESSIONAL REPUTATION
(N = 125)

Perceived Effect	Unde-veloped	Mobility	Fixed	In Process	Total Sample
	Per Cent				
Enhancement of reputation due to institutional or departmental halo	15	27	14	13	17
Due to increased opportunity for research or professional activity	21	40	13	13	21
Detraction from reputation due to institutional or departmental halo	3	0	4	0	2
Due to decreased opportunity for research or professional activity	3	0	4	13	4
Ambiguous effect	11	0	18	13	11
No particular effect	23	20	18	27	22
Do not know or uncodable	24	13	26	20	22
Total	100	100	100	100	100
Number	(72)	(15)	(23)	(15)	(125)

a diminution of prestige as a result of their move, and none saw it as having a mixed effect.

For the first time in this series of tables the pattern of similarity between mobiles and men in process is broken. In Table 30 responses from men in process look more like those from fixed or undeveloped faculty members than they do like those from mobiles. This is probably a function of the question asked, which called for more than a rating or an assessment of fact: it asked men in process to predict the course of a possible future action. Their responses to this request deviated from the pattern shown by those who had already made the decision for Fairlawn. We must conclude that their future behavior might also be expected to be different. From their responses to institutional and departmental rating questions, they might be expected to become mobiles; from their responses to the question on the effect on their prestige of going to Fairlawn, we might expect them on the whole to be fixed with regard to this particular Fairlawn, but to be mobile in the future. It is still too early, three years after interview, to test fully the results of that expectation, but the results of the 1969 mailing mentioned earlier show that, of the men in process when interviewed in 1967, 40 per cent had already left Shadyside by 1969 and that of that group, only one went to the Fairlawn about which he was interviewed in 1967! This totally unexpected and really rather startling confirmation of the predictive power of the prestige algebra and of its discrimination seems to confirm the hope that an instrument especially designed for that purpose would produce reliable predictive data.

It is possible to summarize the discussion of the relation between ratings and labor market outcomes thus far by saying that, in a general way, our findings seem to have been predictable by the prestige algebra. The moves which mobiles made were perceived by the men involved as moves to institutions and departments to which their own professional standings were better suited, that is, the moves were in directions predictable by the algebra. So were the decisions to remain in place. The theory, if that it may be called, seems to hang together: men who perceived status gains (or reductions in status inconsistency) to be made by movement tended to move; those who perceived no gains in movement, or feared loss, tended to remain immobile. Table 31 summarizes the ratings of mobile and fixed faculty members to contrast them with each other. It can be read as the raw data from which a collective prestige algebra would be computed for these two groups of faculty members. (Specific predictions, of course, would have to be made from individual ratings, not from grouped data.) Scanning the table to take summary conclusions from it, it is not difficult to see that, in general, the two groups of faculty members made different ratings which are logically associated with the market behavior used to classify them: mobiles, in general, thought better of their own professional reputations, slightly less of their departments, and notably less of their institutions, were somewhat more ambiguous about the proffering de-

Table 31. SUMMARIZED RATINGS FROM MOBILE
AND FIXED FACULTY[a]

	Frequency with which mobile faculty gave			
To	High Ratings	Medium Ratings	Low Ratings	Total
	Per Cent			
Themselves	33	25	42	100
Employing departments	25	50	25	100
Employing institutions	11	78	11	100
Proffering departments	17	83	0	100
Proffering institutions	25	75	0	100
	Frequency with which fixed faculty gave			
To	High Ratings	Medium Ratings	Low Ratings	Total
	Per Cent			
Themselves	16	10	74	100
Employing departments	25	58	17	100
Employing institutions	44	56	0	100
Proffering departments	29	57	14	100
Proffering institutions	33	56	11	100

[a] Uncodable ratings, multiple ratings on noncomparable scales, and so on are omitted. The table, being composed of different tabulations, should be read horizontally, not vertically.

partments, and thought somewhat better of the proffering institution than did fixed faculty. Note also that no mobile gave either proffering organization a low rating and no fixed faculty member gave the institution where he was fixed a low rating. (These, of course, are the agencies with which the two groups of men will be associated in the future, but 17 per cent of fixed faculty did give their own departments a low prestige rating.) The two most striking differences in group ratings are in self-assessment (where over twice as many high ratings were given by mobiles as by fixed faculty, and only about one-half as many low ones) and in assessment of Shadyside, where fixed faculty gave four times as many high ratings as did mobiles. Given that fixed faculty actually gave somewhat greater proportions of high ratings to Fairlawn, it appears that, for this sample of faculty members, at least, the critical features of the algebra are relative self-assessment and assessment of the job in hand, those who feel their own standings are superior to those of their institutions will be more inclined to be mobile than those who regard their institution's standings as superior to their own.

Prestige, of course, is not all there is to academic mobility. Other variables also influence it, although, as we have seen, the multiple ratings of prestige in which men necessarily become involved when they receive an offer from another institution seem to be predictive of their reactions to it. But certainly the natures of the two jobs which must be compared in employment decision-making (the job held and the one proffered) are also influential, as are the individual's satisfactions and complaints where he is. (For, as we have noted, a push out of a position seems to be required for movement as well as a pull toward another one, and the general similarities between mobile and fixed faculty in assessment of the merits of Fairlawn suggests that push may be more important than pull.) Table 32 shows coder's comparisons of the two positions involved for mobile and fixed faculty on the bases of salary, rank, and specific working conditions. It is readily apparent that mobile faculty members, as a class, received better offers than fixed faculty, and we must assume that this also is related to the former group's willingness to move. All considerations of prestige aside, unless extremely dissatisfied, men are unlikely to leave one position for another which is inferior or even approximately the same. An offer which is markedly superior, however, might tempt them even when status gains were minimal or entirely absent since it would mean an even exchange with regard to status and would produce advantages from other perspectives. The conditions of work coded here include rank increases, however, which is a status variable, so prestige considerations are not entirely absent from the tabulation.

Under the circumstances revealed in Table 32 it would be foolish to assume that the fact that mobile faculty members received markedly superior offers in significantly greater proportions than fixed fac-

Table 32.   WORKING CONDITIONS OFFERED MOBILE
AND FIXED FACULTY

Relative Quality of Conditions Offered in Comparison With Job Held	Mobiles	Fixed	Total Sample
		Per Cent	
Offer inferior to present circumstances	7	9	8
Offer essentially similar to present circumstances	7	17	13
Offer slightly superior to present circumstances	7	17	13
Offer distinctly or markedly superior to present circumstances	73	48	58
Comparison impossible due to incomparable circumstances	0	4	3
Uncodable for other reasons	7	4	5
Total	100	100	100
Number	(15)	(23)	(38)

ulty had nothing to do with their decisions to be mobile. We do not know that it did, but the distributions are sufficiently unlike that the differences are probably not fortuitous. These facts do not tell us anything, however, about motives for leaving Shadyside, although they would help account for the attraction to Fairlawn. Table 33 illuminates some of the reasons for departure. Two features of Table 33 are immediately evident. First, although a quarter of respondents mentioned no complaints or problems about their positions, none of them was among the mobile faculty members. Second, the patterns of complaint or dissatisfaction shown by mobiles is noticeably different from that of other categories of faculty. Forty per cent of mobiles were dissatisfied with the institutional philosophy or educational policies of the institutions which employed them, more than three times the proportion of men in any other category who made such complaints. Also, none of the mobile faculty members was coded as having complaints

Table 33. OUTCOME BY RESPONDENT'S COMPLAINTS OR
PROBLEMS AT THEIR EMPLOYING INSTITUTIONS

Complaint or Problem	Unde-veloped	Mobility	Fixed	In Process	Total Sample
			Per Cent		
Salary, rank, prospects of promotion	11	0	26	27	14
Conditions of personal work	25	20	13	7	20
Institutional philosophy or educational policy	7	40	13	13	13
Administrators or administrative relations or methods	6	20	13	7	9
Geography, climate, location	8	20	4	7	9
Quality of students	3	0	4	0	2
Personal and idiosyncratic matters	6	0	9	20	7
No complaints	33	0	17	20	25
Uncodable	1	0	0	0	1
Total	100	100	100	100	100
Number	(72)	(15)	(23)	(15)	(125)

concerning his salary, rank, or prospects for promotion. Men are motivated to leave positions by dissatisfactions with them, but their dissatisfactions are not immediately self-serving. The mobile men were not happy with the institutions they were leaving, but their pattern of complaints is quite different from that of men in other categories. Men who are not departing either were satisfied or else primarily complained about things very closely related to themselves—the conditions of their work and their salaries. Less than a tenth mentioned the philosophy or policy of their institutions as a significant area of complaint.

These reactions seem quite understandable. Those who are satisfied where they are, and are staying there, are unlikely to have serious complaints concerning things which are unchangeable. Conditions of personal work are perennially unsatisfactory to academic men (the proportion of nonmobiles mentioning them is identical to that of mobiles), and salary is changeable, if not through one's own efforts, then at least through time. But if a faculty member is really out of sympathy with the policies or educational philosophies of his institution or the personalities of its administrators, there is not much he can do about it. If his dissatisfaction becomes severe, he has no alternative but to depart. It is important to reiterate, however, that the dissatisfied and departing men were not complaining about their salaries, rank, or the chance they saw for promotion. The myth, as we have seen before, is that salary is of major significance to the academic man, that he is always unhappy with it, and that salaries are the principal factor explaining his mobility or immobility. A number of items in the data of this study, of which this table may be the most conclusive, demonstrate that this is simply not true. Salary is important for its symbolic function; these data suggest it has little other significance to the men of the better private colleges.

Oddly enough, it was fixed faculty who were most dissatisfied with their salaries—men who had the opportunity to move and rejected it. We know from Table 32 that 65 per cent of them were offered positions at least somewhat superior in salary, rank, and working conditions to those they elected to retain, so their dissatisfaction with their salaries cannot be laid to lack of opportunity to improve them. The data do not permit a demonstrable explanation of the reasons for their complaints about salary, but it is reasonable to conjecture that at least some of them may have expected Shadyside to offer them a greater reward for their immobility than it in fact conveyed.

Other features of Table 33 remain to be noted. More than twice as many mobile men as persons in other categories complained about Shadyside's geography or locale. This, too, is inexplicable in absolute terms, but I suspect that complaints about geography, climate, and locale are a bonus offered the mobile. We know from earlier evidence that men do not move for reasons of geography, but moving for other, more pressing, reasons may afford the luxury of getting away from a locality with which one is dissatisfied. Thus, a faculty member who is leaving his institution because he is dissatisfied with a new direction which he perceives it to be taking, and who feels he is bettering himself professionally by his move as well, may also luxuriate in the knowledge that, as a side effect, he is leaving the northern winter behind him, and his comments on his motives may make that sound more important in his decision than it was.

Finally, it should be noted that personal or idiosyncratic matters were the second most frequent cause of dissatisfaction on the part of men in process and appeared among them between two and three times as frequently as they did among men of other categories. (There were no such complaints among the mobiles.) This may be a feature of the dislocation which we said earlier characterizes a market transaction. Those who have completed their transactions and decided to leave know exactly what their complaints are; they have had to articulate and rationalize them in order to make the psychological break which a mobility decision requires. But men in process have not made up their minds; they are considering departure but have not yet fixed on it. The costs of movement are in the forefront of consciousness, and their principal disaffections are with conditions which they can hope will be put right with time. Under these circumstances, their complaints may seem to them to be personal or idiosyncratic, and they will be apt to voice them in that vein. It is probable that, had the interview found them two months after their decisions were finally made, they would have more closely resembled either mobile or fixed faculty members.

The importance of the prestige system in understanding the academic profession in the United States is difficult to exaggerate. It dominates the universities, and although its influence is not as pervasive in the private colleges, it is clearly operative there as well. For the private colleges the significance of the prestige system is that it is basically university-defined and university-oriented. The academic professions (the disciplines) are dominated by the values of the university, of research and scholarship, and, increasingly, the colleges seem to be accepting those values. The universities, in their graduate schools, train college faculty members, and these, in turn, bring the values they have adopted as their own, and as those of their professions, into the colleges. But the colleges by their natures incorporate other commitments besides those to scholarship. They are basically teaching institutions. And because of some of the practical inconsistencies between the demands of scholarship and those of teaching, the gradual incorporation of disciplinary values has created problems for them. The foremost of these, of course, provide the Janus character described previously.

The fact and operation of the academic prestige system is simply one aspect of the faces of Janus in the colleges. This chapter has shown how that system affects the activities of faculty members and their decisions regarding departure or continuing residence in their institutions. Not shown here, because the study did not focus on the matter and thus the only relevant data are indirect, is the effect of the prestige system and the values it incorporates on the institutions themselves. That effect is profound and is exaggerated by the financial problems private institutions face and by the competition they experience from public institutions, both for students and for functions, as Barzun has pointed out (1964). The effect of the prestige system in this matter is that only the better private colleges are likely to survive the financial crisis, but *better* is increasingly defined by the academic profession and the prestige system itself, that is, by values originating in the universities. The academy has become the hostage of the multiversity, and it is beyond the power of the academy much to affect the situation, for the judgments which will determine it are made elsewhere.

As this chapter shows, institutional reputation, although a standard constantly used in judgment, is based on hazy and often insufficient evidence, but it is real (because it is used). The one objective or empirical factor involved in such reputations which is widely recognized is students—student quality, performance, and ability. Obviously the quality and abilities of a given student body are best known to the faculty members at the institution that student body attends, and this is clearly reflected in our data. But other academics and other persons also have some measure of it and of the postgraduate performance of students attending an institution. When men are asked how they estimate student quality at an institution their answers consistently deal with Graduate Record Examination scores, proportional admission to prestigious graduate and professional schools, amounts of award money granted in graduate schools, and so on. These are centered on as measures of quality because they are objective; of all the things that go into making an institutional reputation, these are among the few that can be measured, counted, compared, and checked. That is their importance as the only simple, readily accessible, and nonsubjective measure of institutional quality possible.

But institutional standing as defined by student success has one interesting quality about it: although what happens to the student during his stay at a college presumably has something to do with how well he will perform in postgraduate work, it is also overwhelmingly associated, for each college as a whole, with the type and quality of students admitted or recruited in the first place. It is probably true, as more than one respondent noted, that there will be at least a few truly outstanding students in even the most miserable academic environments in the country. Fortunately for the human race, talent is not in terribly short supply. But having a few outstanding students and consistently having such large numbers of them over the years that an institution becomes known for them are quite different things. The undergraduate institutions with top reputations (among the public as well as within the profession) are those which consistently graduate large groups of students who perform well on the measures cited above. The reasons, of course, are essentially circular: colleges with "good" reputations are attractive to "good" students and to their parents; both want the student to succeed, and academic success is presumably related to vocational success after graduation. The better the institutional reputation, therefore, the larger the group of applicants with the intellectual, financial, and personal qualities which produce academic success. And the more refined this group is, the better becomes the institutional reputation for producing students who are successful by the only tests which can be applied to them. As one faculty member remarked, "It doesn't seem to matter what we do with them; with the quality of student we get here, they will go on to graduate school and will be successful there."

The implications of the phenomenon are structural: to attract good students in order to build an institutional reputation with which to attract even better students (and with them, more funds for better equipment, buildings, and faculty), the colleges must offer programs which maximize access to and success in postgraduate work. But success in postgraduate work is not decided by the undergraduate colleges but by the graduate and professional schools. To the degree that the college program can influence student postgraduate success (and this,

at this point, is difficult to know—see Astin, 1965, 1963, 1962, 1961),
colleges must orient those programs to the values and demands of the
postgraduate school. The successful academy, then, becomes a graduate prep school. And thus is the hidden face of Janus unmasked: the
domination of the universities extends down through the entire institution of higher education and indeed even into the high schools. This
has been called by some writers the rise of meritocracy, but if it is, it
is merit as defined by only one type of institution, the university.

All this is not necessarily bad, and the reader should not leap
to the conclusion that the situation is socially undesirable. It is yet too
early in the development to guess accurately its final implications for
education and for society. But it does pose problems for the colleges.
They have survived heretofore in part because they offered alternatives
to the educational structures and values of the multiversities. It appears
that they will continue to survive only to the degree that they adopt
them. But this, in turn, may mean the abandonment of many of the
values of the academy which they still hold dear and have institutionalized in their programs and structures and which have given them real
reason for existence. Janus was one of the gods and therefore immor-
tal; it remains to be seen whether that performance can be duplicated
in the workaday world.

Through a Glass Darkly

Findings and Recommendations

ᐳᐳᐳᐳᐳᐳᐳᐳᐳᐳᐳᐳᐳᐳᐳᐳᐳᐳᐸᐸᐸᐸᐸᐸᐸᐸᐸᐸᐸᐸᐸᐸᐸᐸᐸ

The present study did not scrutinize colleges as such; its primary focus was on men and their behavior. It was inevitable, nonetheless, that in the process a great deal would be learned about the institutions in which they were employed and about the social system which encompasses men and institutions alike. It was, of course, with this expectation that the research was begun. The preceding chapters have perforce concerned themselves with matters of detail; the reporting of research data is not conducive to sweeping generalization. Three interrelated conclusions seem reasonably clear, however. First, a college must be comprehended as a social system, as a dynamic, shifting (although generally stable) balance of forces and counterforces, adjustments, and accommodations. Some of these forces are internal, that is, on-campus; some are external although institutionally specific (for example, the board or the local community) ; some are societal. All members of the college are involved in this social system in that their behavior, whether active or passive, affects its balance and direction at particular times. In the social structure of the system, some members tend to be more influential than others—for example, the president, the dean, and campus statesmen—because their positions allow them to exert greater influence on the balance of the system than do the positions of most faculty members. The chief administrators occupy what, on most campuses, are clearly the most influential statuses because they are the authorized leaders and decision-makers and because they have authority over budget and other forms of resource allocation. But even top administrators operate within the limits of the social system of the college, and their effective or functional jurisdictions are limited by other forces such as the direction and influence of faculty conservatism. The faculty is the instrument through which the work of the college is accomplished, and the ability of administration to coerce compliance is very limited. Faculty authority over its own affairs is likewise very limited; its collective influence is usually somewhat greater, but the faculty's principal power is over curricula and student affairs. Conflict in the faculty, while to some extent built into the social structure of the college, is rarely serious and tends to occur over policies rather than over resources (perhaps in part because of the nature of the men who take up teaching in the smaller colleges). Personal reward for faculty is sufficiently high in the better colleges that there is enough to go around, and competition for institutional resources among departments and agencies tends to be kept within bounds. All in all, the better colleges are happy institutions.

The second conclusion is that the colleges are teaching institutions. Not only is this the claim of all of them, the data of the study are persuasive that it is the fact. Teaching is defined in all of them as the basic faculty job, and it is apparent that faculty members accept the definition and act on it. Concern with and for students and the conditions of their instruction is universal. More importantly, adequacy in teaching is for most faculty members a necessary precondition for reward above the minimum and for local prestige. It is possible for a faculty member to acquire power on the campus although known as an unpopular teacher; it is not likely that he will also have the respect of his colleagues and, typically, men believed to be poor teachers are not among the best paid. Judging from student postgraduate performance, the general level of teaching quality at the private colleges seems to be rather high, although student outcomes are greatly influenced by institutional selection policies. Even allowing for this fact, however, there is reason to believe that the quality of instruction at the private college is superior to that typically offered undergraduates at multiversities.

But although the colleges practice what they preach concerning teaching, disciplinary professional norms are a significant influence on faculty members. Locals and cosmopolitans still exist together in some degree of amity on most campuses, but any struggle between them on the better campuses has been resolved in favor of the cosmopolitans. The locals who see professional values and activities as flatly antithetical to the aims of liberal education are older men who will be retiring soon and, although there are institutionally-oriented faculty members among the younger faculty, they are less apt to define professional values as inconsistent with their aims and more apt to share some disciplinary values themselves. It is probably just as well for the colleges that the situation turned out this way, for excessive localism in the past seems often to have been a camouflage for professional incompetence. That cosmopolitanism would eventually become dominant was, of course, inevitable, since the supply of faculty for the colleges is becoming dominated by the great graduate schools where local values are practically unknown. Given the sometimes harsh realities within which they must exist, the better private colleges seem to have made an effective and healthy compromise between the values of localism and those of disciplinary professionalism. They have a declining share of the college student population at a time when the costs of higher education are climbing rapidly. They are in competition for subject matter both with the better high schools and with the graduate schools as the high schools reach up into curricula which were heretofore taught only at the college level and as the graduate schools reach down to put professional curricula into the undergraduate program. And, given that they tend to be judged largely for their ability to turn out "successful" graduates, the very survival of the colleges may have determined the compromise the best among them have (often tacitly) adopted.

That compromise—the adoption of disciplinary professional values within a teaching-oriented framework and curriculum—has not been without cost. The principal financial cost, which has been considerable, has been borne by the institutions as an investment in faculty salaries, teaching equipment, libraries, and so on. A personal psychological cost which has been borne by the faculties may be of similar magnitude—the abandonment of serious professional ambition. For men in most fields, the election of small college teaching as a career means the forfeiture of any ambition for the great rewards their disciplines offer. Outstanding research scholarship with its rewards of fame, fortune, travel, power, and personal freedom is rarely found on the campus of the private college. (It is rare anywhere, but is relatively more common in the universities.) The sacrifice, of course, is one made knowingly and without much apparent regret by the college faculties, and it has a reward of its own in comfort and a style of life unknown on any university campus with which I am familiar. Furthermore, the academic labor market has been sufficiently active since World War II to ensure that any faculty member who decided his choice was wrong had the opportunity to revoke it. In the end the penalty college faculty pay (in addition to the forfeiture of opportunity for the pursuit of much research scholarship) is the necessity of juggling two careers and keeping their hands in at their research in the odds and ends of time during vacations. Their general satisfaction with their jobs indicates that they do not find the requirement onerous.

The third conclusion is that the most serious problems facing the colleges are financial and qualitative. As their proportional share of the college student population continues to decrease, and as education becomes increasingly expensive to offer, some private colleges will necessarily have to close their doors, seek public support, or merge with others in order to survive. Those which remain solvent and independent will still face the problem of maintaining their differentiation from public institutions in order to justify their higher costs to students. They have done this in the past by claiming that they do a better job of teaching, claims which probably can be supported by the better institutions among them. But with increasing competition for students and increasing costs, such claims may require greater justification. Middle-class parents for whom the costs of private education may represent a considerable sacrifice are likely to become more skeptical of making such an investment unless they can be shown that it is worth it. This, in turn, may well accelerate the trend (already apparent among the best) toward defining the private college largely as a graduate preparatory school. And this, in turn, will further strengthen the influence of disciplinary professional values among them as they recruit more highly professionalized faculty members to carry out their new mission.

Such trends, rightly, will not be without their critics. (Nor without further costs, both human and financial.) Widespread complaints about the quality of college instruction from students and academics alike already have institutions of higher education somewhat on the defensive. (Old Guard locals find it a ground on which to make a last-ditch stand.) And the voice of the humanist which has long been raised against the increasing professionalization and institutionalization of teaching will certainly decry it. Professor William Arrowsmith, former chairman of the Department of Classics at The University of Texas, has already done so, with specific reference to the liberal arts college.

> Let me say immediately that I am concerned here with only one kind of teaching . . . with which apparently too few administrators in higher education are concerned. I mean the ancient, crucial, high art of teaching, the kind of teaching which alone can claim to be called educational, an essential element in all human culture, and hence a task of infinitely more importance than research scholarship. With the teacher as a transmitter or conductor of knowledge . . . I have no concern. He is useful and necessary, and because he does the bulk of university teaching, it is important that his job be effectively performed and intelligently evaluated. But so long as the teacher is viewed as merely a diffuser of knowledge or a higher popularizer, his position will necessarily be a modest or even menial one. (1967, p. 57)

> I can think of no more conspicuous failure of leadership than in the liberal arts colleges. With a few notable exceptions, the record of the college is one of failure . . . and it is precisely on the claim to *teach* that the American college stakes its case. Here— in low student-teacher ratios, in college plans, tutorials, etc.—it has spent its money and ingenuity, and it is here that its failure has been spectacular. Why? In my opinion, the colleges have failed as teaching institutions because they have been subverted from within. They have recruited their faculties heavily from the major graduate institutions and these recruits have inevitably altered the tone and finally the function of the colleges. . . . And they are now in the ludicrous position of proudly claiming, on the one hand, that seventy-odd percent of their graduates go on to graduate or professional schools, and, on the other, of com-

plaining that they are being turned into prep schools for graduate study. . . . Instead of cleaving to the Socratic pretensions and traditions, the colleges have tended instead to become petty universities, different . . . only in a slightly higher regard for the teacher and a corresponding tolerance of the student. If the wealthier colleges have managed to recruit able faculty, the poor colleges have fared badly, recruiting second- and third-rate Ph.D.'s, who for their part regard the college as an academic boondocks and lust for the day when they can return to the urban Edens of research. In the meantime they teach the only thing they know—technical expertise—and thereby both corrupt their students and refuse their Socratic opportunities. If I am right, the trouble with the colleges is that they recruit their faculties from uncongenial sources; the well is poisoned. By imitating the universities, the colleges have everything to lose and nothing to gain; neither their funds nor their human resources are adequate to the competition. My solution is dramatically simple. Let the colleges go into business on their own, *against* the graduate universities; let them form their own league as it were and train the kind of man they cannot expect to recruit from the universities. (1967, pp. 65–66)

There will be few who will not vibrate in sympathetic response to at least some portions of what Arrowsmith and similar critics have to say. For, unquestionably, college teaching is often badly done and, unquestionably, it has been allowed to take a distinct second place to research activities in the universities. Yet Arrowsmith is incorrect about the colleges. It is not true, for example, that only the better colleges have been able to hire able faculty and that the lesser ones, therefore, have had access only to "second- and third-rate Ph.D.'s" who constantly hunger for a return to some research Eden. The fact is that the lesser colleges have been hard put to find Ph.D.'s at all, and, as we have seen, at the best colleges the faculties are overwhelmingly satisfied with their positions and do not leave them. No one can argue that a 2 or 3 per cent annual turnover (excluding deaths and retirements) represents some sign of an Exodus in check—especially not under the circumstances of the market this study has revealed. Men who want opportunities to leave their positions have not suffered for lack of them.

More important than Arrowsmith's factual inadequacies, however, are the errors of his two fundamental assumptions, first, that American academies sometime and somewhere offered a Socratic Eden where teachers could "live upon a pure text" (p. 61) for the benefit of their students, an academic state now corrupted by the graduate schools and by demands for professionalization, and, second, that institutions newly reinvented to act that part would now fill a demand and survive. Both of these assumptions, however honorable and however expressive of the ideals of liberal education, are probably false. It seems doubtful that purely Socratic institutions of the type Arrowsmith recommends ever existed anywhere; certainly they are unknown in American history. Our schools have been vocational from the start (Harvard was founded as a seminary), and the nineteenth century German university was hardly thrust upon us. It also seems improbable that colleges offering the program suggested would have the sufficiency of students Arrowsmith seems sure would flock to them. It beggars the imagination to believe that state legislatures could be induced to support such experiments with appropriations and for them to be conducted on a basis of private support seems even less likely. With few exceptions, the private colleges are dependent on student fees for their operation. This means dependence on parents to pay such fees and that, in turn, is likely to mean parents who in one way or another expect some return for their money. That return is overwhelmingly understood and defined in the United States as vocational training or something very like it. Few colleges, it is true, explicitly guarantee vocational placement and success, but there is no question that the public culture of the United States has it that college education helps one get on in life and is necessary for the procurement of a good job or, for women, of a husband who has one.

The hard fact of the matter is that institutions of higher education are luxuries for a culture, expensive luxuries. And their high cost of operation means that, whether ostensibly public or private, they are supported by the public, by the citizens of the society in which they occur. (The real financial difference is that ostensibly public institutions are supported by a broader base through taxation by the state. But even giving to private schools is tax-exempt, so in that sense, and in their own exemptions, private institutions are also partially state supported.) Under these circumstances, institutions of education necessarily must respond to the demands of their constituencies or they will lose them. The understandings of the meanings and functions of education common in a society probably determine what kind of education it will have; the values of a national culture are what produce its school system, not the values of the teachers therein. And the history of education in this country, replete with experiments of one kind or another which failed through lack of support (Robert Maynard Hutchins' University of Chicago comes to mind), indicates that educational innovations which are contrary to the thrust of the common culture are likely to fail. (Another form of failure, of course, is the gradual abandonment of the innovative program in the face of nonsupport and its supplantation by more conventional ones. The New School for Social Research, like New College in Florida, is not so new anymore.) And the common culture of Americans is pragmatic, timebound, and materialistic. In educational expectations it is essentially vocational. We have no objections to liberal or humane learnings, but we expect the consequence of four years of (expensive) college education to be "good for something." And it has—unhappily—been impossible for our humanists to convince the public that pure learning for its own sake is worth anything. It is too much to expect that they should have done so; cultural change is glacially slow and cannot be directed by the conscious efforts of individuals.

In the meantime, the colleges face the problem of survival. For good or for ill, many will pass away or change their natures. Those that do neither will most probably survive by doing even better that which they do well now—acting as graduate preparatory institutions in addition to the other educational and social functions they perform. I am not as convinced as Arrowsmith that this function is iniquitous, but our convictions in the matter seem irrelevant—it works. That is what the colleges' constituencies demand and, given the plight of the colleges, that is likely to be what they get.

There are also three themes which summarize the nature of occupational mobility among the faculties of the better liberal arts colleges. First, the labor market of the private liberal arts college is universal in scope. Although "the" academic labor market for the country as a whole is highly balkanized, there is no special small college market or segment. Probes reported by our sample of market actives came from minor universities, private colleges, and public colleges, in that order of frequency; other sources were reported in very small numbers. Exactly 43 per cent of probes came from colleges and 43 per cent from universities although major universities accounted for only a few of these. Small college faculties are evidently perceived by recruiters principally as a source of teachers, since only 6 per cent of probes were for nonteaching positions. There seems to be little tendency for an exchange of personnel between colleges and business or industry to develop.

Second, although the market for college faculty is universal in scope, it is particular in operation. Although 25 per cent of probes came directly from recruiting agents and had been unforeseen by the recipients, another 26 per cent originated with sources with which the recipients had had some previous contact. Sixty-nine per cent of respondents reported acquaintance with someone on the staff of the proffering institution; in about half these cases the acquaintance was close. Thus, most market transactions involve persons known to one another. This personalism in the market is probably not the consequence of a desire on the part of recruiters simply to hire their friends but is necessitated by the demand for compatibility in new faculty. This demand, in turn, appears to be a requirement or outgrowth of the social structure of the college and cannot be met or satisfied through examination of formal certification available in professional biographies or employment agency records. Thus, contrary to what the candidates themselves believed, it may be that the reason for their selection as candidates by other institutions was that recruiting agents were acquainted with them—that they possessed the academic qualities desired and were also known to meet compatibility requirements.

Third, the labor market for small college faculty was good at the time of study and men did not use it manipulatively. The overwhelming majority of market active faculty did not perceive probes from other institutions as offering manipulative possibilities, and 24 per cent of them did not even inform anyone else of probes received, while an additional 43 per cent informed only their wives. Thus, more than two-thirds of men interviewed did nothing to create the possibility of manipulation. This conclusion, based on what respondents said about their reaction to probes, is supported by the fact that chairmen and deans were not commonly informed of them. Some failure to inform administrative figures may result from fear of punitive reaction among some faculty members, but there is no evidence to indicate that such fears had any foundation in the institutions surveyed.

About a third of probes received resulted in formal offers, and about a third of offers were responded to by the agents of the colleges where respondents were employed with some material encouragement for the candidate to reject the offer—raises, promotion, reductions in load, and so on. For market active faculty as a class, interaction on the academic labor market was a routine part of life; two-thirds of respondents received more than one probe during the study year. Thus, being on the market was in no sense abnormal or indicative of a desire on the candidate's part to leave his employment. Market actives are likely to be visible (that is, to receive probes) for exactly the activities that make them desirable to their own institutions.

The vast majority of offers received by market active faculty proffered practical terms superior to those enjoyed by the men receiving them (62 per cent distinctly superior, 13 per cent slightly superior). But better terms offered did not account for mobility. Pull toward other positions largely consisted of the attraction of what appeared to be superior disciplinary professional opportunities. Financial motives for movement were insignificant. Before mobility occurred, push out of the position held must also have been present and appeared to be of considerably greater importance than pull toward another position in accounting for movement. Among the men surveyed, push out of a position centered in dissatisfaction with conditions of personal work and with institutional policy or philosophy. Dissatisfaction with the speed or prospects of promotion did not account for mobility. There was some tendency for offers to come to men who knew before receiving them what they wanted to do with them; 51 per cent of respondents receiving offers entered the market transaction predisposed either to accept them and leave their jobs or to reject them and remain. Others made their decisions—or found them made for them—during the process of negotiation. Most men receiving offers did not accept them. But rejection of offers does not necessarily terminate the interaction between the candidate and the proffering institution. In 50 per cent of the cases reported it continued after the position had been rejected, usually in relation to the possibility of future acceptance and usually at the initiation of the recruiting institution.

Six conclusions can be made about the labor market for college faculty. First, the process whereby men come into and act in the academic labor market is social and transitive. Men are selected as targets for probes by recruiting institutions for social as well as for intellectual reasons, and they accept or reject such probes for almost entirely social considerations. The series of interactions which constitute a market transaction are transitive in that they must each proceed in a more or less certain way and come to a particular conclusion out of a number of possible alternatives in order for the next stage to occur. A failure in any stage of the transaction terminates the entire transaction for that time, which usually means at least for that academic year.

Second, the labor market for faculty members from better private colleges is good, but there is no evidence that most men active in it are attempting to flee poor working conditions. The colleges surveyed for this report can be described as among the upper middle class of the academic world (if the great universities are the upper class), and the general conditions of work among their faculties are quite good compared with national norms. The principal material rewards of academic life, salary and promotion in rank, are available to all in adequate measure and are closely correlated with length of service. Possession of the Ph.D. degree is prerequisite to normal career advancement, however. The prestige of the degree-granting institution is not important in most instances. Given possession of the doctoral degree, most faculty members at the colleges have only to do their jobs and bide their time. Promotion will occur for them in due course, and adequate, if not munificent, salary will also be forthcoming. Contrary to popular belief, academic rank is similarly distributed among departmental areas—the sciences are not favored in this regard. Neither are scientists more mobile than persons in other fields. Artists are not discriminated against in pay (although they are more apt to lack the doctoral degree than men in other areas), but they are less mobile. Scientists seem to be somewhat better paid than other men, but the differences are not great. In general, college faculty members are treated fairly and without discrimination and are rewarded adequately, even somewhat generously by national standards, although relatively few really high academic salaries can be found among small college faculty. An exception to this generalization is that men without the Ph.D. in academic fields where it is considered normal certification will have lower salaries and slower promotion and market opportunities, although for most of them, as for others, patience will eventually provide reward.

Men who are active in the academic labor market are different from men who are inactive in a number of respects. Market activity is unrelated to either rank or speed of promotion, but actives are paid more highly and activity seems to be causally, although indirectly, related to their high salaries. Actives are better certified (in terms of possession of the doctoral degree) than inactives and are more likely to have taken their degrees at major institutions. Their degrees were also completed more rapidly than were the doctoral programs of inactives. Actives are also more mobile, as would be expected, but 45 per cent of all college faculty remain in their positions at least nine years; market activity drops off sharply after the age of fifty. The evidence supports the proposition that market active and inactive faculty members are drawn from essentially different populations among college faculty. They are differentiated with statistical significance on eight professional and structural variables—departmental affiliation, salary, possession of Ph.D., source of Ph.D., youth, speed with which the Ph.D. was obtained, length of employment and speed of promotion. The dichotomization between them may not be identical with the ideological division into locals and cosmopolitans, but the overlap between the two is likely to be great. As judged by disciplinary professional standards, actives are qualitatively superior to inactives; the labor market today is essentially a professional one and renders what amounts to professional evaluation.

The third conclusion is that, although the labor market for college faculty has been good, mobility is low and most market activity is not serious in the sense of leading to occupational movement. Almost three-fifths of all interactions remained undeveloped, and only about 17 per cent of market active faculty actually became mobile—2 or 3 per cent of the regular faculties of the institutions surveyed. Among college faculty members, the labor market can be said to consist of two markets, a professional disciplinary one, for men with doctoral degrees from major universities and active in their disciplines, and what might be called a classroom market for men without the doctoral degree. The kinds of positions available to the two classes of men are distinctly different.

The fourth conclusion is that neither mobility behavior nor the more general range of market behavior can be accounted for by reference to the classic economic variables. The occupational phenomena which classical economics would lead us to expect would be motives for mobility or market activity—pay and promotion—are unrelated to either. Among mobile faculty members, no complaints were made regarding either variable. Men do not move to secure either more salary or promotion, nor can it be shown in these data that they move for reasons of dissatisfaction with either. Academic men are not importantly motivated by economic considerations. This is not to say that salary and rank are not important to them. Both have immense symbolic significance, and an assistant professor who would not leave his position for a nine-hundred-dollar raise and a promotion might well do so if he discovered that his chairman had recommended for a raise larger than his own a colleague of whom the subject in question thought little. In this hypothetical case the appearance of the matter is that the actor departs because he was dissatisfied with his raise. The fact is that he leaves because his claims to status are not being responded to. The salary is significant only as a measure of his standing in the department, and the issue might equally well have been decided over teaching load, office assignment, or any number of other status symbols.

The fifth conclusion is that men leave their jobs when they are driven out by their inability to continue to live with their dissatisfactions with them. Once determined to leave, or thinking of doing so, they can always improve their conditions, at least in terms of salary and working conditions and often in rank as well, but the lure of better terms is not a principal motive for mobility. The motives or dissatisfactions which create the final frustrations are essentially professional: Primarily, they are unsupportable educational policies, philosophies, or institutional directions; secondarily, they are dissatisfaction with administrative relations or methods; and thirdly, they are dissatisfaction with personal conditions of work. Thus, a fair proportion of academic mobility should be regarded as healthy, at least for the mobile faculty members, since it removes them from a source of serious professional frustration. In some instances it is probably healthy for the institutional metabolism too, since it removes sources of discontent from the institutional body. Most men, apparently, prefer not to be mobile; this implies that their dissatisfactions with their institutions can either be remedied or tolerated; immobility is not an indication of slavish acceptance of the status quo nor is this argument for the health of the institutional metabolism to be regarded as a defense against institutional criticism. "If you don't like it, you can leave" is a poor slogan for a competent administrator or a stable college. But some frustrations and disagreements are not remediable. If an institution is successfully moving in a legitimate educational direction with the support and acquiescence of the majority of its faculty and administration while a few individuals in it simply cannot abide the course it is on, it is not unreasonable to suppose that it may be for the best for both the college and the disaffected men for them to leave. This does not mean, however, that faculty members should either depart or accept without protest illegitimate conditions such as violations by administration of academic freedom or intellectual integrity. Among the institutions surveyed for this research, no such questions arose. Mobility was low and seems, in general, to have worked to the advantage of individuals and at least not to the disadvantage of the institutions they left.

The sixth conclusion is that consideration of personal, departmental, and institutional prestige in one way or another color all market decisions and limit possible choices. Institutional reputation is perceived in a general way, and men usually have only vague ideas about the actual nature of the variables on which it is based. Among small college faculty, institutional reputation is far more important than departmental standing in the discipline, which is usually absent or unknown. In general, institutional reputation is correlated with presumed influence on national educational structures and practices. Departmental reputations are based on the professional prominence of individuals within them. Professional research and writing are the basis of individual prestige in an academic discipline but, lacking accomplishment in these areas, men will use other criteria for self-evaluations. The performance and quality of students are important elements in the rating of colleges where men are employed because students and teaching are central in the private colleges and because they offer the only readily accessible objective measure of institutional quality.

As a group, men who rejected offers to move rated their own institutions highly five times more frequently than those who elected to move, although the two groups thought well of the proffering institutions in similar proportions. Departing men had higher self-evaluations for professional prestige than did fixed faculty; approximately twice as many mobiles claimed some national reputation than did fixed faculty members, and the mobiles perceived their professional standings as being improved by their moves about a third more often than fixed faculty estimated that their own standings would have been improved had they accepted offers. About three-quarters of mobiles reported themselves as moving to distinctly superior terms in their new positions, and all of them had complaints concerning the institutions they were leaving. These centered on the philosophy or policy of the college three times more frequently than did complaints from others and two and a half times more frequently on administrative relations and methods. However, no mobile man complained about his salary, rank, or prospects for promotion at the institution he was leaving.

As the reader may already have decided for himself, the general prospects for even the best private colleges are not particularly good, but the schools will assuredly survive. Lesser institutions will almost certainly have to close or change their present forms; often the financial situations they face presently are precarious, and will not improve unless massive federal intervention of some kind occurs—a prospect not apparently in the offing for the early seventies. The stronger schools will survive because they will further adapt to and promote a function already apparent among them—performance as graduate preparatory institutions. This, since it fulfills a need in society and is in accord with cultural understandings of the uses of higher education, will probably permit the most prestigious private colleges to retain a sufficient share of the middle- and upper-class college market to keep them open and functioning more or less on a business as usual basis. And since business as usual for them is high quality instruction of young people who overwhelmingly go on to graduate and professional schools and compete there very well against the university's own undergraduate products, there is no reason to believe that this accommodation to the times will not prove viable for the colleges.

But this is not to say that it will be without problems for them. The competition among them, and between them and the universities, for students and staff will increase, which in turn will further increase their cost of operation. It is important to note that the competition for staff in which they are engaged is not directed against the major universities. It is not true, judging by the nature of the labor market of the colleges as we have seen it, that private college teaching offers an alternative to a career in the multiversities for the academic man. The strain between the faces of Janus is muted. But the labor market of the colleges was split exactly (except for very minor nonteaching opportunities) between probes from colleges and those from universities, many of them publicly supported. And it is exactly this segment of the national educational structure which is growing most rapidly today— the public colleges and minor universities. It will continue to grow. Thus, we may expect that the demand for the services which the private college faculty member offers will continue to increase for some time to come; his market should continue to be reasonably quick for the same reasons that the private colleges are in increasing financial trouble—greater proportions of students are going to the public colleges and universities. Staffing will get little easier for the private schools and may become somewhat more difficult. (To the degree that undergraduate experience in a private college may be related to willingness to teach in one, this may be exacerbated. Diminishing proportions of younger faculty members now have private school undergraduate experience.)

One set of strains within the colleges may be expected to decrease, although it was probably serious only rarely among the better ones. The struggle for power in the schools between Old Guard and Young Turks—to the degree those terms represent institutionalists or locals and disciplinarians or cosmopolitans—has been decided already and will be completed by the disappearance or metamorphosis of the lesser colleges. The locals are older men and will be retiring soon, and, with the expected emergence of the graduate preparatory emphasis, the cosmopolitan disciplinarians will have carried the day. But while this strain may be expected rapidly to diminish on the campus in the seventies, another will take its place and be emphasized by the new directions we may expect the schools to take; the faces of Janus will become even more evident. As the colleges move more straightforwardly to become graduate preparatory institutions, as they probably must, they will need, in order to prepare students adequately for graduate and professional schools, to seek faculty members perhaps even more than now oriented to their disciplines and to professional activity in them. Such a shift in recruiting emphasis will mean, first, that the colleges will come more directly into competition with the universities, perhaps even with major ones, for staff and, second, that faculty members will be even more torn than they are now between the demands of professionalism and those of the classroom. It will mean, furthermore, that the colleges will have to be willing to provide, in order to keep the men they need, the appurtenances and the time which those men will require for their professional activities.

To the degree that the teaching requirements of high quality undergraduate instruction and the requirements of some kind of success in a professional career really are inconsistent, the faces of Janus are irreconcilable. But to the degree that my earlier contention that what is irreconcilable about the matter is *time* is correct, it will be possible for the colleges to adjust to the situation. The adjustment will not be easy, as it may require some major reorientations in personnel policy and in direction, nor will it be inexpensive, but it can be made. The key to the success with which it will be accomplished will probably lie in the hands, flexibility, imagination, and leadership of top administration in the several schools. The kinds of changes envisioned here are not radical; in many cases they will not even require fundamental changes in direction. But to be successful they will require explicit recognition by and the commitment of campus leadership among both faculty and administration.

One of the single greatest obstacles to the will to effective leadership on the part of either faculty members or administrators is, in my experience, unwillingness to recognize and inability to deal with faculty conservatism and resistance to change. Administrators are probably far more familiar with this conservatism than are faculty members themselves, and therefore they are more willing to recognize it, but it requires wisdom, patience, and generosity, plus willingness to make hard decisions, to deal with it effectively. This resistance to change on the part of faculty members at all kinds of institutions is so widespread and so camouflaged by faculty politics and ideologies that it is very difficult even to convince men that it exists. My own experience (in administration at two huge universities and with faculty committees and politics at institutions of all sizes) has been so consistent that I once formulated McGee's Law of Faculty Conservatism: Any faculty, given the choice between the admission of an unpleasant truth about themselves or the institution with which they are affiliated, the recognition of which will make possible a universally desired progressive change, or the abandonment of a self-congratulatory myth the adherence to which will make the desired change impossible, will invariably elect to maintain the myth.

This statement was devised half in jest and at a time of considerable personal frustration, but whether it is wholly accurate or not, the operative phrase within it certainly is "any faculty, *given the choice.*" If the private colleges are to make the adjustments they may have to make in order to survive, their faculties can probably not be permitted to choose whether or not to make them. They are too likely to elect inaction instead. Thus the first specific recommendation which can be made to enable the colleges to face the likely future with effectiveness is that college administration, specifically presidents and deans, should undertake right now ruthless examination of institutional finance and future and should begin immediately to plan explicitly both what will have to be done in the seventies to enable the college to survive effectively, and how it can best be done. Having undertaken this examination and determined their course of action, the first task of the administration will be the education of its board. If the board cannot be persuaded that the proposals are sound, the only alternatives for the administration are resignation or remaining around to preside over the eventual liquidation which will follow if the original administrative determination has been correct. However, if the board proves educable (and most, in varying degrees, will do so), the administration will then face securing the involvement, education, and cooperation of its faculty, and perhaps of students too. (The latter will prove both more realistic and more malleable.) In the course of this step some typical administrative habits will have to be changed.

The majority of the campuses I visited for this study were still administered more or less on what could be called the Nineteenth Century Autocratic Model. Several, to be sure, had very active faculty "government" organizations which were deeply involved in curricular and student affairs and, to some extent, in advising the administration on matters of policy. (This advising, however, too often seemed to be largely a matter of telling the president what the faculty thought about things, that is, a device merely for communicating opinion.) But it is relatively rare in the colleges surveyed for faculty actually to be involved in administrative decision-making, to be fully informed by the president of the problems he and the institution face, of the options open for solution, and of the likely consequence of the various alternatives. Most presidents—and, following them, too many deans—play it close to the vest when dealing with their faculty members, too often presenting them with *faits accomplis* in matters in which not only do the faculty have legitimate interests but in the decisions on which faculty input might well have aided. The same observations are true in even greater degree of students.

None of this is to propose that administration can or should give up what in many institutions is its legal obligation to make decisions or its power or authority to do so. It is merely to propose that faculty members and students be more fully informed of what decisions are to be made and permitted to assist their administrations in making them. By involving faculty and students (perhaps, at first, only opinion leaders among them) in the problems the institutions face and the alternatives available for their solution, administration can begin to coopt them for the pursuit of the strategies which must be followed for institutional survival.

Another way of saying the same thing is that administration should recognize the systemic nature of the campus. No good college can be long ruled by administrative decree in these times. The authority of the board, president, or dean may be theoretically or legally unlimited, but it is in fact highly circumscribed by the ability of the leader to secure the acquiescence of the led. And the better the quality of the faculty and the student body of the college, the more this will prove true. An administration with what it fears is a hard or unpopular program for change, therefore, will do very well indeed to educate and persuade its faculty and student body of the need for it, and education and persuasion are best accomplished by involvement of those to be educated and persuaded. Once those whose support is necessary for the successful accomplishment of a program have been secured, the persuasion process can be broadened to include the entire membership of "the campus community." At that time absolutism—if unavoidable—can work to secure acquiescence (or departure). Before that time it cannot.

If all the assumptions or conclusions thus far about the nature of the future for the private college and the kinds of changes which will have to be made to accommodate to it are correct, there are, it seems to me, three changes of emphasis which will be required in most of them to accomplish the shift to a specific graduate preparatory function. First, the colleges should begin deliberately to compete with the universities in the recruitment of bright, young, research-oriented scholars who like to teach. These men should be rewarded for their professional activities in the same ways the universities reward them, and they should be encouraged to pursue them as functions of the college, as part of their normal jobs, rather than as part-time and voluntary activities which they may pursue on their own time if they wish. This will have to be done primarily at the expense of teaching time in the college, although travel and actual research expenditures will be involved as well. But adopting such a program at the expense of teaching time does not necessarily mean at the expense of teaching. That it would increase teaching cost is undeniable. If typical loads are reduced from ten to seven hours a week while student loads remain constant, either the number of courses offered will have to be reduced, or else the number of teachers will have to be increased. (The number of courses, incidentally, can usually be reduced without any trouble whatsoever. Most college curricula preserve, like fossil insects in amber, an astonishing number of courses which could be eliminated from the curriculum with no loss in actual subject matter covered and with only minor adjustments among remaining courses. Duplication of courses or course content is a constant danger in any curriculum. Also, many courses could be given less frequently than they are often offered.) The same problems would result from a reduction in class size.

But it can be very sensibly argued that reductions in standard loads from, say, three to two courses a term could be used to improve caliber of teaching and classroom preparation. If it did not, or if the effect were unknown, administration could fairly be charged with not doing its job. In private correspondence, Kenneth Goodrich, dean of Macalester College, pointed out that "load may also be defined by private college faculty as consisting in number of students to be taught rather than numbers of class hours." This would make sense as reflecting both student and faculty perceptions in the small college that it is the relationship between teacher and student which constitutes the teaching relation. *Teaching load,* then, would refer to the burden of student relationships. Its reduction would still result, of course, in either an increase in teachers or a decrease in courses. Something of the like will have to be accomplished in some way. For if the colleges are to become principally graduate preparatory institutions, they will have to have professionally-oriented scholars to teach in them, and the only

way such men can be recruited and retained is to permit them to practice their professions without handicap or serious disadvantage.

The second change in emphasis is that the function of the colleges should be defined and testably established as the pursuit of academic excellence in teaching the disciplinary subject matter. This does
not mean the abandonment of the colleges' traditional goals in humane
learning nor of the hope that something about their programs may
enable their graduates to live richer and more contributory lives than
might be true had they pursued other curricula. But the critics have
yet to prove that academic excellence, even narrowly defined in professional terms, creates philistines at a rate any greater than that with
which our culture produces them anyway. And it can be argued that
the pursuit of excellence within the context of the private college can
have exactly that broadening and liberating effect which the humanists
so desperately seek. The two need not be mutually inconsistent goals.
But the cost of private education is sufficiently high, and will become
sufficiently higher, that its consumers are unlikely to be willing to settle
any longer for pious platitudes. If the colleges claim to be able to offer
students something they cannot receive at the public institutions, the
parents who will have to pay the bill are apt in the future to ask more
pointedly than they have in the past just what that something is. Graduation ceremony invocations about citizenship and preparation for life
will not satisfy them; they are likely to ask for facts and figures to support the claims which are being made to them. It is a very American—
and not unreasonable—request. It can be met by showing that the colleges do, in fact, produce a product which competes at least as well as
does that of the universities on the terms which the public expects and
may have the right to demand, since that is what they are paying for:
success in attainment of vocational and professional goals. The colleges
can probably show that now. It is possible that by making a virtue out
of what seems to be a coming necessity, they may be able to do even
better than that and to show that their product does better. Just doing
as well may actually be good enough—the extra cost of private education can probably be at least partially justified (as long as the student
product is at least as satisfactory as that of public education) on the
grounds that the life experience of the private college is superior. It is
even possible that an investigation of the later lives of private and pub-

lic college students would show significant differences in such indexes of personal disorganization as alcoholism, divorce, and suicide. Whether or not such differences, if found, might not be entirely due to the initial selection process which determines which students go where is another question, one which certainly should be investigated. It seems curious to me, given the length of time in which the merits of private education have been extolled as having some bearing on quality of life, that such investigations have not already been conducted, but perhaps the private schools have been afraid to make them and the public schools have lacked motivation to do so.

An internal change which will have to take place in the private colleges if a program of pursuit of academic excellence is to be adopted will be the rigorous discard of localism or institutionalism in administrative thought and its disregard in the faculty. Localism is essentially defensive and too often an apology for mediocrity or even for incompetence. If all a college has to offer a prospective student is that it is Old Shadyside and that thousands of alumni stretching back into the preceding century have loved it for *being* Shadyside, that will not be good enough. The values of higher education have changed beyond recognition since World War II, and the things that graying alumni harken back to in alma mater will not matter in terms of financial survival in the seventies. To put the matter very simply, for the private colleges the seventies and eighties are going to be rough. There will not be enough money or students to go around, and the lame and the halt will fall by the wayside. College costs can be expected to go up and up, and many parental supporters who now pay their bills with wincing but without question will begin to ask questions and want hard answers. Student expectations, too, are changing radically and rapidly. (Their questions may be even harder to answer than those of their parents, who are, after all, of a generation which took the values of Old Shadyside for granted.) The young people know full well the kinds of competition they will have to face and what they need to survive it, and they want to know that their educations will prepare them for it. Vocationalism is not by any means limited to parents. The questions, in other words, will be asked, and the colleges had better be prepared to reply, for the answers which were good enough in the days when the biggest event on campus in the spring was the Bock Beer Festival will not be good enough for students who may hang themselves if they are not accepted in one of the graduate schools of their choice or for whom scores on the Graduate Record Examination may (out of all proportion) determine their professional futures.

The third change of emphasis is that the colleges should concentrate their program on men by recruiting bright men who are fascinated by their subjects and want to communicate them. It is to be expected that they will want to communicate about them to their colleagues and peers in their professions, and they should certainly be encouraged to do so. But teachers with a rage to teach, to let others know what they know and think and speculate, will never be satisfied by the relatively sterile forms of communication permitted by academic convention. One of the first impulses of the real *discoverers* I have known (and I mean not only men who make startling original discoveries, but also those who find out for themselves things they later learn were already known) is to communicate what has been found to others who may also be interested or who can be interested. All the curricular revision in the world cannot guarantee the production of that electric excitement in the classroom between teacher and students which is generated by a man who is excited by what he knows and wants to communicate that excitement to others. I am convinced that such men are born, not made, but they are not really rare, and the conditions under which they function best can be deliberately created. Those conditions are not mysterious: such men need to be given the time and encouragement to do their work and think about it and to be provided with the opportunity to communicate what they think to people who can be made to understand. The classroom—if it is filled with the kind of students who inhabit the better colleges—provides the latter opportunity. But the colleges must provide the time to work and think. Under such circumstances the college program is likely to take care of itself. The teachers themselves have a very great stake—how great preceding chapters have shown—in the performance of their students, and they can be trusted to ensure that the students receive the kind of training they need. And in their necessary (to them) interaction with students, student needs will be adequately expressed and can be assured of being fulfilled. When excited teachers and excitable students are permitted to come together in ways of their own deciding, education will inevitably result.

It seems appropriate to address a final word to the administrators and faculty members of colleges of the type surveyed here. The academic labor market is problematic for them in numerous ways and, for administrators at least, is likely to become more so before the leveling off predicted by Cartter occurs. The discoveries of this study seem convincing that the better colleges have nothing to fear from the labor market or from faculty activity in it. For a variety of reasons, in fact, it can be argued that colleges should encourage their faculties to professional activity in full recognition that it will lead to activity in the labor market. Professional visibility invites inquiries from other institutions; there are no two ways about that matter. But the appropriate administrative reaction to this state of affairs is not to discourage exploration of other possibilities but to encourage it. Institutional loyalty is not a myth, but it cannot be demanded; it must be earned by the way the institution treats its men and women. It can be neither coerced nor bought. When men explore other opportunities and decide to reject them, they should be rewarded for the rejection, not punished for the exploration. The psychology of learning is clear enough: with every rewarded decision to remain in place, the ties that bind men to their schools are made stronger, while decisions not to move which are ignored or even scorned through lack of institutional response reinforce the attractiveness of that which was proffered and rejected. The lessons of this report are plain: men will usually leave positions only when they are driven out of them, but the things that drive them out are social and psychological, not material, as, in general, are the things that keep them in place.

And when the market, as it does, selects some odd men out, it is probably cheaper, as well as more humane, not to ignore them entirely unless there has been a specific decision made on good grounds that they are to be urged out. The deliberate strafing of the immobile, or even overlooking them simply because they have no power to force the institutional hand, although it poses no danger from them particularly, offers a symbolic threat to faculty who are not in their position. "If they treat anyone that way," the musing runs, "what protection will *I* have when I am through or old?" There are excellent arguments to be made from the perspective of faculty morale, solidarity, and common decency, that men once given tenure should be accorded cost-of-living raises along with everyone else and promoted at least to associate professor within reasonable time. These things are often easily and quite honestly accomplishable if the administrator looks for areas of service to the college in which the unproductive researcher or ineffective teacher can be successful. The financial cost of such policies may actually be lower than the hidden costs of turnover or faculty apprehension, and the human costs are unquestionably less. A college of humane learning, a liberal arts college, if it is to be either liberal or humane, can afford no less.

Methods of the
Research

For the sake of those who may have been led by introductory text-books to believe that scientific research problems spring full-blown from the brow of the investigator, it is useful to trace the genesis of the Career Decision Study from its beginning in a research undertaken in the fall of 1962 on the influence of fringe benefits on newly recruited faculty members at the University of Texas. This work, for various reasons, was never completed, but it did not expire without issue for, by the spring of 1963, having interviewed twenty or thirty newly recruited faculty members at the university, I had become fascinated by some of the market behavior patterns my interviews revealed. This fascination led me to propose a new collaboration on faculty mobility phenomena to Theodore Caplow, with whom I had worked a few years before. We did, for a time, collaborate and produced a proposal for a research on the academic labor market of the major universities which would be focused on the job decisions of the potentially mobile professor (unlike the *Marketplace* study which investigated turnover in departments and the institutional response thereto). By September of 1963 a project proposal for the study had been completed and was in submission to various foundations. By April, 1964, the proposal had been shelved for reasons of cost, Caplow's inability to participate further, and my own impending departure from the university to a small college position from which it would have been impossible to conduct the massive investigational operation then planned.

The abandonment of this particular project did not mean the abandonment of the problem, however. Once in residence at Macalester College it seemed appropriate to rewrite the proposal in much reduced scale (suitable for handling by one man alone and to the structural requirements of the smaller institution) and to redirect its focus from the major university to the private college. The problem thus remained the same but with the additional bonus, under these circumstances, of being aimed at a segment of the institution of education about which much less was known sociologically.

The actual work of research (as opposed to planning and design) may be said to have begun about August 15, 1966, when I wrote to the administrative officers of several Minnesota colleges asking them to rank order a number of midwestern institutions, excluding their own, for academic excellence. The average ranking for each college was then computed and the twelve institutions obtaining the highest average ranking were selected as the potential sample for the study. Letters were then sent to the presidents of the twelve institutions explaining the study and asking their cooperation. Simultaneously, preparations were going forward for a pilot study to be conducted during the fall semester at my own institution, Macalester College, utilizing Macalester faculty as respondents. Permission for this work had kindly been given me by the administration of the college when I submitted my proposal for the Career Decision Study, and a letter had been sent to each faculty member explaining the research and asking cooperation. Pilot studies for field research, of course, are conducted for numerous reasons. In this case, the most important reason was to obtain interview data, actual answers to questions, which could be used to develop computer coding categories and instructions for the data which would be gathered the following semester by the master study. A secondary, although little less important, reason for undertaking a pilot study was to give a final test to the interview schedule. A final reason for the pilot study was to give me experience in actually using the interview schedule in real interviews about real events, to train myself in its use and the results to be expected of it. As a result of pilot study experience, numerous modifications were made in the interview schedule with some questions being omitted, some added, and some rearranged in the order in which they were asked, and some new items of information being called for.

A subpurpose of the pilot study was to test the utility of the tape recorder as an interviewing instrument. At the time of the *Marketplace* study (1957) there had seemed reason not to use tape recording in interviews because of difficulties in transcription and fear that respondents would be inhibited by it. But a decade later the tape recorder had not only come of age mechanically but, with the advent of transistors, had been miniaturized to a startling degree. Recorders were now familiar features in many homes, as everything from musical instruments to toys. Respondents, thus, might be expected to be less shy with them than might have been true earlier. Transcription equipment, too, had come a long way in the ten years, and many secretaries were now familiar with it. The pilot study showed that interview subjects were not generally reluctant to be recorded and that the problem of editing irrelevancies was not as insurmountable as Caplow and I had feared when preparing the *Marketplace* study. The pilot study use of the recorder showed that its drawbacks were clearly outweighed by its advantages.

The drawbacks of tape recorder use in interviewing are that two machines are required for work of any duration, one to transcribe and one to record, one of which must be carried about by the interviewer. This means that it must be relatively light, should be battery-powered, and requires carrying extra tapes and batteries and keeping careful notation of what is on each tape. More importantly, a recorder sufficiently sensitive to pick up low sounds and muffled words across a desk will also pick up the normal background racket of offices and office buildings which an interviewer using pencil and paper screens out of his perception. Interview tapes from this study faithfully record notes and voices from music practice rooms, groans of antique elevators, bubbling from aquaria, recitations from nearby classrooms, fire engines, hammering and other construction noises (including one nearly unintelligible interview conducted in the vicinity of an air hammer), and a variety of miscellaneous sounds which defy description. Worst of all the drawbacks of the taped interviewing for this study was the continual, and apparently uncorrectable, breakdown of the Scandinavian transcription machine which, although purchased new for the study, proved touchy, delicate of adjustment, and unreliable. The advantages of tape-recording interviews, however, are considerable. Perhaps most importantly, recording frees the interviewer to concentrate on what the subject is saying, to examine responses as they are made, to notice clues to assumptions or events which require probing not foreseen by the interview schedule, and to pick up apparent inconsistencies in the narrative which sometimes prove valuable when explored.

Eleven of the twelve colleges responded promptly to my letters, graciously granting permission for the study. The letters requesting cooperation had included a brief occupational biography (to indicate to the college presidents my competence to undertake the work) and a summary of the goals of the study. No inducements of any kind were offered to secure cooperation other than the promise that copies of the final report would be made available to participating institutions. Complete anonymity for institutions and individuals was assured. Six of the presidents replied with complete cooperation, designating a dean or other official through whom details could be arranged, and one or two put their facilities and offices entirely at my disposal. Five others offered tentative agreement pending a personal visit for explanation of details. These visits were completed by mid-October and the participation of all eleven institutions assured.

Having obtained the cooperation of the eleven, I wrote again requesting rosters of their full-time, regular faculty members in the three professorial ranks. This request, oddly enough, was not well responded to, and it took me until December to obtain the last of the rosters which I did receive. In four cases none ever was forthcoming, and I had to make shift from the list of faculty in the college bulletins. Rosters in hand, I began in mid-January to write faculty members at the participating institutions. The letters sought the cooperation of the recipient in returning to me a postcard on which he was asked to check one of three sentences describing his labor market experience so far during that same academic year (1966–67). The options offered were "I have been asked to submit credentials or to interview as a candidate for another position this year," "I have been probed about being a candidate for another position this year but have not yet been asked to submit credentials or to interview," and "As yet I have not been asked to be a candidate for another position." About ten days after the first mailing a second was made to those individuals who had not yet replied to the first, and ten days after that, a third. Each mailing included postal reply cards. The response to the first mailing was 70.3 per cent replies, an extraordinarily high rate for mailed forms. The second mailing raised this response rate to 90.5 per cent, and the final follow-up produced a total average response of 97.2 per cent with a range from 88 to 100 per cent among the several colleges.

The plan was to interview only those individuals responding that they had been asked to submit credentials or to interview for another position, for these persons, it seemed to me, would have most fully experienced the operation of the academic labor market. Part of the interview would elicit from them information about their academic backgrounds and accomplishments. For those who replied on the postcard that no market activity had occurred during the study year, similar occupational information would be gathered, where possible, from the college personnel files or, when this information was considered confidential by the institution, by direct mailing of a brief questionnaire (four such instances occurred). The study would, thus, have a market active group of faculty interviewed, and an inactive control group against which the characteristics of the former could be compared.

The work required from the institution only two items of cooperation after the original list of faculty had been obtained. Once on campus I needed a faculty telephone directory and access to a campus telephone and someone to whom to give the list of market inactive faculty and the forms to be filled out about them from faculty personnel records. In the schools which had agreed to do this chore for me, no problem was encountered with the latter requirement. Oddly, obtaining access to the campus telephone proved, on several campuses, to be a considerable problem. In some cases, private offices with telephones were graciously made available for my use, but in five or six others the request for the use of a phone was impossible to fulfill on any basis of privacy, and I had to resort to public campus phones located in hall-ways, student lounges, or, in one instance, outdoors. Once at the tele-phone armed with my roster of market active faculty, I simply called men on the list, introduced myself with a reminder of the mailed in-quiry, and requested an interview with them. There were a few cases where the subjects, although willing and available, had cited incidents which had occurred the year previous to the study period and were not, therefore, eligible. Because of absence of mind on my part, I kept no record of these changes in the roster for the first half of the interview-ing period and thus cannot give an exact figure for the proportion of true eligibles reached by interview. An informed guess would be from 88 to 94 per cent. Once committed to being interviewed, most respon-dents talked freely and answered my questions fully and, I think, frankly. The average length of interviews was forty-eight minutes, with a range from ten minutes to over two and a half hours.

Interviewing academic men presents few conventional hazards. The greatest, in my experience, are the threats to quality of yield from boredom, inattention, and fatigue, and these problems are only par-tially forestalled by the tape recorder. Information interviewing of the kind reported here requires of the interviewer both considerable per-sonal knowledge of the subject under investigation and continual alert-ness to his subjects' narratives. The covert clue in a narrative is sig-nificant. This may be an allusion to materials or subject matter not yet discussed, an offhand comment, or even so tenuous a lead as a nuance of wording or pronunciation indicating hidden affect. (For example, "I knew what it meant if *he* said that.") The interviewer, if he is to maximize the detail and meaning of the information he is gathering, must be sufficiently alert to the significance of what the respondent is saying either to pounce on such leads at the time they are given to explore them further or to note them on paper or in memory in order to return to them at some more propitious time in the interview. De-pending on the situation and the interviewer's perception of the re-spondent's affectivity about the matter, such hidden leads may be ap-proached directly with further questions or indirectly with questions designed to explore the territory uncovered but without approaching the specific subject directly.

In any event, boredom or fatigue and consequent inattention

to the details thrown off in any narrative will reduce the richness of the material gathered and can mean that, even though all the questions on the schedule are asked and answered, the answers turn out to be far less valuable than they might have been. Unfortunately, both boredom and fatigue are inevitable in circumstances of the kind in which the materials for this research were gathered. There are two reasons for this phenomenon. The first is repetition. In any interviewing task where the questioner repeatedly asks the same questions of similar people who have had similar experiences, once he is thoroughly familiar with the kinds of answers he is likely to get, all of his subjects begin to sound alike and their stories seem remarkably the same. (In my own experience in more than one study this point is reached at about the thirtieth or fortieth interview or in the second or third institution visited.) Once this feeling of having heard it all before sets in, alertness diminishes and the truly unique possibilities in any given interview are not likely to be noted and explored.

The second reason for the onset of inattention during interviews is interviewer anomie. When the research situation takes the interviewer away from home ground and familiar surroundings and, for long periods of time, makes him a stranger in strange places, seeing and interacting only with strangers, and doing so, further, on an essentially role-playing basis where he cannot express his own personality and interests but must constantly repress his individuality in order to elicit unbiased responses from others, he is apt to suffer mild psychic disorientation. The consequence of this is that he hurries through the unpleasant situations where the factors of this disorientation are emphasized (the interviews) and addresses his attention mostly to those periods when he can be himself—his meals and evenings in his room. (In an earlier interviewing experience where I had had to be on the road for periods of from four to six weeks at a time, this anomie became so pronounced that clear declines in interview quality were perceivable by coders as correlated with trip duration. There were even some objective indications, as time passed, that the decline began to set in ever earlier in successive trips as the recurrent anomic experiences became more familiar. Knowing this feature of the problem I helped avoid it during the present research by making frequent interviewing trips of short duration with returns to home base in between to break the monotony and strangeness of the interviewing experience. This seemed to relieve the situation considerably.) Fatigue becomes a problem relative to anomie, at least in my own case, because, as feelings of anomie set in, I tend to stay up late at night in order to have some time to myself, with consequently inadequate sleep and fatigue the following day. This problem is exacerbated, of course, by strange beds and uncomfortable quarters, awkward travel schedules, inclement weather, poor meals, and so forth. Woe to the traveler who must depend for his principal sustenance on college eating facilities!

A second hazard to interviewing is less significant because more directly under the interviewer's control and can be described as knowing too much. This is particularly relevant when the researcher must live, for a time, within the social situation he is studying and when it is a relatively limited one like a small college campus. On the small campus, the interviewer's presence and purpose there become known through word of mouth among the faculty or, as sometimes occurred in this research, through administrative announcement. If the other persons in the situation are aware of the purpose of the research and are personally interested in it, curiosity is a natural result. One may, thus, know too much in several senses. He may be quizzed by informants or casual acquaintances concerning what he is learning about Shadyside and be forced, if he is dealing with confidential materials, to refuse to divulge his information with consequent threat to his relations with the parties to the conversation, some of whom he may yet have to interview. This can usually be handled with tact, however, and few will push too hard at a confidentiality which protects their colleagues and, by extension, themselves. Probably the most serious problem of knowing too much occurs in interviews where the interviewer, having spoken to many persons on the campus, sometimes about the same events, may have information which the respondent does not and inadvertently lets it slip, with consequent discredit to his reputation for reliability. The problem is particularly vulnerable to anomie wherein the volunteering of personal information on the part of the subject invites reciprocity on the part of the interviewer. I know of no sure safeguard against this eventuality and handled it myself only through the practice, which becomes habitual, of pretending always to know nothing of any situation a respondent described.

This impression can be easily conveyed by asking him for fuller information, thus suggesting one has never heard of the situation or person under discussion. It rarely occurs to the subject under these circumstances to interview the interviewer about what he knows of the matter since the interviewer is, after all, a stranger, and—despite the possible expertise conveyed by his function—may be presumed to be ignorant if he has given clues to this effect.

A potential hazard with which any interviewer must expect to deal under almost any circumstances is hostility or even overt aggression from his respondents. The degree to which this is a threat, of course, is largely dependent on the interviewer's experience, personality, and, perhaps, ego strength. Experience is the best armor against it because it teaches that success in the interview situation is possible even with very defensive or very aggressive subjects, although the handling of them in order to ensure interview success is sometimes difficult. And, under some circumstances, the rough must be taken with the smooth: on one occasion of interviewing academic men (in another study), I was punched in the nose and pushed bodily out of an office. Such extreme reactions, fortunately, are rare, and none even remotely comparable occurred during this research.

Student reaction to interviewing of this type is not a hazard. Although carried on, usually, during regular terms, the study and the interviewer are invisible to the student population. They are used to seeing anonymous people in business suits strolling through their campus (book salesmen, trustees and friends of the college, alumni, parents, and business recruiters), and they ignore them as beneath notice. On one occasion, however, while eating lunch in a college cafeteria, I did become visible to at least one small segment of the student body. The campus was a "liberal" one with beard and sandal the norm and guitars and recorders were not infrequently carried. A group of young men had been lounging at a table next to mine and, after a lengthy discussion of me, one approached. Student (slouching into seat at my table): "Is that a radio you have there?" McGee: "No, it's a tape recorder." Student: "Are you fuzz?" McGee: "Good lord, do I look like a cop?" Student (flatly): "Yes." McGee: "Well, I'm a sociologist." Student (rising to leave): "Oh, yeah, I've heard about guys like you." I did not quite know what to make of this incident and do not now. It was, however, the only time my presence on a campus was in any way noticed or responded to by a student.

The process of data preparation and analysis is a simple one to describe but it occupied a longer period of time, and took many more hours, than the interviews themselves. As suggested earlier, the object of the interview was to secure on tape the respondent's answers to a partially predetermined set of questions, the interview schedule. The schedule, of course, was the product of a long planning process and was designed to elicit from subjects the information which would enable me to answer the questions which would fulfill the general objectives of the work. But all the endeavor up to this point in the research process—my exit from a faculty office tape recorder in hand—was in one sense only the first step of the data collection process. For the conversation on that tape had to be first transcribed onto a new interview schedule form and then, much of it, coded for putting onto punched cards and statistical analysis. The tape, thus, was just the raw form of the principal data of the study. (There were, of course, other types of information gathered.)

During the interview process I used a blank interview schedule, on which I had noted basic information about the respondent (rank, age, and so on), to check off the questions as I asked them, and on which to make notes. Upon my return to base at the end of the week, completed forms and tape reels were left with the project secretary for transcription. The secretary had one of the most trying jobs in the research—the transcription of raw tapes into usable interviews. This was accomplished by a double process of transcription. She would first literally transcribe what she heard on the tape, indicating every pause and hesitation, every stutter and mispronunciation. The purpose of this tedious effort was to provide me with an absolutely accurate script of the interview from which to work. I would check this script while listening to the taped interview myself, looking both for inaccuracies of transcription and for places where the wording had not been clear to the typist. Having made this check, I could then edit the transcript, removing from it as much irrelevance, social chatter, false starts, and so on as I liked. The edited script was then returned to the secretary for final typing on blank interview forms.

Crittenden's commentary (Appendix B) evaluates the coding

process. The actual process of data analysis was carried on in three different ways: logical, statistical, and thematic. The logical portion of the analysis consisted of the assignment of specific topics, questions, blocks of information from the interview, and so on, to specific topics and problems defined by the research proposal. Statistical analysis was largely accomplished through use of an IBM counter-sorter and computer which enabled me to manipulate rapidly and in large numbers the cards on which information had been coded. This is basically a counting and comparison process in which persons with one set of characteristics are contrasted with other persons or sets of characteristics. The determination of frequency and likelihood of certain combinations thus demonstrated is statistical and, essentially, mechanical; the interpretation of the meaning of any combinations found is one aspect of sociological analysis. Thematic analysis consisted of the apprehension of themes or recurrent content patterns in the interview material and their recovery through simple content analysis or card sorting. For this form of analysis a secretary retyped sequentially answers to interview questions so that great lists were developed consisting of all of the answers to each question, each answer being identified by the school and department of the individual making it. Reading these lists made it possible easily to identify categories of answer which typified responses to particular questions in specific schools or disciplines or which were typical regardless of institutional or disciplinary affiliation. Once identified in this way, these themes or patterns of typical answer could then be sought out and counted, and their frequencies and variations identified.

Once I was armed with materials prepared in these ways, writing the report was comparatively easy. The original research proposal defined and outlined the report of the data which had to be made. For this to be meaningful, certain introductory materials were obviously necessary, and from these two requirements, the table of contents of the report (and, hence, its content outline) was determined. Thus, what had to be said and the order in which it was to be said were determined before I ever set pen to paper. Needless to say, it was impossible to foresee and to have prepared each statistical and thematic analysis which appears herein; the need for many became apparent only during the course of actual writing, but, nonetheless, the major tabulations and analyses necessary were predictable, prepared, and assigned their places in the outline before writing began. It is, perhaps, a pedantic and uncreative way to go about writing a book. It remains a useful one for reporting and analysis of this type.

Actual and Reconstructed
Coding Procedure

By Kathleen Stones Crittenden

ᘓᘓᘓᘓᘓᘓᘓᘓᘓᘓᘓᘓᘓᘓᘓᘐᘐᘐᘐᘐᘐᘐᘐᘐᘐᘐᘐᘐ

Although research has been addressed to human sources of error in the interview situation and in the experimental laboratory,[1] relatively little attention has been given to errors stemming from the coding process in social scientific research. Coding error typically is dismissed with a passing word of warning in the methodological literature. (See Riley—1963—for a typical treatment of coding error.) Yet it might be argued that the success or failure of the entire social scientific enterprise rests largely on the degree to which symbolic phenomena can be converted successfully into scientific data that can be treated quantitatively. Recent evidence suggests that coding error may be sufficiently high to warrant special care for its elimination (Sussman and Haug, 1967). In this discussion I shall use the term *coding* to refer to the process by which persons assign data to categories in the research enterprise. "Through coding, the raw data are transformed into symbols—usually numerals—that may be tabulated and counted (Selltiz

---

[1] For examples of research on the interview situation, see Hyman and others (1954), Hyman (1955), and Richardson and others (1965). Researches into sources of error in the experiment are reported in Rosenthal and Fode (1963), Rosenthal (1966), Friedman (1967), and Orne (1962).

228

and others, 1962, p. 401). Generally defined, coding includes a number of relatively straightforward tasks such as the assignment of numbers to precoded, fixed-alternative responses to questionnaire items, as well as the more typical tasks found in the Academic Janus Study involving categorization of respondent's answers to open-ended questions in an interview.

Coding is a basic measurement procedure. The investigator chooses to code his data in order to simplify them and to abstract certain essentials from them in order to bring them to bear on certain concepts. Each code designation comprises a measure by which a particular case is classified relative to other cases with respect to a given property, for example, Age: (1) 0–10, (2) 11–20, (3) 21–30, and so on, where numbered categories represent code classifications into which different responses may be sorted. The coding task always involves explicitly or implicitly, first, a set of data, second, a specification of the size of the units of data to be taken into consideration for each part of the coding task, third, a set of categories, fourth, a set of code designations, one for each category, and fifth, a set of rules for assigning the data to the categories. The nature of the coding task varies with the particular characteristics of each of its five elements.

Since the purpose of any coding procedure is to produce scientific data, the literature stresses that coding results must be objective or reproducible. The requirement of objectivity derives from the general scientific criterion of intersubjectivity—the extent to which independent scientists can perform the same procedure on the same empirical phenomena and arrive at the same results. With respect to the coding task, objectivity requires explicit specification of the variables employed, the categories for each variable, and the operational definition of each category. Objectivity also requires that the set of categories used for a variable satisfy certain logical criteria: the set of categories should be derived from a single classificatory principle and should be mutually exclusive and exhaustive. The last requirement of objectivity for the coding task concerns the appropriateness of the coding instructions for the data to be coded. "The most logically constructed and theoretically elegant scheme of analysis will not produce objective results if it does not in fact 'fit' the material being analyzed. . . . Reproducible coding will be possible only when the system of classification is properly adapted to the material being coded"

(Cartwright, 1953, p. 438). The requirements of objectivity are difficult or impossible to satisfy fully in most coding situations, particularly
those in which the data are verbal materials. Difficulties derive from
both the requirement of explicit specification of the operational definition of each category and the logical requirements concerning the category set.

Two units of analysis are involved in the operational definition
of a category—the recording unit and the context unit (Berelson,
1954). The recording unit is the specific segment of the content that
is characterized by placing it in a given category. For questionnaire
or interview data, the most commonly used recording unit is the answer
to a question. Occasionally, however, a respondent may answer a question before it is asked or in response to another question. In such a
case, the social scientist legitimately may feel that the answer should
be coded as if it had appeared in proper sequence. Such a procedure,
which may be quite justifiable in terms of the particular situation involved, may be difficult to specify in easily reproducible terms. The
context unit is the largest portion of the content that may be examined
by the coder in categorizing a recording unit. "Designation of the context unit is often left quite vague or to the individual coder's judgment.
Since the major purpose in setting up a context unit larger than the
recording unit is to provide better bases for perceiving the 'meaning'
of the recording unit, there seems to be some justification in allowing
the coder to seek clarification throughout the material. Such a procedure, however, sometimes greatly reduces the reliability of coding"
(Cartwright, 1953, p. 459).

Another aspect of the operational definition of a category involves specification of the indicators by which the coder determines
whether a given unit of data should fall within the category. "If it were
possible to list all the variations of content which indicate a given category, such a list would provide a complete operational definition of
the category. Unfortunately, most categories with which social scientists deal cannot be defined in actual practice by an exhaustive listing
of indicators" (Cartwright, 1953, p. 437).

The investigator who attempts to develop an exhaustive list of
theoretically equivalent segments of any natural language finds his task
multiplied to the point of virtual impossibility. The problem is that the
subtleties, ambiguities, and inconsistencies which humans manipulate

and understand without difficulty virtually defy determinate, exhaustive specification. At some point the researcher must decide that the operational definition of his category is sufficiently complete for him to proceed with the work at hand. Instead of attempting a complete list of indicators, typically the investigator defines his categories by means of examples from the data. The examples should include responses that fall at the boundaries of the category as well as responses that typify its core meaning. Having established a rationale for a given set of indicators, the investigator then relies on the ability of trained, sophisticated coders to respond to the indicators in a systematic way. Good coders are sensitive to verbal materials. They must be able to detect subtle differences in meaning but also to neglect differences that are irrelevant for a specific coding task. It is helpful if they are familiar with social scientific concepts. In addition, some methodologists stress the importance of communicating to the coders a full understanding of the purposes of the research project in which the coding task occurs. Unfortunately, coder expertise is difficult to specify in the interests of reproducible procedure.

The logical requirements of objectivity with respect to the category set are also difficult to satisfy. In order to satisfy the criterion of exhaustiveness for a category set to be applied to empirical data, the researcher frequently must employ such residual categories as "other," "not applicable," "information missing," "no answer," or "uncodable." Use of these residual categories violates the requirement that a category set be based on a single classificatory principle. In short, objectivity is approachable for the coding task, but its complete realization cannot be ensured. Since the degree of objectivity in a particular coding situation is not directly measurable, the researcher seeks to assess indirectly the likelihood that a given set of coded results may be viewed as intersubjective, as resulting from an objective procedure. Hence, there has been continued concern on the part of social scientists with such concepts as reliability and validity.

The concern for objectivity in the general coding situation may generate contradictory demands with respect to the actual coding procedures employed in a specific research context. Hence the investigator is free to (and must) decide which of the requirements of objectivity are most appropriately emphasized in the coding of his data, given the goals of his research. The advantages and disadvantages of any specific procedures he chooses must be weighed carefully with respect to their implications for objectivity and the research goals. The coding procedures in the *Academic Janus* study are described here in terms of the explicit or implicit choices made by the principal investigator between alternative forms of the basic components of the coding task. I became involved in the study when I became interested in coding problems and offered to exchange coding supervision and services on the study for access to the coded data for my research on the coding process.

The set of data to be coded consisted of transcribed interviews with open-ended answers to questions. Mailed questionnaires might have been chosen instead of interviews; a fixed-answer format might have been substituted for open-ended questions. Either of these alternatives would have yielded a simpler coding task. Questionnaires generally are more economical than interviews, and they eliminate the difficulties of coding transcribed spoken language. On the other hand, skillful interviewing may yield more information than do questionnaires. The interviewer himself gains insight through interacting with and observing his respondents. Fixed-answer questions yield valid information only if the appropriate response categories are known in advance. Since the goals of the study were exploratory and descriptive, not oriented to hypothesis-testing, appropriate data would emphasize maximum information yield over objective coding procedure. The use of open-ended interviews was consistent with this relative emphasis. The sizes of the units of data to be taken into consideration for each coding decision were made explicit in the study. For each coding item, the recording unit was specified in the coding instructions as the answer to a particular question. The context unit was invariably the entire interview. Coders were instructed always to read the complete interview before coding any items.

The set of coding categories for each coding item was made exhaustive through the use of residual categories such as "uncodable," "do not know," "not applicable," "not asked," and "unclassifiable." In short, if a unit of data did not fit into one of the substantive categories, it was automatically assigned to an appropriate residual category. The category set was exhaustive by virtue of the fact that a code was required for every coding decision. The residual coding categories required for exhaustiveness precluded satisfaction of the requirement that the categories be derived from a single classificatory principle. Mutual exclusiveness for a set of categories was a natural condition for some coding items and was contrived for other items through the use of such qualifiers as "primary," "most important," or "first mentioned." Only one code for each coding decision was allowed, so some rule for choosing a best category was required in order to perform the coding task. Sometimes, however, the data did not permit unambiguous determination of, for example, a person's primary reason for something. In such cases, forcing coders to choose a best category may have yielded unreliable codes. Such unreliability, it must be noted, resulted not from classification of the reasons but from attempting to determine which reason was primary. An alternative coding scheme might have been to specify one reason for each coding item, with coding categories of "mentioned" and "not mentioned." Such a scheme might yield a more objective coding scheme but would not allow the investigator to distinguish between reasons that were clearly trivial and those that were important. During the coding stage, the coding instructions were modified several times to better fit the data. (Such modifications would not have been possible if the investigator had employed a fixed-answer format.) Ultimately, however, there is no a priori suitable criterion for judging the suitability of a category set for a set of data.

The set of code designations bears little mention here. An integer suitable for punching into a data card was assigned to each coding category. In general, the coder's task is simplified if identical categories on more than one coding item are designated by the same code, for example, consistent designation of "uncodable" by 9. This practice generally was followed in defining code designations. The rules for assigning data to categories consisted mostly of examples and guidelines either communicated orally to the coders during the briefing sessions or agreed on by the coders during the coding stage. In the initial view of the primary investigator, the names alone of most coding categories were clear and definitive enough not to require additional rules. As it turned out, the proper use of the categories was not as obvious to the coders as to their employer; additional guidelines were required. The rules for assigning data to categories were not specified explicitly in writing prior to the coding task because they were not known in advance and because the need for them had not been anticipated. The need for trained, sophisticated coders was recognized on the basis of the pilot study coding experience. Coders for the *Janus* data were in-telligent, trained in the social sciences, familiar with academia, and fully informed of the goals of the study.

Two female coders were hired in accord with Professor Mc-Gee's desire to have coders who were advanced graduate students and who had considerable knowledge of the workings of the academic sys-tem. On the same day, I met with McGee to discuss his conception of coding error. The gist of his position, quite compatible with mine, might be paraphrased as follows: When coding requires interpretation on the part of the coder, we can speak of error only when the coder makes an obvious mistake—that is, what he considers to be an obvious mistake. Unreliability resulting from differing interpretations among coders cannot then be viewed as error. I discussed with McGee the procedures to be used for training the coders. We agreed to record the training sessions and to go through at least one interview aloud using the coding instructions and discuss the coding decisions with respect to that interview. The first coder briefing session, attended by McGee, the two coders, and myself, lasted two hours. Two more sessions were necessary to complete preliminary briefing on the entire set of coding instructions. Each session lasted two hours and was attended by the same four persons. Excerpts from the transcript of the briefing sessions are reported below.

McGee: . . . The ones that checked that they had been asked to submit credentials or interview, I came and interviewed about the ex-perience, how did this come, what did they do about it, who did they talk to, and so on. These things [interview typescripts] that you'll see have been edited. You may not think so, but they have been. What we're going to do now is code them for IBM. I know from the pilot study that the coding is sticky. The face sheet info, the first page here, is perfectly standard factual stuff—salary, rank, how long they've been there, this kind of thing. But a lot of the coding that I want to do called for interpretation on the part of the coder where he has to read the answer and then interpret it to mean one of several things, and that's why we have to have a fairly sophisticated training period here to at least get ourselves together. . . . With the pilot study staff, my secretary last year, she and I started doing this just to see how it worked. I'd code it, then give it to her, and she'd code it separately. She'd dropped out to get married, so she knew practically nothing about the social structure of academics, and when we started out we were getting less than 50 per cent agreement, just in terms of number of agreeing items. Some of these were just errors on my part, or on hers, where we'd simply mark down the wrong thing, but in many cases, she'd have, say, two, and I'd have five, and so I'd say, "Okay, explain why this was a two on this answer," and she'd explain it where it would make perfect sense from her point of view, whereas my five also made perfect sense from my point of view, and then you're really in trouble, where the codes can mean radically different things or where the same answer can mean radically different things. This we really can't do anything about, because the kinds of interpretations that I want to make are fairly sophisticated, some of them, and it'll just be a matter of our getting together on what we mean, what the questions mean. Now what I thought I'd do today is to take an interview and go through it, item by item, reading the question and the response, going to the code sheet and saying, "Okay, now how do we code this?" And simply all four of us go through it once and argue about interpretation, and so on. . . . Column five, subject's rank—he is an assistant professor, so you would punch or write in two. If he were a full professor, you would put zero; if he were associate, you would put one. Everybody will have one of these three ranks. There are no others represented in this. The rank on the face sheet here where it says name, rank, will be the one you'll punch.

McGee: Department, I think this is now exclusive, these items here—natural science, social science, humanities and/or language, other and/or unclassifiable, education. I don't think we can get anybody who doesn't fall into one of these categories. I don't remember anybody that wouldn't, anyway. Now, what *other or unclassifiable* means is in terms of this particular group. If you can't fit them into natural science, social science, humanities or language, or education, then they're other or unclassifiable.

Coder A: What do you stick in the first two?

McGee: Natural science would include physics, chemistry, biology, and in this case, I would think math.

Crittenden: You don't have any engineers or anything like that?

McGee: No, there won't be any engineers. We might get a geographer.

Coder A: Where does he go?

McGee: Well, of course, the geographers themselves argue about this. And the physical geographers are really more like geologists; social geographers are much more like sociologists. I'm not even sure we have any geographers. Certainly not more than one or two.

Crittenden: What, besides sociology, goes into social science?

McGee: Anthropology, economics, political science; *I* would classify history there.

Crittenden: Psychology?

McGee: Psychology.

Coder B: Not history under humanities?

McGee: Well, that's one we can talk about. History and geography are two of the really marginal ones, because the field itself classifies itself differentially. My own feeling is that both history and geography ought to be called social science. Education, of course, would be anything in a department called something education—elementary education, secondary education. That means education with a capital E.

McGee: Now, source of earned doctorate, here's a dandy. The categories are major university, minor university, professional or technical school, small college, foreign institution, no doctorate. I will give you a list of schools that you can consider major universities. The criterion that I used to pick these was that they had put out two thousand or more nonmedical doctorates by the fall of 1965. . . . Here, I'll give you a little book put out by the American Council on Education that lists every accredited institution in the country. A lot of these you'll be able to inspect, and you'll know. Shadyside is a small college.

Coder B: How about Fairlawn? It's called a university.

McGee: Okay. Fairlawn's a good one. Fairlawn calls itself a university, and let's say you've never heard of it. . . . Fairlawn, for example, is named Fairlawn University because at one time it had a medical school, which technically makes it a university; it gives professional degrees, or it gave them. It no longer does. They still grant the master of social work, master of education, and perhaps master of arts in teaching. I would say they are not a university because by every other criterion you find they are a small private college. Oh, wait a minute! The book classifies them. There's a Roman numeral code where there are numerals like IIIC, and in the front of the book, it tells you what the code means. And we will accept their definition. That's the simple way.

Coder A: So if it's not on your list of major universities and it says in that book it's a university, we'll take it as a minor.

McGee: Then it's a minor university, right.

Coder A: What's a teachers college?

McGee: Professional or technical school.

Coder A: Do you still consider Shadyside a teachers college, which it was when it changed its name?

McGee: No. If it's called Shadyside, it's a private liberal arts college. If it's somebody-or-other state college of education, that's a teachers college. If it's something-or-other polytech, it's a technical school.

Crittenden: Is there no such thing as a large college?

McGee: Not for our purposes. Can you think of one?

Crittenden: Well, as far as that goes, the state college; many of these have like twelve thousand students.

McGee: By God, you're right. I think we'd better add a category. Don't you?

Crittenden: Want to make it six?

Coder A: Let's squash these down so that it would be four.

Crittenden: What about something like Columbia Teachers College?

McGee: That would be professional or technical.

Crittenden: Even though it's a part of Columbia? I think the Columbia Teachers College gives doctorates, but it's part of Columbia University.

McGee: Oh yeah. Absolutely. Well, what about that? Now that's a case I hadn't thought of. If it was Boondocks State Teachers College, it would be a technical school. On the other hand, Columbia is a major university.

Crittenden: Also, some of these universities have divinity schools attached, that give D.D.'s.

McGee: Oh yeah. We'll get some of them. I hadn't foreseen this. My intent was that these things would be transitive, that for instance in the case of Columbia Teachers College, that the fact that it was Columbia, that the teachers college was located within the framework of a major university. . . . My feeling would be that we'd classify it as a major university because it's the intent to find out the influence of the prestige of the school. And Columbia in this case is more important than what college within Columbia the degree came from. If it's a college within a larger unit which is also represented in the coding, take the largest one, if it's on the same campus anyway.

Crittenden: Then Purdue at Ft. Wayne isn't. . . .

McGee: Purdue at Ft. Wayne is not Purdue. We treat it as if it were independent. But I do think we need the category state college. Small college really means private college. Let's change small to read small college, private, and . . . Now for coding purposes would it be better to move no doctorate down to six and let state college be five, or just add state college as six? Does it make any difference?

Coder A: Would you ever want to collapse the college types?

McGee: That would be possible.

Coder A: In which case then you would have it as four.

Crittenden: And then move everything else down. Why don't we make state college, or public college. . . . I guess there are some pretty large community colleges.

McGee: Listen, let's distinguish private colleges from public colleges. How's that?

Crittenden: Okay.

Coder A: That's what, four?

McGee: And make public college four.

Crittenden: Then you want to eliminate the small from private college.

McGee: We'll strike out small and make it private college or public college, and that becomes four, foreign institution becomes five, and no doctorate becomes six.

Coder B: And we do the same, then, on column thirteen?

McGee: Yeah, foreign institution becomes five; no doctorate becomes six.

These excerpts pertain to only a few of the simpler coding items, but they should illustrate the point that, even for relatively straightforward variables, it is difficult to anticipate all the requirements that a set of empirical data will make on a set of coding categories. The third version of the coding instructions was used in the coder briefing sessions, the first two having been invented for use on pilot study data. During the training sessions, coding categories were altered and added, as illustrated in the above excerpts. The rules for assigning data to categories were communicated orally through heavy use of examples and, in the case of some items, eventual provisional formulation of determinate procedural rules for coding a unit of data. *Provisional* is applied here to indicate that these formulations of coding rules were held until a unit of data was encountered for which the rules were not adequate. When such an anomalous empirical unit appeared, the coding categories and rules were modified as required. The coders kept notes concerning the coding rules on their individual copies of the printed coding instructions. Periodically, checks were made to ensure that the notes of individual coders indicated roughly equivalent understanding of the use of the categories.

At the end of the third coder briefing session, the first ten interviews were distributed to be coded independently by the two coders and by McGee. When the three coders (including McGee) had finished coding ten interviews, the results were compared. In cases where all three coders agreed, the code was assumed to be final unless there was a change in the coding categories. Then the four of us met to resolve and discuss the cases of disagreement. The discussion revealed the need to make additional changes in the coding categories for some items. Most of these changes involved forming separate categories for "do not know, not applicable, insufficient information" and for "uncodable" for a number of coding items.

For one typical interview in the first group, coding disagreements were encountered on thirty-seven of the sixty-seven items. To gain insight into the nature of their coding differences, the coders classified the disagreements into four types—disagreements based on lack of sufficient information, disagreements requiring a change in the coding categories, disagreements resulting from differences in judgment among the coders, and disagreements resulting from acknowledged error on the part of one or more coders. Slightly more than half of the disagreements arose from difficulties in the coding categories, and more than one-third resulted from differences in judgment. Less than 3 per cent were the consequence of mistakes.

All the coding disagreements for the first group of interviews were resolved through discussion, and final codes were assigned. The remaining 115 interviews were coded in groups of five. Comparison of results, resolution of disagreements through discussion, and assignment of final codes were completed for each set of interviews before coders were given the next set of interviews to code. McGee served as a third independent coder until twenty interviews had been coded, at which time he was satisfied that the coders were approaching and performing the task as he would. A few changes in coding categories were implemented during discussion of the second group of interviews; no further modifications were made after that time. Elaboration of the categories with examples encountered in the data, however, continued throughout the coding process. As a result, the coding task involved the production, rather than simply the application, of a detailed set of coding instructions. It might be said that the rules governing the coding task were neither specifiable nor known in their entirety before completion of the task. Even the final set of coding instructions produced in the coding task probably are not sufficiently determinate to generate a code for every problem that might be encountered in a new set of interviews. The term *final* may be applied to the coding instructions only because all interviews in the study were coded. It seems probable that this may be the normal state of affairs in coding information of this kind.

In the present study, the terms *reliability* and *unreliability* refer to characteristics of the relationship between coders in their coding results. These terms are employed without regard for the accuracy of coding results or the degree to which those results correspond with a specified criterion. The terms *validity* and *invalidity* are used here to refer to some characteristics of the relationship of coding results to a specified criterion. Two measures of intercoder reliability have been employed in this analysis. The first, the proportion of intercoder agreement (PA) is computed by dividing the number of coding units identically coded by two coders by the total number of units coded. This measure may assume values from zero (no agreement) to 1.0 (total agreement). Depending on the number of coding categories and on the total distribution of codes for each coder, some agreement between coders might be expected on the basis of chance. Hence for some purposes it is desirable to employ a second measure of intercoder reliability which corrects for chance agreement. Such a measure, called R in this analysis, has been formulated by Cohen (1960). R may be interpreted as the proportionate improvement over maximum possible unreliability or, conversely, as the proportion of intercoder agreement after chance agreement has been removed. R reaches a maximum value of 1.0 under the condition of perfect agreement between coders. The measure assumes a zero value when the actual level of intercoder agreement equals the level of agreement to be expected on the basis of chance. When the actual level of intercoder agreement is less than the level expected by chance, R assumes a negative value.

In the absence of a suitable external criterion for establishing a set of "correct" codes in the Academic Janus Study, the final codes assigned in the study are employed in this analysis as the criterion set for assessing the validity of the initial codes assigned by each of the two coders. It will be recalled that whenever the two coders agreed on their initial coding of a particular unit of data, the initial codes were assumed to be correct. With a few exceptions, this procedural assumption eliminated the possibility of discovering cases of "incorrect agreement" between the coders. As a result, the validity scores of the individual coders may be inflated somewhat, but this inflation should be equal for the two coders. Of course, it might legitimately be argued that the final set of codes does not provide an adequate standard for judging validity since it is based to some degree on intercoder agreement. However, any criterion one might use for judging coding validity is necessarily arbitrary. In general, if the correct codes were known in advance, there would be no point in performing the coding task.

Once the set of criterion codes has been specified, validity is assessed by comparing the responses of a given coder with the corresponding criterion codes. Two coefficients of coding validity have been used in this study. One is the proportion of criterion agreement, that is, agreement between a given coder's responses and the criterion codes. Some agreement between coder and criterion responses would be expected on the basis of chance, depending on the number of coding categories and the total distribution of correct codes.[2] The second validity measure, V, corrects for this chance agreement. (V = [P. Actual Criterion Agreement − P. Expected Criterion Agreement]/[1.0 − P. Expected Criterion Agreement].) Parallel to the interpretation of R, V may be interpreted as the proportionate improvement over maximum possible invalidity or as the proportion of agreement between criterion and coder responses after chance agreement has been re-

---

[2] Assuming that the distribution of coder responses ideally should approximate the distribution of criterion codes, the proportion of agreement that might be expected on the basis of chance is the sum of the squared proportions of the criterion responses which fall in each of the coding categories.

moved. V reaches a maximum value of 1.0 when criterion and coder responses agree perfectly. V equals zero when the actual level of agreement equals the level expected by change. When the observed level of agreement is less than the expected level, V is negative.

None of the sixty-seven coding items, no matter how straightforward, is characterized by perfect agreement between the two coders. Intercoder agreement varies from a high of .976 (on the item of age) to a low of .381 (on features at the employing institution which were seen as the primary reason for not accepting an offer). Intercoder reliability ranges from .971 to .263. If arbitrarily we were to specify .90 as the minimum tolerable level of intercoder agreement, only fifteen of sixty-seven items would qualify! Validity levels are somewhat higher. The low reliability levels may be taken as indicative of the difficult and judgmental nature of the task of coding such data. The data involved in the *Janus* study are typical of much of the data obtained in sociological research through the use of open-ended interviews. That these data *are* typical and that there is no known procedure for ensuring that they will be reliably coded provide sufficient reason for researching the coding situation.

The coding stage in the *Janus* study lasted several months. Disagreements between coders were resolved after each set of five interviews was coded. It seems reasonable to inquire whether such a general coding procedure is characterized by improvement in coding performance over time. Since the first group of interviews coded contained ten interviews as opposed to five in each of the following groups, the ten interviews were randomly assigned to two groups of five interviews for this analysis. The 125 interviews coded were thus divided into 25 groups numbered according to the order in which the groups were coded. Table 34 summarizes the overall levels of intercoder agreement and criterion agreement by group. Intercoder agreement levels vacillated considerably from one group of interviews to the next and showed little tendency to increase over time. Criterion agreement, on the other hand, started at exceedingly low levels and increased dramatically during the coding process. See Figure 1 for a graph of the two aspects of coding performance over time. These results suggest that improvement in the performance of the individual coders over time may not be reflected in increased intercoder reliability levels.

Errors stemming from the coding process in any scientific study

Table 34. INTERCODER AGREEMENT AND CRITERION
AGREEMENT OVER TIME

Interview Group[a]	Intercoder Reliability PA[b]	Mean Coding Validity $\overline{PA}$[c]
1	.648	.540
2	.749	.543
3	.716	.740
4	.785	.845
5	.758	.848
6	.752	.884
7	.678	.833
8	.884	.928
9	.684	.820
10	.770	.902
11	.749	.893
12	.758	.893
13	.788	.903
14	.737	.851
15	.791	.910
16	.809	.928
17	.779	.901
18	.710	.869
19	.761	.916
20	.722	.910
21	.821	.943
22	.731	.884
23	.743	.910
24	.776	.934
25	.764	.955

[a] Groups are numbered in the order in which they were coded, except for groups 1 and 2, which were coded at the same time. In general, the group was completely coded before any other group with a higher number. Each group consists of five interviews.

[b] PA refers to the overall proportion of intercoder agreement for a given group of interviews.

[c] $\overline{PA}$ refers to the mean overall proportion of criterion agreement for two coders for a group of interviews.

FIGURE 1.   Intercoder Agreement and Criterion Agreement Over Time

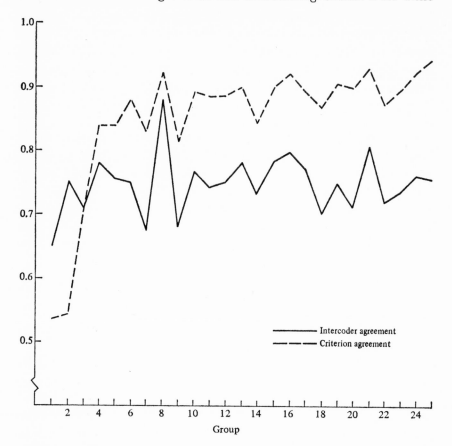

impose restrictions on the analysis and interpretation of the coded results. Social scientists have shown relatively little concern for the di-
agnosis or elimination of coding error in their studies. As a result, the
reliability and validity of coded data analyzed by social scientists have
remained largely unexamined. In the *Janus* study, detailed records of
the coding process were kept to enable determination of reliability and
validity levels. The initial levels of coding reliability and validity in the
study are alarmingly low but may not be peculiar to this work and may,
indeed, typify much current research.

It is appropriate at this point to explore the effect of coding
error on analytical results. Coding error in a nominal coding system,

as opposed to higher levels of measurement, has an all or none character. Any given unit of data either is placed in a certain category or it is not. This has two implications. First, in general, it cannot be assumed that coding errors will balance or cancel each other. Second, there are no such things as small or large errors, slight or major disagreements. Any disagreement between coders in their coding results is simply one disagreement; any misclassification is simply one error, no more and no less. In general, the distorting effect of a given level of coding error increases with the number of variables considered simultaneously in a statistical analysis. The univariate distribution for a coding item may or may not be affected by misclassification of specific units of data on that item. A bivariate distribution, on the other hand, makes more stringent demands with respect to correct classification of specific units on that item. Coding error in one of the variables in a bivariate distribution may either inflate or deflate the apparent association between the variables. With cross tabulations on more than two variables, there is an even greater risk that coding error will distort the true relationships between variables.

In keeping with McGee's promise to use essentially simple tools, statistical analysis of the coded results in the *Janus* study was limited to tabulation of frequency distributions, univariate and bivariate, and use of the chi square test of independence for some bivariate tables. In view of the initial coding reliability and validity levels found in the study, the simple statistical tools employed seem preferable to more sophisticated procedures. Even the limited statistical tabulations done in the study were applied largely to variables characterized by relatively high coding performance levels. More important than these considerations was the fact that the principal investigator himself interviewed all the subjects in the study. Therefore, the investigator's interpretations and analyses were informed by his firsthand experience in the field and by the original interview transcripts as well as by statistical analyses performed on the coded data. Obviously, the reliability of coded data is less serious a concern to the investigator who has other sources of empirical information about his subject matter than to the researcher who must rely on a single source.

A warning note concludes this appendix. The reader should hesitate to conclude that the initial levels of coding reliability and validity reported here for the *Academic Janus* study are atypically low.

Until contrary empirical evidence is presented, it must be assumed that these data and coding procedures represent the best of their kind, for coder training was severe. The burden of proof rests with the researcher who does not examine or does not report levels of coding reliability for his data.

C

Interview Schedule

Actor: Name; rank (time)'; department; institution; longevity (year and rank)'; age; salary; duties; degrees (source and year); dates of promotion; undeveloped, crisis, mobility, fixed.

Respondents: chairman; peer; spouse; yield.

I. Social Gravitation Index

1. When I contacted you earlier, you indicated that you had had an opportunity to take another job this year. Where was that?
2. What was the very first contact you ever had with that department or institution? When?
3. Have you ever worked there as a student or faculty member? When? For how long? In what capacity? Circumstances of departure?
4. Are you acquainted with any members of that department? Who? How closely? How were they met? Is the acquaintance current? (If "no"): Do you know anyone who is acquainted with anyone there? Who? Where? How known?
5. How do you think [proffering institution] selected you? Do you know what their specific job requirements were? How closely do you fit that description?

II. Events Preceding the Formal Offer

6. What did the first contact you had about *this job* actually consist of? Who initiated it? When?

247

7. Did this have any relevance to your problems here? What problems? How was this a solution?

8. Did you tell anyone about this at the time? Who? How? Where did (this/these) conversation(s) take place? How did (he/they) respond?

9. Did you take this up with your chairman or dean? How? When? Where did the conversation occur? How did (he/they) respond?

10. Was there anyone from whom you deliberately *kept* knowledge of this? Who? Why?

11. What happened next? When? Who initiated it? Repeat as necessary to question 12 or 14 as appropriate.

III.   The Formal Offer

12. Were you ever made an official, or formal, offer of a position there? In what form? Who initiated it? What were the terms? When was it received? What did you do when you received it? First person told; how, when, why, where? Why was *he* told first? Did you take *this* up with your chairman or dean? When? Where? What was his response? Did you inform anyone else of this development? Who? When? How? Where? How did (he/they) respond? Did anyone else participate in an official manner? Who? How? When? Was there anyone whom you kept from knowing about this? Who? Why?

13. What happened next? When? Who initiated it? Repeat as necessary to question 14.

IV.   The Decision
(if appropriate, skip to question 21)

14. What did you decide to do? When? Why? What factors were weighed in consideration? What were the specific attractions and negative features of the offer, of remaining?

15. Besides those people you've already mentioned, did you speak with anyone else about this? Other colleagues or people off campus? Who? How? Where? Reactions?

16. When do you think your mind was actually made up? Was there a specific turning point in your considerations?

17. Did you tell anyone your decision right away? Who? When? Why was *he* told first?
18. Was there anyone from whom you were still keeping all knowledge of this? Who? Why?

V. Events Following the Decision

19. When and how did you inform [proffering institution] of your decision?
20. What was their reaction or response? When?

VI. Events Terminating the Sequence

21. What was the last contact you had with [proffering institution]? When? Who initiated it?
22. Was anyone else involved in this or did you inform anyone else? Who? How? When?

VII. Post-Sequence Events and Afterthoughts

23. Has anything happened here since then as a result of all this? What? How did it occur? When? Was anyone else involved?
24. Now that it's all over, how do you feel about it? Do you have any reservations about the outcome? What? Why?

VIII. Prestige Ratings

25. How would you classify [proffering institution's] national standing? What are the bases of the rating? Why are those factors significant?
26. How would you classify the department there in terms of its reputation in your field? Bases?
27. How would you classify this institution's national standing? Bases?
28. How would you classify the department *here* in terms of its standing in your field? Bases?
29. How would you describe your own personal prestige or reputation in your field? Bases?

30. Would your (acceptance/rejection) of the [proffering institution] offer have affected your reputation in your field? In what ways?

IX. Other Opportunities

31. Have you had any offers or probes this year other than the one we've been discussing? Where from? When? What did it consist of?
32. At what point did the matter get dropped? How? Why?
Name of closest colleague in institution
Remarks

Bibliography

ALLEN, D. F. "Changes in the Role of the American University Professor." Ph.D. dissertation, University of Texas, 1962.

ARROWSMITH, W. "The Future of Teaching," in C. B. T. Lee (Ed.). *Improving College Teaching*. Washington, D.C.: The American Council on Education, 1967.

The Association of Governing Boards of Universities and Colleges, *The Role of the Governing Board*. Washington, D.C., 1967.

ASTIN, A. W. "Effects of Different College Environments on the Vocational Choices of High Aptitude Students," *Journal of Counseling Psychology*, 1965, *12*(1), 28–34.

ASTIN, A. W. "Differential College Effects on the Motivation of Talented Students to Obtain the Ph.D. Degree," *Journal of Educational Psychology*, 1963, *54*(1), 63–71.

ASTIN, A. W. "Productivity of Undergraduate Institutions," *Science*, 1962, *136*(3511), 129–135.

ASTIN, A. W. "A Reexamination of College Productivity," *Journal of Educational Psychology*, 1961, *52*(3), 173–178.

BARZUN, J. *The American University: How It Runs, Where It Is Going*. New York: Harper and Row, 1968.

BARZUN, J. "College to University—and After," *The American Scholar*, 1964, *33*(2), 214–216.

BARZUN, J. *The House of Intellect*. New York: Harper and Brothers, 1959.

BARZUN, J. *Teacher in America*. Boston: Little, Brown, 1946.

BERELSON, B. *Graduate Education in the United States*. New York: McGraw-Hill, 1960.

BERELSON, B. "Content Analysis," in G. Lindzey (Ed.). *Handbook of Social Psychology*, Vol. I. Cambridge, Mass.: Addison-Wesley, 1954.

BEVAN, J. O. *University Life in the Olden Time*. London: Chapman and Hall, 1914.

251

BOROFF, D. *Campus USA*. New York: Harper and Brothers, 1961.

BOYER, E. L. "A Fresh Look at the College Trustee," *Educational Record*, 1968, *49*(3), 274–279.

BROWN, D. G. *The Mobile Professors*. Washington, D.C.: The American Council on Education, 1967.

BROWN, D. G. *Academic Labor Markets*. Washington, D.C.: U.S. Department of Labor, Office of Manpower, Automation and Training, 1965a.

BROWN, D. G. *The Market for College Teachers*. Chapel Hill: University of North Carolina Press, 1965b.

BYSE, C. AND JOUGHIN, L. *Tenure in American Higher Education*. Ithaca: Cornell University Press, 1961.

CAPLOW, T. AND MCGEE, R. *The Academic Marketplace*. New York: Basic Books, 1958.

Careers of Ph.D.'s, Academic Versus Nonacademic: A Second Report on Follow-Up of Doctorate Cohorts, 1935–1960, publication No. 1577, Career Patterns Report Number Two. Washington, D.C.: National Academy of Sciences, 1968.

CARTTER, A. M. "Future Faculty: Needs and Resources," in C. B. T. Lee (Ed.). *Improving College Teaching*. Washington, D.C.: American Council on Education, 1967.

CARTTER, A. M. *An Assessment of Quality in Graduate Education*. Washington, D.C.: American Council on Education, 1966.

CARTWRIGHT, D. P. "Analysis of Qualitative Material," in L. Festinger and D. Katz (Eds.). *Research Methods in the Behavioral Sciences*. New York: Dryden Press, 1953.

The Chronicle of Higher Education, August 31, 1970, pp. 1–2.

CLARK, B. R. *Educating the Expert Society*. San Francisco: Chandler, 1962.

COHEN, J. "A Coefficient of Agreement for Nominal Scales," *Educational and Psychological Measurement*, 1960, *20*, 37–46.

CRANE, D. "Scientists at Major and Minor Universities: A Study of Productivity and Recognition," *American Sociological Review*, 1965, *30*(5), 699–714.

DEMERATH, N. J., STEPHENS, R. W., AND TAYLOR, R. R. *Power, Presidents, and Professors*. New York: Basic Books, 1967.

DIEKHOFF, J. S. *The Domain of the Faculty in Our Expanding Colleges*. New York: Harper and Brothers, 1956.

DODDS, H. W. *The American President: Educator or Caretaker*. New York: McGraw-Hill, 1962.

DYKES, A. R. *Faculty Participation in Academic Decision-Making*. Washington, D.C.: American Council on Education, 1968.

FERRISS, A. "An Hypothesis on Institutional Mobility of Teachers in Higher Education," *College and University*, 1966, *42*(1), 2.

FRIEDMAN, N. *The Social Nature of Psychological Research: The Psycho-*

logical Experiment as a Social Interaction. New York: Basic Books, 1967.

GOTTLEIB, D. "Process of Socialization in American Graduate School," *Social Forces,* 1961, *40*(2), 124–131.

GOULDNER, A. W. "Cosmopolitans and Locals: Toward an Analysis of Latent Social Roles, I," *Administrative Science Quarterly,* 1957, *2*(3), 281–306.

GOULDNER, A. W. "Cosmopolitans and Locals: Toward an Analysis of Latent Social Roles, II," *Administrative Science Quarterly,* 1958, *2*(4), 440–480.

GUSTAD, J. W. *The Career Decisions of College Teachers,* Research Monograph Series #2. Atlanta: Southern Regional Education Board, 1960.

HARGENS, L. L. AND HAGSTROM, W. O. "Sponsored and Content Mobility of American Academic Scientists," *Sociology of Education,* 1967, *40*(1), 24–38.

HARTNETT, R. T. *College and University Trustees.* Princeton: Educational Testing Service, 1969.

The Hazen Foundation, New Haven, Conn., *The Student in Higher Education,* 1968.

HOFSTADTER, R. AND METZGER, W. P. *The Development of Academic Freedom in the United States.* New York: Columbia University Press, 1955.

HUGHES, R. M. *A Study of the Graduate School of America.* Oxford, Ohio: Miami University Press, 1925.

HYMAN, H. *Survey Design and Analysis.* New York: The Free Press, 1955.

HYMAN, H. AND OTHERS. *Interviewing in Social Research.* Chicago: University of Chicago Press, 1954.

JENCKS, C. AND RIESMAN, D. *The Academic Revolution.* Garden City: Doubleday, 1968.

JENCKS, C. AND RIESMAN, D. "Where Graduate Schools Fail." *Atlantic Monthly,* 1968, *22*(2), 49–55.

KERR, C. *The Uses of the University.* Cambridge, Mass.: Harvard University Press, 1963.

KIDD, C. V. *American Universities and Federal Research.* Cambridge, Mass.: Harvard University Press, 1959.

KNUDSEN, D. D. AND VAUGHN, T. R. "Quality in Graduate Education: A Reevaluation of the Rankings of Sociology Departments in the Cartter Report," *American Sociologist,* 1968, *3*(1), 12–19.

KOERNER, J. D. *The Parsons College Bubble: A Tale of Higher Education in America.* New York: Basic Books, 1970.

KRAUS, C. A. "The Evolution of the American Graduate School," *Bulletin of the AAUP,* 1951, *37*(3), 497–505.

LAZARSFELD, P. F. AND THIELENDS, W. *The Academic Mind.* New York: The Free Press, 1958.

LEE, C. B. T. (Ed.). *Improving College Teaching*. Washington, D.C.: The American Council on Education, 1967.

LEWIS, L. S. "On Subjective and Objective Rankings of Sociology Departments." *American Sociologist,* 1968, *3*(2), 129–131.

MC CARTHY, M. *The Groves of Academe*. New York: Harcourt Brace Jovanovich, 1951.

MC GEARY, M. N. "Appraising Professors," *Bulletin of the AAUP,* 1947, *33*(4), 695–701.

MARSHALL, H. D. *The Mobility of College Faculties*. New York: Pageant Press, 1964.

NEWBURN, H. K. *Faculty Personnel Policies in State Universities*. Missoula: Montana State University, Office of the President, 1959.

ORLANS, H. *The Effects of Federal Programs on Higher Education*. Washington, D.C.: The Brookings Institute, 1962.

ORNE, M. T. "On the Social Psychology of the Psychological Experiment: With Particular Reference to Demand Characteristics and Their Implication," *American Psychologist,* 1962, *17,* 776–783.

PARSONS, T. "Professions" in D. L. Sills (Ed.). *International Encyclopedia of the Social Sciences,* Vol. 12. New York: Macmillan and Free Press, 1968.

RICHARDSON, S. A. AND OTHERS. *Interviewing: Its Forms and Functions*. New York: Basic Books, 1965.

RIDGEWAY, J. *The Closed Corporation: American Universities in Crisis*. New York: Random House, 1968.

RIESMAN, D. *Constraint and Variety in American Education*. Garden City: Doubleday, 1958.

RILEY, M. W. *Sociological Research: A Case Approach*. New York: Harcourt Brace Jovanovich, 1963.

ROSENTHAL, R. *Experimenter Effects in Behavioral Research*. New York: Appleton-Century-Crofts, 1966.

ROSENTHAL, R. AND FODE, K. L. "Three Experiments in Experimenter Bias," *Psychological Report,* 1963, *12,* 491–511.

RUML, B. *Memo to a College Trustee*. New York: McGraw-Hill, 1959.

SANFORD, N. (Ed.). *The American College*. New York: Wiley, 1962.

SELLTIZ, C. AND OTHERS. *Research Methods in Social Relations*. New York: Holt, Rinehart, and Winston, 1962.

SHICHOR, D. "Prestige of Sociology Departments and the Placing of New Ph.D.'s," *American Sociologist,* 1970, *5*(2), 157–160.

SNOW, C. P. *The Two Cultures and the Scientific Revolution*. New York: Cambridge University Press, 1959.

STALLINGS, W. H. AND SINGHAL, S. "Some Observations on the Relationships Between Research Productivity and Student Evaluations of Courses and Teaching," *American Sociologist,* 1970, *5*(2), 141–143.

STECKLEIN, J. E. "Research on Faculty Recruitment and Motivation," in

Studies of College Faculty. Boulder, Colo., and Berkeley, Calif.: Western Interstate Commission for Higher Education and the Center for the Study of Higher Education, 1961, 25–27.

STECKLEIN, J. E. AND ECKERT, R. E. *An Exploratory Study of Factors Influencing the Choice of College Teaching as a Career.* Minneapolis: University of Minnesota, 1958.

SUSSMAN, M. B. AND HAUG, M. R. "Human and Mechanical Error—An Unknown Quantity in Research." Paper read at the American Sociological Association meeting, San Francisco, August 1967.

U.S. News and World Report. "The Coming Crisis in Private Colleges," 1967, *63*(12), 58.

VEBLEN, T. *The Higher Learning in America: A Memorandum on the Conduct of Universities by Business Men.* New York: Hill and Wang, 1957.

WILSON, L. "Prestige Patterns in Scholarship and Science," *Southwestern Social Science Quarterly,* 1943, *23*(3), 305–319.

WILSON, L. *The Academic Man.* New York: Oxford University Press, 1942.

WOODBURNE, L. S. *Faculty Personnel Policies in Higher Education.* New York: Harper and Brothers, 1950.

WOODRING, P. *The Higher Learning in America: A Reassessment.* New York: McGraw-Hill, 1968.

Index

A

Academic excellence, 20–21
Academic origins, 75–77, 91–92
Academy, idea of, 33–34, 50, 190
Acceptance of offer, 148–150, 173–174
Accreditation, 7, 9
Actives. *See* Market actives
Administration: attitude of toward market activity, 121–122, 125, 128, 132–133, 148, 200, 214; as factor in mobility, 139, 142, 200; and faculty relationship, 4, 15–16, 20, 43, 72, 144, 208–209; genius of, 23; incompetence of, 20; leadership for change of, 207–209, 212–215; nineteenth-century style of, 209; policy of, 139, 143–144; power of, 192, 209; and teaching/research conflict, 36
Admissions policy, 55, 163, 189, 212
Advising, student, 37, 54–55
Age: and academic origins, 75–77; among market actives, 84–85; and salary, 74–75
Aggrandizement Effect, 161, 165
Algebra, prestige of, 159, 177, 181, 183
Alumni, 48, 212
Anonymity, 11
Anthropology, 59
ARROWSMITH, W., 195–198
Artists, 59, 67, 69–70, 83

B

Assistant professors: and age, 60; and mobility, 93; Ph.D.s among, 62; probes of, 110–111, 124–125; promotion of, 63–65; salary of, 61
Associate professors: age of, 60; mobility of, 94; Ph.D.s among, 62; probes of, 110; promotion of, 63–65; salary of, 61
ASTIN, A. W., 190

B

BARZUN, J., 52–53, 188
Blind probe letter, 77
BROWN, D., 2–3
Budget, 14, 23; conflict over, 43; and dean, 17; power of, 15, 21–23; problems of, 51–52, 56; and university departments, 18
Bush league institution, 107n, 154

C

Candidates, active, 104–106
CAPLOW, T., 37, 114, 158, 216, 218
Cardinal Richelieu type, 48
Career Decision Study: analysis of, 226, 245; characteristics of institutions in, 7–9, 217; coding of, 228–246; conduct of, 9–11; expectations of, 107, 120, 122, 191; getting cooperation for, 10, 217, 219–220; goals of, 2, 232;